THE HOME OFFICE, 1782–1801

Duke Historical Publications

TO MY PARENTS

THE HOME OFFICE, 1782–1801

R. R. NELSON

Durham, N.C.
DUKE UNIVERSITY PRESS
1969

L.C.C. card no. 73–86481

PRINTED IN THE UNITED STATES OF
AMERICA BY KINGSPORT PRESS, INC.

CONTENTS

PREFACE

In 1782 administrative and political reasons dictated the rearrangement of the office of Secretary of State. The old Northern Department became the Foreign Office, and the Southern Department the Home Office. To the Secretary of State for Home Affairs fell a large number of duties, great and small. Communications from subjects to the king, all the way from addresses from the University of Oxford to requests for permission to ride through the royal parks, passed through his hands. With his colleague in the Foreign Office, the Home Secretary directed the Secret Service, both in Great Britain and abroad. He presided over the maintenance of domestic order—in a period of turbulence and fear and was also the custodian, so to speak, of the king's capacity as the fountain of mercy. The Secretary oversaw the conduct of Irish and Scottish affairs, and was colonial secretary for what remained of the Empire. Diplomatic responsibilities of the Home Office continued to encompass relations with the four Barbary Coast states. Military duties included correspondence with the English militia units, and, before 1794, the direction of mobilization and the conduct of military operations. To the Home Office was annexed the Alien Office, not to mention supervisory or other relationships with such servants of government as the State Paper Office; various secretaries, translators, and decipherers; the king's messengers; the Signet Office; and the *London Gazette*.

I have not felt able to go into the substantive operations of many of these multifarious duties. The Nootka Sound controversy alone would make a volume; Ireland at least two. I have had to content myself with an outline of the personnel and organization of the Office, with its finances and procedures and a suggestion of its relationships with other governmental departments, but I have discussed for various reasons, including my own interests, some matters in detail, particularly the Secret Service and the preservation of public order.

During the twenty years covered by this study—the terminal year of 1801 is rationalized by the assignment of the colonies to the War Office and the resignation of the Duke of Portland—there was a trend toward the regularization of finances in the Home Office and the elimination of ancient and irregular perquisites that had once constituted the stipends of the personnel. In this period, too, the Office seems to have become increasingly involved in the process of governing, pointing to a future time when central government assumed a new, or reassumed an Elizabethan, part in the functioning of society. The long transition, *pace*

G. R. Elton, from the king's household to the modern bureaucracy, was about at an end. It is worth remarking, too, that the civil service in the eighteenth century had attained some of the more cherished goals of bureaucrats everywhere: nearly absolute security of tenure and the sacred practices of seniority.

No monograph, I believe, has examined the Home Office as an institution during the early years of its new name. The accounts by Sir Edward Troup[1] and Sir Frank Newsam[2] deal almost exclusively with the office in the twentieth century, and Sir Austin Strutts's article is but a brief, though good, survey.[3]

Since, to me, history is primarily the study of people, I have not hesitated to add a few pages in order to rescue from oblivion a few worthwhile and interesting characters; if they do not appear in flesh and blood, at least their skeletons serve as an outline of their lives. Although I was unable to identify every person mentioned in the text, biographical references to many are in the footnotes. Names appearing in standard reference works available in most libraries seldom receive full identification unless relevant to the text. If the name of someone appears in a footnote followed only by the year of death, the *Gentleman's Magazine* for that year is the source.

R. R. N.

Sioux Falls, May 1968

1. *The Home Office* (The Whitehall Series; London, 1925).
2. *The Home Office* (The New Whitehall Series; London, 1954).
3. "The Home Office: An Introduction to Its Early History," *Public Administration*, XXXIX (Summer, 1961), 111–30.

ACKNOWLEDGMENTS

I am greatly indebted to Dr. and Mrs. J. G. C. Spencer Bernard for permission to examine and cite from the papers of Sir Scrope Bernard at Nether Winchendon House, Aylesbury, Buckinghamshire, and for their gracious hospitality while I remained there. I should like to thank Lady Bonham Carter for permission to examine and cite from the papers of William Wickham, deposited in the Hampshire Record Office. I am also indebted to the Right Hon. the Earl Fitzwilliam and the Trustees of the Wentworth Woodhouse Muniments deposited at the Sheffield City (Central) Library for permission to cite from the papers of Edmund Burke.

The staff of the Public Record Office, who provided me with documents for many months, deserves my thanks. The staff of the Institute of Historical Research were unfailingly courteous and helpful, and I wish to express my appreciation to them. I should also like to thank the staffs of the following institutions for their assistance: the British Museum, the William L. Clements Library (particularly Mr. William Ewing), the Duke University Library, the General Register House in Edinburgh, the Hampshire Record Office, the Kent Archives Office (especially Dr. Felix Hull), the Brotherton Collection at the University of Leeds, the National Library of Scotland, the Manuscripts Division of the University of Nottingham, the Literary Division of Somerset House, and the Sheffield City (Central) Library.

In addition to the archivists of several county record offices, the following persons were kind enough to provide me with information about various collections of papers: Lady Agnew of Pinehurst, South Ascot, Berks.; J. E. Chapman, Esq., of Leck Hill House, Cowan Bridge, Lancs.; the Hon. Eve Chetwynd of Watford, Herts.; Professor Alfred Cobban of University College, London; Major General Robert Charles Moss King, C.B., D.S.O., O.B.E.; Miss Agnes Betty Clare Nepean of Rivergate, Shaldon, Teignmouth, Devon.; Miss Olivia Nepean of Winchester, Hants.; Mrs. E. Hews of Orchard House, Oxford; Brigadier W. F. K. Thompson; Sir Reginald Tyrwhitt, Bt.; and the Right Hon. the Earl of Winchilsea and Nottingham.

Mr. Ian Christie was good enough to allow me to attend his seminar at the Institute of Historical Research, 1965–66, and was always generous with his time and advice.

I am most indebted to Mr. W. B. Hamilton for having suggested this study to me and for his advice and assistance throughout the years that I have been at Duke University. Dr. Donald McAdams kindly read and criticized the first draft of the book. And I must thank Dr. C. R. Middleton for considerable search for me on a number of points.

Without the constant encouragement and generosity of my mother and father this book could never have been written.

R. R. N.

My indebtedness to Professor Hamilton has increased from his having undertaken the final editing of the manuscript while I am in military service. Mrs. Elizabeth McConnell has patiently and exactingly typed the final manuscript. Both deserve my deepest and most sincere thanks.

R. R. N.

Rach Kien, Long An, Vietnam
17 July 1968

THE HOME OFFICE, 1782–1801

INTRODUCTION

The post of king's secretary, held by a person entrusted with the "secret" seal of the sovereign, emerged during the Middle Ages. In the course of decades, it acquired official status, power, and prestige. By 1540, the date after which two men usually held the office concurrently, the title "His Majesty's Principal Secretary of State" designated the holder of the office. The word "principal" distinguished the Secretaries of State from the Latin and French secretaries, who were usually no more than translators. The Tudors came to rely upon their Secretaries of State to signify their wishes to private citizens, government officials, and foreign heads of state and their representatives. This Secretary, who carried out the commands of the king in council or the king in Parliament, thus became one of the chief executive officers of the British government and held a seat in the Privy Council and (in the eighteenth century) in the Cabinet. Like the Chancery and the Exchequer, the office of Secretary followed a course of political and administrative evolution that led from a post within the royal household to a great office of state.[1]

The importance of the Secretary of State arose from his possession of the signet, one of the king's royal seals. The delivery of the seals to the Secretary signified his appointment, although the issue of letters patent continued into the nineteenth century.[2] By statute every grant or gift that passed under the great seal of England, such as

1. Two excellent studies of the Secretary of State cover the period from 1558 to 1782: Florence M. Grier Evans (Mrs. C. S. S. Higham), *The Principal Secretary of State: A Survey of the Office from 1558 to 1680* (Publications of the University of Manchester: Historical Studies, XLIII; Manchester, 1923); and Mark A. Thomson, *The Secretaries of State, 1681–1782* (Oxford, 1932). See also G. R. Elton, *The Tudor Revolution in Government* (London, 1953).

2. A Secretary of State actually received three seals—two signets and a cachet. The distinction between the use of the two signets, one smaller and one larger, during the eighteenth century is not clear. It may have been the same distinction as the one described by Anson for the signets in the early twentieth century. Sir William Anson, *The Law and Custom of the Constitution*, Vol. II: *The Crown*, edited by A. B. Keith (4th ed.; 2 pts.; Oxford, 1935), Pt. 1, 182–84.

patents of nobility, appointments to major offices, and grants of land, had first to pass the signet. The Secretary might also use the signet to seal warrants issued under the king's sign manual, which did not pass the great seal. The subjects of such warrants included military commissions, instructions to colonial governors, appointments of minor officials, and directions to government departments, such as to the Ordnance to issue arms and other supplies from the Tower of London. The countersignature of the Secretary on a warrant certified his approval of the document, and meant that Parliament could hold him responsible for his advice to the king.

Though after 1540 two men normally served simultaneously as Secretaries of State (and at present there are nine), the office is and always has been a single unit. Any Secretary may perform the duties of his colleagues. The arrangement of business reflects administrative convenience and may be altered at will by the king and his ministers. After 1689 one Secretary headed the Northern Department and one the Southern Department. The former corresponded with British envoys in the Empire, Holland, Scandinavia, Poland, and Russia. The Southern Department transacted all business relating to France, Switzerland, Italy, the Iberian Peninsula, and Turkey, as well as Ireland, the Channel Islands, and the colonies. Both dealt indiscriminately with domestic affairs, although the Northern Department usually had control of Scottish business.[3] A third Secretary of State, added in 1768, had responsibility for the colonies until a statute abolished the office in 1782.

This study of the office of the Secretary of State begins in March 1782, when a reorganization altered the distribution of duties of the two Secretaries. On March 27, 1782, the Southern Department became the Home Office, and the Northern Department the Foreign Office. The title of the new Secretaries varied in common usage, but technically it remained "His Majesty's Principal Secretary of State." The Attorney General, Richard Pepper Arden, informed the Home Secretary, Lord Sydney, that "I much doubt whether there is any such officer known as Secretary of State for the Home Department. The two Secretaries of State are his Majesty's principal Secretaries of State and the distinction of Home and Foreign are mere arrangements of office but either of them may as I apprehend do any part of

3. Thomson, pp. 2–3.

the duty."[4] Almost at once, however, the terms Home Secretary and Foreign Secretary came into common usage.

The plans for the administrative reorganization of the offices developed during the meetings held by the Rockingham Whigs, Lord Shelburne, and others in February and March of 1782, preceding the imminent fall of the government of Lord North.[5] The alteration in the duties of the Secretaries occurred at this time for three principal reasons. The abolition of both the office of Secretary of State for the American Colonies and of the Board of Trade necessitated a redistribution of their functions. A second cause was the jealousy and suspicion between the two men destined to become the new Secretaries—Lord Shelburne and Charles James Fox. Then, too, Shelburne, Edmund Burke, and others had long been interested in the reform of the finances and administration of government offices. The first explanation is self-evident, but the last two deserve more attention.

The division of authority for foreign affairs had been a source of friction more than once during the seventeenth and eighteenth centuries, when one Secretary had attempted to interfere in the areas of responsibility of his colleague. It had proved, for instance, quite beyond the Duke of Newcastle, while Secretary for the Southern Department (1742 to 1744), to refrain from meddling in the Northern Department. When he finally became Secretary for the Northern Department in 1748, it was equally impossible for him to keep his hands off the Southern Department.[6] The domineering personalities of Fox and Shelburne and their suspicion and jealousy of each other would unquestionably have precluded their sharing responsibility for foreign affairs in the Rockingham ministry.[7] Less than one hundred days after they took office it was found that they could not even remain in the same Cabinet.

In addition to the political considerations, the far more logical division of authority between foreign and home affairs must have influenced the decision to alter the business of the offices. In 1771 George III had seriously considered a major reorganization exactly

4. August 29, 1784, Mold [Flintshire], H.O. 48/1. All designations such as H.O., F.O., C.O. refer to classifications of documents in the Public Record Office (P.R.O.), London.
5. John Norris, *Shelburne and Reform* (London, 1963), pp. 144–50.
6. Thomson, pp. 90–94, 159–60.
7. For example, Lord Edmund Fitzmaurice, *Life of William Earl of Shelburne, Afterwards Marquess of Lansdowne* (2nd ed. rev.; 2 vols.; London, 1912), II, 92.

on the lines of the one that occurred in 1782. He wrote Lord North that

a thought has occurred to me . . . whether Lord Rochford could not transact the whole department of Foreign affairs, which is the case in every other Court, and then Lord Suffolk [who could not read French] might have the home departments which would be composed of all domestick affairs with the addition of Scotland and Ireland.[8]

In 1782 the King may not have been averse to the alterations he himself had earlier suggested.

The reasons for this major administrative change must, however, remain suppositional. No comment by contemporaries seems to be extant. The sole relevant document is a circular that Fox, as Foreign Secretary, sent to the British envoys:

The King having, on the resignation of the Lord Viscount Stormont, been pleased to appoint me to be one of His Principal Secretaries of State, and at the same to make a new arrangement in the Departments by conferring that for Domestic Affairs and the Colonies on the Earl of Shelburne, and entrusting me with the sole direction of the Department for Foreign Affairs, I am to desire that you will for the future address your letters to me.[9]

However obscure the precise details behind the reorganization, the effect of the change became readily apparent. The new Home Office gave up all responsibility for foreign affairs, except that relating to Algiers, Morocco, Tripoli, and Tunis. In return it assumed the Northern Department's responsibility for Scotland and for all the domestic affairs that the two Secretaries had formerly shared. Colonial affairs also fell within the Home Office's jurisdiction. The chief clerk of the Office summarized the business of his department as it was in 1785. It

comprises whatever relates to the internal Government of Great Britain, Ireland, Jersey, Guernsey, Alderney, Sark, the Isle of Man, the colonies in North America, the West Indies, the East Indies, Africa, and Gibraltar; Revenue and Admiralty business are of course excepted: but all other matters such as Crown grants, army commissions, church preferments in His Majesty's gift, approbations of Lord Lieutenants' appointments in the Militia, and business relative to criminals, pass through this office,

8. Jan. 16, 1771, *The Correspondence of King George the Third, from 1760 to December 1783*, edited by Sir John Fortescue (6 vols.; London, 1927–28), II, 205–206.
9. March 29, 1782, printed in Anson, Pt. I, 180, italics omitted.

and are laid by the Secretary of State before His Majesty for His royal signature or approbation.[10]

He should have added conduct of diplomatic relations with the four Barbary states and, though it burgeoned after 1789, correspondence with both county and London magistrates on the preservation of public order. The Home Office also had principal executive responsibility for the conduct of war during the final year of the American Revolution and at the beginning of the wars of the French Revolution, as well as the Russian and Nootka Sound mobilizations in between. The chief clerk purposely omitted Secret Service activities.

The Home Office often served as the executive spur or starting point for much of the activity of the government, for it conveyed the commands of the king and his ministers to many of the great departments of state. The law officers of the Crown—the Attorney General and Solicitor General—and sometimes the Lord Chancellor—submitted opinions on legal points when requested to do so by the Office.[11] The judges were frequently consulted on matters relating to the pardoning of criminals.[12]

Correspondence with the Treasury, the Privy Council, and after its reconstitution in 1786, the Board of Trade consumed much time. The Home Office submitted to the Treasury (after 1795) all its own financial accounts, disbursements for Secret Service, estimates of expenses in the colonies and some accounts of colonial officials, London police accounts, disbursements by the consuls in the Barbary states, and various petitions from private or public persons. The Treasury, which invariably paid all debts of the Office itself, referred many claims to the Secretary for his opinion on the advisability of paying them.[13] Most of the business with the Privy Council and the Board of Trade involved the interchange of ideas and correspondence on colonial affairs, but occasionally dealt with grain shortages and other domestic affairs.[14]

Communications with the Post Office concerned the notification

10. Great Britain, Parliament, House of Commons, *First Report of the Commissioners Appointed by Act 25 Geo. 3, c. 19, to Inquire into the Fees, Perquisites, and Emoluments which are, or have been lately, received in the several Public Offices therein mentioned: The Secretaries of State, 11 April 1786,* H. of C. 309, Appendix 2, pp. 19–20. *Parliamentary Papers, 1806,* VII. Henceforth *Parliamentary Papers* is abbreviated *PP.*

11. H.O. 48/1–10; H.O. 119/1, covering 1782–1801.

12. H.O. 47/128.

13. H.O. 35/1–23 (letters from the Treasury); H.O. 36/1 and S.P. 44/330 (letters to the Treasury).

14. H.O. 1–5, 14–15.

that clerks should have franking privileges, or more important, that letters to or from certain persons should be intercepted.[15] Correspondence with the Foreign Office usually involved the petitions of foreign ministers and ambassadors for the release of their nationals held in English prisons or colonial disputes involving French or Spanish possessions in the West Indies.[16] The rather extensive contact with the Customs stemmed primarily from the need to control the movement of aliens after the beginning of the French Revolution, but occasionally pertained to the capture of smugglers.[17]

With the various military departments the Home Office had extensive business. The Secretary for War, created in July 1794, communicated with the Home department on military affairs in Ireland and the colonies.[18] When the Home Secretary was responsible for the war (either from 1782 or from 1792 to 1794), he had much correspondence on general military affairs with both the Secretary at War[19] and the Commander-in-Chief (vacant from December 1783 to January 1793).[20] Some correspondence between the last two and the Home Office pertained to the movement of troops within Great Britain, especially during riots. Irish military affairs also consumed considerable time, as did the communications among various military departments, the lord lieutenants of counties, and other military commanders relating to the militia and volunteer corps.[21] The Home Office prepared all warrants directing the Ordnance to issue arms and equipment from its stores,[22] and frequently corresponded with it regarding ordnance equipment for the colonies and the Channel Islands.[23]

Connections with the Admiralty usually consisted of the Home Office's giving directions to it regarding ships and equipment for various tasks in the colonies and elsewhere and sending instructions concerning the convicts confined on hulks at various ports, but in wartime the Office sent orders directly to admirals.[24] Correspondence with the Navy Office, the Commissioners of Transportation, and the Commissioners of Victualling invariably dealt with supplies for convicts to be transported to Australia.[25]

15. H.O. 33/1; H.O. 42/206–14. 16. H.O. 32/1–8. 17. H.O. 42/206–14.
18. H.O. 30/1–3. 19. H.O. 50/378–90; H.O. 51/146–54. 20. H.O. 50/1–10.
21. H.O. 50/17–39, 313–29, 330–56; H.O. 51/7–12, 104–105. 22. H.O. 51/140–44.
23. H.O. 50/364–74: out-letters are scattered in H.O. 43/1–13.
24. H.O. 29/1–4; H.O. 28/1–27, 57–63. 25. Scattered in H.O. 43/1–13; H.O. 42/1–57.

With other government departments the Home Office had little to do. Correspondence with the Lord Chamberlain involved the messenger corps or the issuing of plate to colonial governors. With the Chancery, Exchequer, many of the boards of revenue, the paymaster general of the forces, and others there seems to have been virtually no contact.

With Parliament the Home Office had a special relationship throughout the two decades concerned in this study. A reform of the finances and procedures of many government departments was the cause of this relationship. Agitation for such reform began in response to certain failings that appeared during the course of the American Revolution. One central problem lay with the tangled financial structure of the government. No First Lord of the Treasury had been able to make a survey or even a good guess as to the expenses of government during any one year, and could not, therefore, draw up a proper budget and organize his planning accordingly. Government departments had too much independence both in their financial affairs and, to some extent, in the manner in which they conducted their particular business.

Following the fall of Lord North, the Rockinghams introduced several reform measures, of which Edmund Burke's economical reform bill is the best known. Shelburne continued many of the reforms and added or suggested others during the short period that he remained at the head of the Treasury.[26] During the coalition government of Fox and North from April to December 1783 William Pitt

> proposed a bill & carried it thro' the H of C. obliging the Commissioners of Accounts to enter upon an enquiry into the Establishments, business & Emoluments of the several public offices in order to judge what reform could be made in them. The Bill was thrown out, but he [Pitt] feels himself bound not to drop the idea, altho' he thinks it expedient not to put it into the hands of the Commissioners of Accounts. He has therefore ordered a Commission to be made out to three Persons, who are the two Comptrollers of Army Accounts & a Mr. Baring a considerable Merchant who are to execute this business.[27]

26. Norris, *Shelburne and Reform,* chaps. x–xiii; J. E. D. Binney, *British Public Finance and Administration, 1774–92* (Oxford, 1958) , chaps. i–ii.

27. W. W. Grenville to Scrope Bernard, Dec. 23, 1784, quoted in Mrs. Napier Higgins, *The Bernards of Abingdon and Nether Winchendon: A Family History* (4 vols.; London, 1904) , III, 74–75.

According to the provisions of the Act[28] the commissioners began to hear evidence in November 1785. On September 10 they requested certain information from the Secretary of State for the Home Department, who replied on November 3.[29] Later that month the commissioners began to summon all the personnel of the office to give testimony, an undertaking that lasted into December. The commissioners made ten reports on various offices, of which the first concerns the Home and Foreign offices.[30] In 1789 they presented their reports to the Privy Council, but it did not consider them until January 1792. The Council ordered the reports sent to the Secretaries for possible additions and corrections.[31] The Secretaries did not submit their final replies, it appears, until February 23, 1795. Four days later the Privy Council issued an order enacting all the recommendations of the commissioners that had been approved by the Secretaries.[32]

In 1797 a select committee of the House of Commons investigated the extent to which the various offices had complied with the recommendations of the commissioners in 1786. The committee printed its findings in thirty-six reports. The sixteenth concerns the Home Office, and also contains a copy of the order in council of 1795 that effected the reorganization.[33] Evidence of the scope and importance of these parliamentary inquiries into the office of the Secretaries of State appears in nearly every chapter of this book.

28. Great Britain, *Statutes at Large,* 25 Geo. III, c. 19 (1785).
29. Lord Sydney to the commissioners, H.O. 43/2.
30. The ten reports were first printed in 1792, but without the valuable appendices (*PP 1792–93* [103], X). The reports were reprinted in 1806 with appendices (above, n. 10).
31. Jan. 12, 1792, H.O. 42/10.
32. Privy Council Register, P.C. 2/142.
33. *Sixteenth Report from the Select Committee on Finance. Expenditure of the Public Revenue. Secretaries of State. Reported by Charles Abbot, Esquire, 19 July 1797,* reprinted by order of the House of Commons in the First Series of reprints of *Reports from Committees of the House of Commons, 1715–1801* (16 vols.; London, 1773–1803), XII, 296–327; hereafter *Sixteenth Report, 1797.*

Chapter One

SECRETARIES OF STATE

Six men held the seals of the office of Secretary of State for Home Affairs during the twenty years from 1782 to 1801. The first of these, and the first man to be designated Home Secretary, was William (Petty), second Earl of Shelburne, created Marquess of Lansdowne in 1784. Following a brief but notable military career, Shelburne entered politics as a supporter of Lord Bute, but with Henry Fox as his real mentor. In 1761 he succeeded to his father's peerage and entered the House of Lords, where he soon attached himself to the elder Pitt. From 1766 to 1768 he served with little distinction as Secretary of State for the Southern Department. After his resignation in 1768 he opposed the government of Lord North till its fall in 1782. Sir Lewis Namier described him as

> a keen reformer, patron of Priestley, Bentham, and Richard Price, he was an aristocratic forerunner of the "philosophic radicals." He had some real friends among those who knew him best, but generally was disliked by men of his own standing, social or political, and especially by those who served under him. . . . The deeper contradictions and involutions of his character made him appear insincere: he was distrusted and his political career was wrecked by his unpopularity.[1]

Shelburne received the seals of office and was sworn before the Privy Council on March 27, 1782.[2] The most important features of his incumbency concerned his direction of the negotiations for the Peace of Paris,[3] his plans for reforming the procedures and policies of the Home Office, and his special relationship with King George III. Unfortunately the brevity of his tenure prevents any detailed evaluation.

Between 1768 and 1780 Shelburne formulated extensive plans for

1. Sir Lewis Namier and John Brooke (eds.), *The History of Parliament: The House of Commons, 1754–1790* (3 vols.; London, 1964), III, 271–72.
2. Privy Council Register, P.C. 2/127. 3. See Chapter X.

the reform of public offices,[4] and had he been at the Home Office longer than three months and a few days he probably would have inaugurated and carried out many changes both in procedure and in policy. His designs for the remaining colonies were particularly ambitious.[5] Prior to his appointment as Secretary he made a critical survey of the personnel of the Southern Department, the defunct Colonial Office, and the old Board of Trade in order to "retain those of the best abilities in each, and make a complete and perfect establishment out of the three."[6] In effect, however, the core of the old Southern Department remained. Only one clerk, William Duck, retired,[7] although the chief clerk, Richard Shadwell, retired on May 31, 1782.[8] Three clerks migrated from the Colonial Office,[9] and Grey Elliott, acting secretary, solicitor, and clerk of reports to the Board of Trade, eventually became Undersecretary of the Plantation Department, which formed part of the Home Office.[10] Shelburne's plans for further reorganization are unknown.

King George's outrageous partiality to Shelburne over the Marquis of Rockingham perhaps gave Shelburne the distinction of being the most powerful Secretary for the Home department during the period.[11] Shelburne looked upon himself as a colleague, not as a subordinate, of Rockingham. In early April 1782 the King wrote that "when Ld Shelburne was with me he expressed an uneasiness lest I should yield to the importunities of Lord Rockingham, which would reduce him to a Secretary of State acting under the former, instead of a colleague. . . ."[12] Shelburne himself described his association with Rockingham in similar terms: "I have manifested from the beginning [the desire] of keeping the present systems together, and of gratifying him, and the impossibility of his considering me as

4. Norris, *Shelburne and Reform,* chaps. iv–xii.

5. Helen Taft Manning, *British Colonial Government After the American Revolution, 1782–1820* (New Haven and London, 1933), pp. 17–18; Vincent T. Harlow, *The Founding of the Second British Empire, 1763–1793* (2 vols.; London, 1952–64), I, chap. vi.

6. William Knox, *Extra Official State Papers* (London, 1789), p. 24; Historical Manuscripts Commission, "The Manuscripts of Captain Howard Vicente Knox," *Report on the Manuscripts in Various Collections* (6 vols.; London, 1901–9), VI, 283.

7. Thomson, *Secretaries of State,* Appendix XI, p. 179.

8. The information on all clerks mentioned hereafter will be found in Appendix I.

9. William Pollock, Eardley Wilmot, and George L. Palman.

10. For Elliott and the Plantation Office, see Chapter X.

11. The tone of the correspondence between George III and Shelburne throughout this time clearly demonstrates the King's favoritism. *Correspondence of George III,* V, 407–509; VI, 1–73.

12. To Thurlow, April 5, 1782, *ibid.,* V, 443.

an ordinary Secretary of State, from our having always kept separate lines, as well as from the circumstances attending the formation of the present Ministry."[13] It is not surprising to find that on July 4, three days after Rockingham's death, Shelburne became First Lord of the Treasury.

On July 10, Thomas Townshend succeeded Shelburne at the Home Office. Townshend, who was created Baron Sydney in March 1783, also served as Shelburne's chief spokesman in the House of Commons, principally upon the peace negotiations, which dominated the business of the Home Secretary. Following a vote of censure in the House prompted by the coalition formed by Lord North and Fox, who had quitted the Cabinet when Shelburne became First Lord of the Treasury, Shelburne resigned February 24, 1783.[14] William Pitt (Chancellor of the Exchequer), Townshend, and other ministers carried on the headless government until late March, when they too resigned.

The King, much to his disgust, appointed to office the members of the coalition. On April 2, 1783, the Duke of Portland became First Lord of the Treasury, but was only titular leader. Fox, the real power, took the Foreign Office, and Lord North accepted the Home Office.[15]

Sometime in March 1782 North informed his father that he hated the thought of taking the seals, but Portland and Fox insisted. He never again wanted to be in the Cabinet, provided that he could quit it with honor and justice.[16] All evidence confirms North's lack of interest in public life and Fox's domination of the coalition.[17] North spoke only once in the Commons on a matter relating to his office.[18] His correspondence with the King was infrequent, formal, and cold.[19] The sole step of any importance taken by North as

13. To the King, April 29, 1782, *ibid.*, 502–3.
14. Fitzmaurice, *Life of Shelburne,* II, 252.
15. Memorandum by the King, dated April 1, 1783, but obviously of a later date, *Correspondence of George III,* VI, 328–29.
16. To the Earl of Guilford, Tues. morning, North MSS, Kent Archives Office; printed in full in Alan Valentine, *Lord North* (2 vols.; Norman, Okla., 1967), II, 358–59.
17. Valentine, II, 349–92; Reginald Lucas, *Lord North, Second Earl of Guilford, K.G., 1732–1792* (2 vols.; London, 1913), II, 240–41; Baring Pemberton, *Lord North* (London, 1938), pp. 370–89.
18. The speech on June 27, 1783, concerned American Loyalists. William Cobbett (compiler), *The Parliamentary History of England from the Earliest Period to the Year 1803,* XXIII, 1050–53, 1056; hereafter cited as Cobbett, *Parl. Hist.*
19. *Correspondence of George III,* VI, *passim.*

Secretary was at the behest of Grey Elliott—the establishment of the Plantation Department within the Home Office.[20]

On the evening of December 18, 1783, following secret negotiations with William Pitt, George III sent the Undersecretary of the Home Office, Evan Nepean, with a curt notice to North to deliver up the seals of his office and to inform Fox to do the same.[21] Nepean arrived at North's house about eleven at night to find North, Fox, and others at dinner. Although the party was incredulous at the announcement, North gave the seals to Nepean, who returned them to the King.[22]

On the next day William Pitt became First Lord of the Treasury and his cousin Richard (Grenville), third Earl Temple, received the seals of both the Home and Foreign offices. Temple intended to retain those of the Home Office and also serve as leader in the House of Lords, but on December 22 he resigned for unknown reasons. He may have feared actual impeachment for having read the King's threatening message in the House of Lords on Fox's India bill, which had led to the defeat of that bill. Or he may have resigned simply to quiet the clamor over the incident.[23] The King, although he created Temple Marquis of Buckingham in 1784, never forgave him, but Pitt remained on good terms with him. Temple later served as Lord Lieutenant of Ireland.[24] The sole records of Temple's term as Home and Foreign Secretary are the copies of letters that he signed dismissing members of the coalition and letters to John Lee, the Attorney General, and the Earl of Derby, Chancellor of the Duchy of Lancaster, signifying to them that he would lay their resignations before the King.[25]

Pitt had much difficulty finding men willing to accept posts in a government that seemed unlikely to last. He even turned to the discredited Lord Sackville (formerly Lord George Germain), who

20. Elliott to North, Sept. 18, 1783, H.O. 42/3; North to the Lord Commissioners of the Treasury (hereafter the Treasury), Oct. 30, 1783, H.O. 36/4.

21. George III to North, Dec. 18, 1783, 10:43 P.M., *Correspondence of George III*, VI, 476.

22. The accounts vary somewhat but the best is probably Burges': *Selections from the Letters and Correspondence of Sir James Bland Burges, Bart.*, edited by James Hutton (London, 1885), pp. 64–65.

23. E. Anthony Smith, "Earl Temple's Resignation, December 22, 1783," *Historical Journal*, VI (1963), 91–97. Smith favors the last-mentioned view, which was also the view of Pitt's tutor and biographer, Bishop Tomline, *Memoirs of the Life of the Right Honorable William Pitt* (4 vols.; London, 1821), I, 231–32.

24. Smith, p. 97.

25. H.O. 43/1. The dismissals are dated Dec. 19, and the letters to Lee and Derby the 20th.

refused him.[26] On September 23 Pitt finally prevailed upon the Marquis of Carmarthen to take the Foreign Office[27] and virtually coerced his brother's father-in-law, Lord Sydney, to take once again the seals of the Home Office. Thomas Orde, who accepted the post of Secretary to the Treasury, wrote that Sydney

very kindly acts as a volunteer in this office, because there is no other to be found, declaring however that he very much disliked the employment both on account of the business and expense of it, and hoped, that he should have an opportunity of giving it up in exchange for a more quiet one, and requiring less outgoings.[28]

Sydney himself wrote to Shelburne the day after taking office, surmising that Shelburne must be surprised to find himself receiving a letter from the office to which Sydney had first introduced him.

Your astonishment cannot exceed mine. I certainly never wished and have done all I could to avoid returning to it. But I am looked upon as one, who is ready to go aloft in a Storm. Under the present circumstances I thought it my Duty to undertake the Task. . . .[29]

Sydney's initial dislike of office seems to have colored his entire tenure. Lord Carmarthen reported a conversation in which the Duke of Richmond, Master General of the Ordnance,

could not help lamenting to me a want of confidential communication in the Cabinet, and of the dilatory proceedings in some of the departments; he told me in confidence that Pitt had express'd a wish of his (the Dukes) taking the Seals of the Home department, and of giving the Privy Seal to Lord Sydney [but that Richmond declined the arrangement].[30]

William Smith, an American Loyalist residing in London prior to being appointed Chief Justice of Quebec, saw Sydney frequently and recorded his impression of him:

Lord Sydney has a bad Utterance, & but a moderate Understanding. I should imagine him very unfit for his present Station. His thoughts are on the Surface, very scattered. He seems to be candid, he is reputed to be honest, but I can't believe him industrious or vigilant, certainly not pro-

26. J. Holland Rose, *William Pitt and National Revival* (London, 1911), pp. 154–56.
27. Francis Godolphin (Osborne), fifth Duke of Leeds, *The Political Memoranda of Francis Fifth Duke of Leeds,* edited by Oscar Browning (Camden Society Publications, n.s., XXXV; Westminster, 1884), 90–92.
28. To Shelburne, Dec. 23, 1783, Fitzmaurice, II, 280–81.
29. December 24, 1783, copy, Sydney Papers, William L. Clements Library, Ann Arbor, Michigan.
30. Leeds, *Political Memoranda,* p. 102.

found; and he wastes Time at all his Audiences by talking himself, and upon Subjects not relating to Business.[31]

Smith later commented that

Lord Sydney has an obstructed utterance that don't arise from the Fault of the Tongue but a scattered Mind & Impotence of Language. Yet there is some Sense in all that he says.[32]

It is too harsh to describe Lord Sydney as an incompetent Secretary of State, but he was certainly not an energetic one. Fortunately the years from 1784 to 1789 were relatively quiet. The volume of correspondence was far less than for any other time during the twenty years of this study. Sydney seems to have made few if any innovations in the office.

Politically, Sydney was not within Pitt's inner circle. Although the Duke of Rutland, Lord Lieutenant of Ireland, liked Sydney, he remarked that his separation from the Cabinet would not "weigh a feather."[33] Sydney had been a regular speaker in the House of Commons, sometimes with good effect. He ably led the defense of the peace preliminaries in February 1783 while serving as Home Secretary; the diarist Nathaniel William Wraxall "never saw him display so much animation nor heard him manifest such ability."[34] After entering the upper house he seldom spoke, although he did defend Pitt's Irish commercial propositions in 1785[35] and made one lengthy speech during the Regency crisis in 1788.[36] As Wraxall observed, however, "Sydney, when removed to the Upper House of Parliament, seemed to have sunk into an ordinary man."[37]

Sydney's term as Home Secretary approached its close in the spring of 1789. Early in that year he antagonized Lord Buckingham, Lord Lieutenant of Ireland, and also discovered that all the dispatches from Ireland came first not to him but to Buckingham's brother, William Wyndham Grenville, who, though holding no

31. Diary for Oct. 23, 1784 [William Smith], *The Diary and Selected Papers of Chief Justice William Smith, 1784–1793,* edited by L. F. S. Upton (2 vols.; Publications of the Champlain Society, XLI and XLII; Toronto, 1963–65), I, 154.

32. Diary for June 13, 1786, *ibid.*, II, 104–105.

33. To Thomas Orde, July 1786, H.M.C., *Report on the Manuscripts of His Grace the Duke of Rutland, K.G., preserved at Belvoir Castle* (4 vols.; London, 1888–1905), III, 320–21; hereafter H.M.C., *Rutland.*

34. *The Historical and the Posthumous Memoirs of Sir Nathaniel William Wraxall 1772–1784* [1789], edited by Henry Wheatley (5 vols.; New York, 1884), II, 424–25.

35. Cobbett, *Parl. Hist.*, XXV, 821, 830–34. Ireland was under Home Office jurisdiction.

36. *Ibid.*, XXVII, 1292–93.

37. Wraxall, *Memoirs,* IV, 5; see also Burges, *Letters and Correspondence,* pp. 66–67.

office relevant to Irish affairs, served as one of Pitt's closest advisers. On May 2, 1789, Grenville informed his brother:

> Lord S[ydney] has taken great offence, from the circumstance of having at last found out that your despatches to him come over enclosed to me. I could wish, therefore, that for the *very short time* that your correspondence with him is likely to continue you would alter this, as nothing material is likely to arise that can render it necessary, and I am desirous just at this particular moment to avoid any altercation with him. This jealousy on his part, and a just sense of mine of his conduct towards you, has entirely broke off all communication between us with respect to Irish, or indeed any other, business.[38]

Pitt was seeking to staff his offices with more efficient men and with men personally closer to him, such as Grenville. Sydney had served the purpose in 1783 by accepting office, but had outlived his usefulness by 1789. Never having wanted to be Secretary, he probably felt no obligation to exert himself either as administrator or politician. On June 5 he resigned the seals. In return for his services he received the sinecure post of Chief Justice in Eyre South of the Trent for life, valued at £2,500 a year, and a step in the peerage to viscount. His son John Thomas Townshend, who had served as Undersecretary in the Home Office, was appointed Lord of the Admiralty.[39]

William Grenville, who resigned as Speaker of the House of Commons to accept the seals of the Home Office on June 5, 1789, differed from his predecessor both as a politician and as an administrator. Though only twenty-nine years old in 1789, Grenville had served without Cabinet rank as Pitt's principal adviser on foreign affairs for several years.[40] His frequent speeches in the House of Commons, though not great orations, usually contained careful argument and commanded respect.[41] Prior to coming to the Home Office, Grenville had gained considerable experience as joint pay-

38. Duke of Buckingham and Chandos, *Memoirs of the Court and Cabinets of George III* (2nd ed. rev.; 4 vols.; London, 1853–55), II, 155. For the dispute with Buckingham see *ibid.*, pp. 131–37, and H.M.C., *Report on the Manuscripts of J. B. Fortescue, Esq., preserved at Dropmore* (10 vols.; London, 1892–1927), I, 437–57; hereafter *Dropmore Papers*. Grenville had wanted to supplant Sydney by early 1788. Grenville to Buckingham, April 1, 1788, Buckingham, *Court and Cabinets of George III*, I, 366–73.

39. Sydney to the King, June 4, 1789, *Later Correspondence of George III*, edited by Arthur Aspinall (5 vols. projected; Cambridge, since 1962), I, 421–22; n. 1, p. 422.

40. J. H. Rose, *William Pitt and National Revival*, pp. 317, 326, 405; Leeds, p. 101.

41. Sir Leslie Stephen and Sir Sidney Lee (eds.), *Dictionary of National Biography* (21 vols. and supplements; since 1885), VII, 576–81; hereafter cited as *DNB*.

master general of the forces and as member of both the Board of Control (for India) and the Board of Trade. It was as a man of business (in the eighteenth-century sense of governmental administration) rather than as a politician that Grenville excelled.

Almost immediately after taking office in 1789 he made several useful innovations in the record-keeping procedures. He directed that précis or brief summaries be made of all incoming and some outgoing correspondence with virtually all colonial governors and officials. The Secretary or any interested Cabinet member could then examine the essence of a particular dispatch at a glance.[42] Charles Goddard, whom Grenville brought into office with him, served him as both précis writer and private secretary. Both positions came to be so useful that they were retained on the permanent establishment.[43] Grenville was also the first Secretary to use a register for letters that circulated among members of the Cabinet. By this means the Office could be certain that every interested official had seen a particular dispatch and also know its location at any given time.[44] Although minor, these innovations greatly increased the efficiency of the Office at a time when correspondence began to increase in volume.

What other plans Grenville might have had for the Home Office are unknown, for two years after he became Home Secretary he moved to the Foreign Office. When the Duke of Leeds resigned the seals of that office on April 21, 1791, the King sent them to Lord Grenville,[45] who had been created a baron in November 1790. Since Grenville's paramount interest lay in foreign affairs, Pitt naturally wanted him to move to the Foreign Office; but Henry Dundas, Grenville's intended successor at the Home Office, could not accept the seals without resigning from Parliament and standing at a by-

42. The C.O. papers are indexed by colony; hence, the précis for each colony appears as a subdivision under the name of the colony. The précis for the Bahama correspondence 1789–1806, for example, is in C.O. 24/8–12. C.O. 5/268 contains a volume that served as a general index for incoming colonial dispatches. C.O. 5/269 was an abortive attempt to make a précis of all dispatches received. The indexing of outgoing dispatches does not appear to have been followed at all times.

43. Chapter IV has further information on both positions.

44. C.O. 324/61; H.O. 97/1–2. After January 1794 the practice seems to have been to send the dispatches to the King as usual, but then to deposit them in the "Reading Room" where ministers might come to examine them. "State Paper Office Delivery Book," C.O. 324/61.

45. The King to Pitt, April 23, 1791, quoted in Phillip Henry (Stanhope), fifth Earl Stanhope, *Life of the Right Honourable William Pitt* (4 vols.; London, 1861–62), II, Appendix, p. xiv.

election.[46] To avoid this, Grenville held the seals of both secretariats until June 18, two days before the end of the parliamentary session, when Dundas became Home Secretary.[47]

Henry Dundas, while at the Home department, bore the heaviest work load of any of the Secretaries. Although seventeen years Pitt's senior, he served as his right-hand man on India and managed Scottish elections on behalf of the government—both of which duties he continued to perform while Home Secretary. As well as being Secretary, he was concurrently a commissioner of the Board of Control (and its president after June 1793), lord advocate of Scotland, and treasurer of the Navy.[48] His energy and capacity for mastering a huge amount of material in a short time served him well when the full effect of the French Revolution struck England. Disaffection and open sedition forced the Secretary to act with unprecedented frequency in his capacity as preserver of public order in Great Britain. The passage of the Alien Act in 1793, to control the movement of foreigners within England, added a new department and an additional responsibility to the Home Office. When France declared war on England in February 1793, Dundas became executive director and planner of the war. The new military duties placed a severe strain upon the Office, but Dundas did much to improve its efficiency by replacing ineffective clerks and adding a much needed librarian and keeper of criminal registers to the payroll.[49] Dundas' ineffectiveness as a war minister has somewhat marred his reputation, but his tenure as Home Secretary left every evidence of administrative ability and competence.

Although the Home Office could probably have continued to function well enough under the burden of conducting the war,[50] the necessity of finding places for the Portland Whigs, who were about to join Pitt's government, dictated the separation of the war business from the Office and the creation of a Secretary for War, July 11,

46. Pitt to the King, April 29, 1791, *Later Correspondence of George III,* I, 529.

47. Pitt originally asked General the Lord Cornwallis to be Home Secretary. Dundas was to serve only until Cornwallis could return from India, but the general declined the offer because he did not believe that he had an absolute prerequisite for a Cabinet member—the ability to speak well. Cornwallis to Pitt, Jan. 23, 1792, *Cornwallis Correspondence,* edited by Charles Ross (3 vols.; London, 1859), II, 144–45.

48. Holden Furber, *Henry Dundas, First Viscount Melville, 1742–1811* (London, 1931), chaps. i–v, gives an able and fair account of Dundas.

49. See Chapter III.

50. Dundas certainly thought so. Dundas to Pitt, July 9, 1794, Wimbledon, P.R.O. 30/8/127 (Chatham MSS); copy in G.D. 51/1/24/3, General Register House, Edinburgh.

1794.[51] Dundas moved to the new department, and William Henry Cavendish (Bentinck), third Duke of Portland, aged fifty-six, became Home Secretary. He had been Lord Lieutenant of Ireland during Rockingham's administration, April to August 1782, and First Lord of the Treasury during the coalition. At Rockingham's death he became head of the Whig party.[52]

Historians as well as some of Portland's contemporaries have often represented him as weak, vacillating, and incapable of decisive action.[53] This description does not apply to the Duke while he served as head of the Home Office. His habit of writing on the backs of official letters received in the Office conclusively proves that he read and personally drafted answers to great numbers of letters each month. On the back of one letter is the notation in Portland's hand that his draft should be kept in the office as "it was so late that I kept no copy of my answer."[54] His letters appear succinct and forceful, although his style and indirectness occasionally antagonized people.[55] While in office, he carried out the reforms recommended by the parliamentary commission of 1786 and followed Dundas' plans to retire ineffective clerks.

Turberville has observed that Portland had no "illusions as to his own abilities; he was devoid of personal ambition. As he was not ambitious for himself, so he was never jealous."[56] Portland's evenness of temper and lack of jealousy probably explain why he could lead the Whig party, which contained as diverse and independent a collection of men as one might find, and also serve in the Cabinet of William Pitt, a strong-willed man who liked his own way. Once Portland joined the Cabinet, there does not appear to have been a

51. J. H. Rose, *William Pitt and the Great War* (London, 1912), pp. 271–72. The negotiations became entangled, because Portland refused the Home Office shorn of the colonies, and Dundas did not want to lose the patronage of the colonies and Scotland. Dundas finally gave in to the importunities of Pitt and the King. The relevant letters may be found in H.M.C., *Dropmore Papers,* II, 595–98; Stanhope, *Life of Pitt,* II, 254–55; *Later Correspondence of George III,* II, 222–23; and J. Holland Rose, *Pitt and Napoleon: Essays and Letters* (London, 1912), pp. 250–51.

52. P.C. 2/138; *History of Parliament,* II, 84–85.

53. The sketch in the *DNB,* II, 302–304 is, however, quite fair to Portland, as is the lengthy account by Arthur Stanley Turberville, *A History of Welbeck Abbey and Its Owners* (2 vols.; London, 1939), II, chaps. iii–xiv.

54. The Reverend David Hughes to Portland, Jesus College, Oxford, Sept. 7, 1800, H.O. 42/51.

55. For example, *Cornwallis Correspondence,* III, 262–66; Henry Richard Vassall (Fox), third Baron Holland, *Memoirs of the Whig Party During My Time,* edited by Henry Edward, fourth Baron Holland (2 vols.; London, 1852–54), I, 165–66.

56. Turberville, *History of Welbeck Abbey,* II, 319–20.

single instance of his acting treacherously toward Pitt, whom he formerly opposed for nearly twelve years. His judicious exercise of the enormous police power that he possessed by virtue of his office during the disorders in England commands respect.[57] In accordance with some arrangements made by Henry Addington, who replaced Pitt as First Lord in February 1801, Portland resigned as Home Secretary on July 30, 1801, to become Lord President of the Council.

Although the preceding pages have shown that seven different men served as head of the Home Office from 1782 through mid-1801, the basic duties that each performed as Secretary of State did not alter significantly during the period. The responsibilities of the Home Secretary may be divided into three general categories: administrator, Cabinet minister, and servant of the king. As administrator he directed the work of his office; as minister he participated in the decisions of state; and as servant of the king he received and carried out the wishes of the sovereign. Unlike most modern Secretaries, he did not always speak for his department in Parliament.

The Secretary had responsibility for the general direction and supervision of the department of which he was head. It does not appear that any person in the Office made major decisions without the knowledge of the Secretary. Although there may be some question as to how much work Lord Sydney actually did, the other Secretaries read most of the incoming letters, made many of the final decisions, and often drafted the replies. The Secretary gave directions to the Undersecretaries, who in turn supervised the clerks.[58]

The Secretary laid most important business before the Cabinet. The registers of dispatches circulated among the ministers attest to the prevalence of interdepartmental consultation, especially on colonial and Irish affairs. At least, it appears, the other ministers saw, if they did not actually consider in the Cabinet, a large number of

57. See Chapters VII and VIII. The records I saw show no trace of the £20,000 to £30,000 said to have been borrowed by Portland from H.O. funds. (*Later Correspondence of George III,* III, xxi, 566 n.) Perhaps he had repaid the sum by Sept. 1801, when his secret service accounts were audited.

58. The correspondence between Grenville and his Undersecretaries in the Spencer Bernard MSS makes this procedure quite clear. The MSS are in the possession of Dr. J. G. C. Spencer Bernard of Nether Winchendon House, Aylesbury, Buckinghamshire. I am indebted to him for permission to examine and cite from them. The National Register of Archives has a report on these MSS. Further details on the departmental duties of the Secretary appear throughout the book. Chapter II describes more exactly the relationship of the Secretary and Undersecretaries.

dispatches to and from the Home Office. When the Cabinet met, it probably deliberated on the most critical decisions and left the Home Secretary to implement the decisions. Many times Pitt and the other ministers probably perfunctorily examined the dispatches sent in circulation, approved the course of action recommended by the Home Secretary, and returned them to him for execution. The influence that any Home Secretary had in the Cabinet depended more upon his personal qualities and his standing with Pitt than upon the office he held.

Communication with the sovereign always constituted a major duty of the Secretary of State. The Secretary himself, rather than any of his subordinates, generally corresponded with the king, and he submitted nearly all significant incoming and outgoing dispatches for the King's information and approval. Considering the diligence of George III, he probably read most of the material that passed before him. A general examination of King George's correspondence reveals that he sometimes objected to a particular course that the ministers intended to follow, or occasionally suggested some amendment to a dispatch. Most often, however, he gave his ready approval.

Much of the correspondence between the Home Secretary and the king concerned formal or routine matters. The Secretary submitted all warrants to the king for his approval and signature; seldom was there any difficulty respecting them. Often the king received from the Secretary accounts of debates or votes in the Houses of Parliament. The Secretary arranged meetings of the Privy Council to enable the king to give the royal assent to bills passed by the Irish parliament and of the "grand" or "nominal" cabinet to hear the report of the recorder of London on capital convicts. He also made appointments for individuals, or representatives of counties, cities, boroughs, corporate bodies such as the South Sea Company, the universities, companies of artisans and merchants, and others to present addresses or petitions to the king. The Home Office prepared replies to those addressed requiring a response. Addresses to the king on the throne,[59] such as those presented by Parliament and

59. Nearly all petitions and addresses are in H.O. 55. See also Portland to the King, Nov. 28, 1795; and reply, Nov. 29. *Later Correspondence of George III*, II, 433; same to same, Dec. 7, 1795, *ibid.*, pp. 436–37.

convocations of the provinces of Canterbury or York traditionally received answers; those presented at the royal levee did not require replies.[60] Since the answers were largely formal in nature, their preparation by the Home Office entailed only clerical work. The king also signified through the Secretary of State his pleasure regarding the many applications from persons requesting permission to pass through the gates of the Horse Guards and ride through St. James's Park to avoid the crowded streets. If the king approved the request, the Secretary directed the Gold Stick in Waiting at the Horse Guards (the commander of the First Life Guards) and the ranger of St. James's Park to grant the necessary permission.[61]

The emoluments that the Secretaries received for their services were handsome but certainly not exorbitant. From 1782 to 1795 the income of the Secretaries came from a variety of sources. The king's civil list paid the basic salary of £5,580, and the patent appointing each Secretary of State carried with it a salary of £100. In addition the Home Secretary received 55 per cent of the Home Office's share of fees. (Half of the fees went to the Foreign Office.) The two Secretaries of State also divided equally part of the profits from the *London Gazette*—the official government newspaper. In 1784, for example, Lord Sydney received about £2,520 in fees and about £300 from the *London Gazette*. His gross receipts for 1784 amounted to about £8,500.

From the gross receipts of office each Secretary had to pay certain expenses. Taxes and other charges on the salary consumed over £1,600, and a tax of one shilling in the pound (or 5 per cent) on the fees (but not on the *Gazette* profits) took another £112. Sydney disbursed £112 for coals, candles, and miscellaneous items for his office and paid almost £900 in salaries to the clerks and others in the office proper, and another £800 to the Undersecretary and clerks in

60. See Portland to the King, Oct. 3, 1800, *Later Correspondence of George III*, III, 421–22, for an interesting dispute over the different manner of presenting addresses.

61. The relevant letters are scattered in H.O. 42 and 43. Most requests were granted, but in 1791 Grenville restricted access to the Park to persons engaged in public business (Grenville to the Earl of Shrewsbury, Feb. 23, 1791, H.O. 43/3). Lord Fife complained that he had repeatedly asked permission, but still had "to go through the horrid Streets of Westm[inste]r. . . ." (Fife to Dundas, June 5, 1792, Mar Lodge, H.O. 42/20.) In 1799 fifty-two persons, mostly government officials, had permission to pass through the Park in carriages (Earl of Euston, ranger of St. James's Park, to Portland, April 30, 1799, H.O. 42/47). The Gold Sticks for this period were the fifth Marquis of Lothian (1737–1815), 1777–89; Lord Dover (1724–92), 1789–92; the third Earl of Harrington (1753–1829), 1792–1829.

the Plantation Department. These expenses reduced his income in 1784 to the net sum of £5,000.[62]

The absence of the account books for the years before 1791 makes it difficult to ascertain the exact receipts and expenses, but they were probably similar to those of 1784. There is no reason to suppose that the expenses rose or decreased significantly; as the salary remained the same, only the fees and *Gazette* receipts could fluctuate. The average *Gazette* receipts remained at almost exactly what they had been in 1784—£300.[63] The average of the fees received net by the Secretary of State was £1,830 per annum, £700 less than in 1784. In an average year, therefore, the Home Secretary netted about £4,300.[64]

In compliance with the recommendation of the commissioners appointed by Parliament in 1786, with which the Secretaries of State concurred, an Order in Council in February 1795 directed the Secretaries to surrender their rights to the salaries and fees that they had previously enjoyed, in return for a salary of £6,000 per annum clear of all deductions. The grant was made retroactive to January 12, 1792, for Grenville and Dundas, and to July 11, 1794, for Portland.[65] The fees formerly received by the Secretaries went into a common fund along with nearly all other fees collected by the offices. From this fund the Secretaries and other officers received their salaries.[66]

The position of Home Secretary was nearly always held by men of the first standing. Shelburne, North, and Portland were the leaders of particular factions in coalition governments. Grenville and Dundas were Pitt's closest associates and advisers. Sydney perhaps had

62. *First Report, 1786,* pp. 5–6; Appendix 2, p. 20. Sydney had not received his fees as of the date of the report. The percentage of the fees received by the Secretary is figured from *Sixteenth Report, 1797,* Appendix C.4, p. 321. All figures are rounded off.

63. *Sixteenth Report, 1797,* p. 302 n.

64. *Ibid.,* Appendix C.4, p. 321. The figures are derived by dividing the fees received by the Secretaries in half for a given year, deducting £300 (the amount of *Gazette* profits, since they were not taxed), deducting the amount of the 5 per cent tax, and then averaging the amounts received between 1785 and 1790.

65. *Ibid.,* Appendix A.1, pp. 309–11. Grenville, then Foreign Secretary, renounced his salary for 1794 and fees of office from January 12, 1792, to January 5, 1795, amounting to £12,006. Dundas, Secretary for War, relinquished his salary from January 12, 1792, to January 12, 1795, but retained the fees; nevertheless, he gave up almost £8,000 by so doing. Portland relinquished a little over £3,360—the amount of fees which he had received in excess of his salary from July 11, 1794, to January 5, 1795 (*ibid.,* p. 303; Appendix E.1, 2, 3, pp. 321–22).

Legally the three Secretaries could have retained the entire receipts, but that would certainly have appeared greedy. Grenville also renounced from his salary the amount of the income from his sinecure office of Auditor of the Exchequer. H.M.C., *Dropmore Papers,* II, 511–13.

66. *Sixteenth Report, 1797,* Appendix A.1, p. 310.

less political status than the others. All came from prominent families—as would be expected in an eighteenth-century ministry. Being head of the Home Office was but part of their public life, for all were members of Parliament and of the Cabinet. Most simultaneously held at least one additional public office. Ability as a speaker in either House of Parliament was not a requisite for office; only Grenville and Dundas spoke with any regularity.

All six men (Temple being excluded) were competent. Sydney was unenergetic, but the others conscientiously carried out their duties. Only Shelburne, however, can be considered imaginative. In the cases of Grenville, Dundas, and Portland, ability to master the details of office procedure, industry, and resoluteness (born perhaps of a confidence in their class and traditions) compensated for the absence of constructive imagination.

Chapter Two

UNDERSECRETARIES OF STATE

Ordinarily two Undersecretaries of State served in the Home Office at any one time. Nineteenth-century terminology labeled one as "permanent" and the other as "parliamentary," but this classification does not hold true for the preceding century.[1] Although the commissioners in 1786 recommended that the Home and Foreign offices always retain a permanent Undersecretary despite changes in administration,[2] the Secretaries objected, because they wanted the option of either continuing or removing the Undersecretaries whom they found in the offices. The Secretaries conceded, however, that in practice one Undersecretary in each office generally did remain, and that the arrangement had advantages for the business of the offices.[3] During this period there were, in fact, two permanent Undersecretaries, Evan Nepean from 1782 to 1794 and John King from 1794 to 1806. They technically lacked the security afforded by the modern civil service, but both remained in government service most of their lives.

Although there is good cause for labeling one of the Undersecretaries as "permanent," there can be no justification for referring to the other as "parliamentary." Of the nine men who successively held the second Undersecretaryship, three did not even sit in the House of Commons; the other six were not active parliamentarians. John Thomas Townshend, for example, the Undersecretary from 1784 to 1789, sat in the Commons after April 1786, but evidently never made a speech.[4] His successor from 1789 to 1792, Scrope Bernard,

1. Joseph Haydn, *The Book of Dignities,* 3rd edition revised by Horace Ockerby (London, 1894), pp. 227–28, lists the Undersecretaries in the late eighteenth century under those two classifications. The distinction is not valid even for the first two or three decades of the nineteenth century. For example, see *The Diary of Henry Hobhouse,* edited by Arthur Aspinall (London, 1947), p. v.

2. *First Report, 1786,* p. 10. 3. *Sixteenth Report, 1797,* Appendix A.1, p. 309.

4. Namier and Brooke, *History of Parliament,* III, 553–54.

spoke once about Home Office affairs.[5] After 1792, only one Undersecretary, Charles Greville, sat in Parliament, and he for only two months.[6]

George Canning, when he was considering taking a public office in March 1795, made the following observation about the Undersecretaryships in the Home Office:

> I mentioned [to Pitt] one of the under secretaryships of State in the Duke of Portland's department, which was now vacant. . . . I knew that these offices had not of late years been considered as Parliamentary ones, having been filled chiefly by private men, but I considered that as no objection, or at least as one of no great Weight, & the Business of the Secretary of State's Office was I thought such as would at once open to me great opportunities of general information, & assign to me also, in some measure, in the House of Commons, that sort of province, which I have described as so desireable.[7]

Canning, however, went to the Foreign Office; the Home department continued to have Undersecretaries who were politically inactive. Specialization of departmental functions had not reached the point where the Secretary of State required an Undersecretary specifically to assist him in preparing official business to be presented in Parliament. More strikingly, no Undersecretary had to represent the Home Office in the House of Commons, although for over eleven years in this period the Secretary of State sat in the House of Lords. For this second Undersecretary the adjective private rather than parliamentary would be more applicable.

Two Undersecretaries worked in the office of the Secretary of State for the Southern Department in March 1782. Sir Stanier Porten had been there since December 1770, and before that in the Northern Department for two years. Shortly before the change of ministers in early 1782, Porten requested a pension that had been promised to him as early as 1778. The King consented,[8] and Porten

5. Bernard spoke on May 12, 1791, on the Canada Act. John Debrett (compiler), *The Parliamentary Register or History of the Proceedings and Debates of the House of Commons [and the House of Lords]*, XXIX, 409, 413; hereafter cited as Debrett, *Parl. Reg.*

6. Greville sat as M.P. for Petersfield Borough from January 12, 1795, until the dissolution of that Parliament on May 20, 1796. Great Britain, Parliament, House of Commons, *[Official Returns of the] Members of Parliament* (2 vols.; London, 1878), II, 193. He became Undersecretary on March 14, 1796; consequently, he sat for only two months while in the Home Office. There is no record of his having spoken in the House. Thomas Brodrick, William Wickham, and Edward Finch Hatton did not have seats.

7. Dorothy Marshall, *The Rise of George Canning* (London, 1938), p. 109.

8. The King to Lord North, March 25, 1782, *Correspondence of George III*, V, 413.

retired on March 27, when he supposedly told Lord Shelburne "God be thanked I am not to be under you again."[9]

John Bell served as Porten's colleague in the Southern Department. He had been a junior commissioner of the Office for Sick and Hurt Seamen from 1756 to 1763, and first commissioner of that office from August 1773 to January 1781, when he accepted the appointment as Undersecretary with the understanding that he would succeed Porten as "what is considered the fix'd and Resident" Undersecretary. He replaced Porten ostensibly on March 27, 1782.[10] The additional work arising from the incorporation of the duties of the old Colonial Office proved too much for Bell's eyesight, and being nearly sixty years old, he asked Shelburne for permission to retire upon a promised pension. Shelburne apparently consented.[11] Bell's last day in office seems to have been April 23, 1782.[12]

Immediately upon being appointed Home Secretary, Shelburne brought with him into office a new Undersecretary and a remarkable man—Evan Nepean. Although Bell technically replaced Porten

9. H.M.C., "Knox MSS," *Various Collections,* VI, 283; Porten, the uncle of Edward Gibbon, served as commissioner of customs 1782–1786. He died on June 7, 1789. *DNB,* XVI, 167. 10. "Case of Mr. Bell" [Feb. 28, 1783], H.O. 42/2.

11. *Ibid.*; Bell to Shelburne, April 9, 1782, Shelburne MSS, Vol. 168, Clements Library.

12. The last letter signed by Bell was on this date. Bell to Matthew Lewis, H.O. 50/378. Thomas Orde entered the office on the following day. Shelburne evidently did not get Bell a pension, but told him that he must return to the Sick and Hurt Office to seek reinstatement ("Case of Mr. Bell," H.O. 42/2). There is no record of his appearing on that establishment at the time of the report in 1788 (*Seventh Report of the Commissioners Appointed to Inquire into Fees . . . in Public Offices: The Sick and Hurt Office, 20 March 1788,* H. of C. 309, pp. 507–47; *PP 1806,* VII).

Bell, the son of William Bell of East Greenwich, Kent (probably the commissioner of the Sick and Hurt Office of that name), was admitted to Lincoln's Inn on April 16, 1741, and called to the bar on June 19, 1747; he declined a call to the bench on December 14, 1772. He married on December 8, 1753, Jane Bradshaw of Watford, Hertfordshire, in the chapel at Lincoln's Inn (*The Records of the Honourable Society of Lincoln's Inn. Admissions from* A.D. *1421 to . . .* A.D. *1893, and Chapel Registers* [2 vols.; London, 1896], I, 422, 644; *ibid., The Black Books* [4 vols.; London, 1897–1902], III, 339, 413, 427).

John Bell married the widow of his cousin. She was born on December 3, 1717, and died on October 24, 1771. Bell's friend, the great Dr. Samuel Johnson, wrote the inscription for the tomb of his deceased wife. Bell died on August 4, 1797, at his house in Fludyer Street, Whitehall, aged seventy-two, and was buried in the church at Watford. Robert Clutterbuck, *The History and Antiquities of the County of Hertford* (3 vols.; London, 1815–27), I, 266–67; [James Boswell] *Boswell's Life of Johnson,* edited by George Birkbeck and rev. and enlarged by L. F. Powell (6 vols.; Oxford, 1934–64), II, 204, n. 1; *Gentleman's Magazine,* LXVI (Aug., 1796), 706.

Bell's brother William (1731–1816) was domestic chaplain and secretary to Princess Amelia (1710–1786), aunt of George III. Through her influence he became a prebendary of Westminster in 1865 (*DNB,* II, 176–77; John Venn and J. A. Venn [eds.], *Alumni Cantabrigienses: A Biographical List of All Known Students, Graduates and Holders of Office at the University of Cambridge, from the Earliest Times to 1900* [10 vols.; Cambridge, 1922–54], Pt. II, VI, 219).

as permanent Undersecretary, it was Nepean who remained in the post under five different Secretaries till July 11, 1794, when he followed Dundas to the new War Department as his Undersecretary. Precisely how he came to know Lord Shelburne is not certain, but Shelburne's friend and follower Captain John Jervis probably recommended him.[13] Nepean had served as purser aboard Jervis' ship in 1780, and enjoyed his friendship thereafter.[14]

Nepean came from a Cornwall family, apparently of small fortune. One brother entered the Royal Engineers and another the Army. Both eventually rose to the rank of lieutenant general. Nepean went to sea, where he served as purser aboard several ships, including Jervis'. In 1782 he acted as secretary to the port admiral at Plymouth before coming to the Home Office.[15] On June 6, 1782, he married Margaret Skinner, only daughter of Captain William Skinner and granddaughter of General William Skinner of the Royal Engineers, Chief Engineer of Great Britain.[16] He had four sons and one daughter; two of the sons and possibly the daughter were born while he was Undersecretary in the Home Office.[17]

Nepean's service in that office bears out his reputation for diligence, energy, and hard work. William Knox found him "intelligent, attentive and obliging."[18] In 1791 Grenville wrote to his brother that the death of George Augustus Selwyn

> gives me the disposal of his office in Barbadoes, of between £400 and £500 per annum, but it can be held only by a resident. I feel myself bound, in the first instance, to offer [it] to Nepean, who is killing himself by his labour here, to give it to any proper person who will vacate anything for it here.[19]

Buckingham replied that "Nepean has clearly the first claim upon your goodness. . . ."[20] William Huskisson, upon his first meeting Nepean in regard to his appointment as head of the new Alien Office, wrote to a friend that he "had constantly met with the

13. Jervis was knighted May 28, 1782, promoted to admiral in 1787, and created Earl of St. Vincent in 1797. He sat for one of Shelburne's boroughs. *History of Parliament*, II, 682. 14. *DNB*, XIV, 222–23. 15. *Ibid.*

16. *DNB*, XIV, 222–23 and XVIII, 350–51.

17. *Burke's Genealogical and Heraldic History of the Peerage, Baronetage and Knightage* (99th ed.; London, 1949), pp. 1474–75.

18. *Extra Official State Papers*, p. 26.

19. To Buckingham, Feb. 4, 1791, Buckingham, *Court and Cabinets of George III*, II, 188.

20. Feb. 6, 1791, H.M.C., *Dropmore Papers*, II, 29; see also David Parry, Governor of Barbados, to Nepean, May 19, 1791, C.O. 28/63.

greatest civility from Mr. Nepean the Under Secretary, no less remarkable for his indefatigable attention to business, than for his upright & honorable conduct."[21]

From 1789 to 1792 Nepean's extremely poor health prevented his regular attendance at the Office. In late 1789 he wrote to his colleague Scrope Bernard from Bath, where he had gone for his health: "London for ever! I am never easy when I am out of it, and you may be assured that [I shall] not continue here a moment longer than I am obliged so to do. I found myself completely tired of this abominable place the first day."[22] After early January 1790 he seems to have improved,[23] but in the autumn of 1791 he found himself so unwell that he had to leave town.[24] In early December he departed for the West Indies to seek a better climate for the winter.[25] He held two sinecure offices in Jamaica in reversion to the incumbent, who died about this time, but it was undoubtedly his health rather than any punctiliousness in observing the law requiring actual residence to hold such offices that brought him to the West Indies.[26] He returned to England by June 1792.[27]

Although Nepean's health gave way in late summer 1792 and his going abroad again was mentioned,[28] he does not appear to have left. By February 1793 his friend Alexander Davison could write, "I am glad to tell you our friend Nepean is in perfect health, and instead of the extraordinary load of business [of war] he has had upon his shoulders affecting him, it has had a contrary effect."[29] Davison later remarked that Nepean's time was so occupied "that it is melancholy at times to see him. I may without exaggeration say almost the whole official business is now thrown upon his shoulders, and it is the astonishment of every person how he holds . . . out."[30] But Nepean

21. To William Hayley, Whitehall, Sept. 12, 1793, Huskisson Papers, British Museum Additional MS 38,754, ff. 77–78.

22. Nov. 8, 1789, Bath, Spencer Bernard MSS, O.E. 7/3.

23. Mrs. Margaret Nepean to Bernard, St. James's Place, Jan. 13, 1790. *Ibid.*, O.E. 7/6. Nepean was unwell as of the date of this letter, but seems to have attended the office with regularity until the autumn of 1791.

24. Nepean to Bernard, Sept. 20, 1791, *ibid.*, O.E. 7/7.

25. The last letter signed by him was on November 30, 1791, H.O. 37/1.

26. Manning, *British Colonial Government*, p. 94.

27. The first letter is dated June 7, to Justice Bond, H.O. 43/4.

28. Dundas to Grenville, Aug. 30, 1792, H.M.C., *Dropmore Papers*, II, 306; Sir John Jervis to Nepean, Nov. 9, 1792, H.O. 44/41.

29. To John Graves Simcoe, Lieutenant Governor of Upper Canada, *The Correspondence of Lieut. Governor John Graves Simcoe*, edited by E. A. Cruikshank (5 vols.; Toronto, 1923–1931), I, 287. For Davison (1750–1824), see *DNB*, V, 624–25.

30. To Simcoe, April 29, 1793, *ibid.*, I, 320.

31. *Ibid.*, pp. 193–94, 415.

remained well for the rest of his years at the Home Department.[31] His career continued to be distinguished and successful after he left the Home Office on July 11, 1794. In 1802 he received a baronetcy.

During the twelve years that Nepean served as Undersecretary he had five different colleagues.[32] After the retirement of John Bell, Shelburne appointed Thomas Orde, later Lord Bolton, as Undersecretary on April 24, 1782. Edmund Burke suggested, probably quite correctly, the reason for this appointment:

> Lord Shelburne . . . is furnished with the most active member of the committee of secrecy [on the affairs of the East India Company] (Mr. Orde) which not only gives him the means of accomplishing his ends, but connects him with the advocate Dundas whose peculiar object (I know) is to be a principal governor in that department.[33]

Dundas had, indeed, brought Orde to the Home Office for the express purpose of introducing him to Shelburne.[34] When Shelburne became First Lord of the Treasury in July, Orde followed him to serve as secretary to the Treasury.[35]

Orde exchanged offices with Henry Strachey, who had been at the Treasury and now moved to the Home Office. Strachey has been called a "quasi civil servant." He was private secretary to Lord Clive from 1764 to 1775, secretary to the Howe commission to America, 1776–78, clerk of deliveries at the Ordnance, 1778–80, and chief storekeeper, 1780–82. The knowledge of American affairs that he gained while secretary to the Howe commission may be the reason for his appointment to the Home Office, which had responsibility for the peace negotiations in Paris.[36] He went to Paris to strengthen the British peace commission, and except for one return to London for

32. William Knox, Undersecretary in the old Colonial Office, certainly assisted in the business of the Home Office for a month after the reorganization in 1782, but Shelburne explicitly told him that his office had been suppressed and that no new Undersecretary in the Home Office had replaced him. Knox should not, therefore, be considered as having been on the Home Office establishment. H.M.C., "Knox MSS," *Various Collections,* VI, 285; [Knox] *Extra Official State Papers,* pp. 2–37, especially pp. 26–37 for the suppression of his office.

33. To the Marquis of Rockingham, April 27, 1782, *Correspondence of Edmund Burke,* edited by Thomas Copeland and others (5 vols. to date; Cambridge and Chicago, since 1958), IV, 448–50.

34. Knox to Shelburne, April 23, 1782, but in error for April 26, H.M.C., "Knox MSS," *Various Collections,* VI, 183, 285.

35. Orde's later career may be followed in the *History of Parliament,* III, 232–34, and the *DNB,* XIV, 1133–35.

36. *History of Parliament,* III, 487–89; *DNB,* XXII, 1236–37.

instructions, remained in Paris from October 28, 1782,[37] till at least the first week in December.[38] John Adams described him as "as artfull and insinuating a Man as they could send. He pushes and presses every Point as far as it can possibly go. He is the most eager, earnest, pointed Spirit."[39] Strachey did not long remain at the Home department. In April 1783 the coalition appointed him to his former office of clerk of deliveries at the Ordnance,[40] and George Augustus North, Lord North's twenty-five-year-old son, replaced him as Undersecretary. The Home Office papers have little trace of this man. In any case, his stay was brief, for he left office when Lord North was dismissed on December 18.[41]

Nepean served as sole Undersecretary from the time of North's dismissal to February 19, 1784, when Lord Sydney appointed his son John Thomas Townshend,[42] who was two days short of his twentieth birthday. Young Townshend did not take an active part in the business of the Office. From June to December 1785 he was on the Grand Tour of Europe.[43] He left the Office with his father in June 1789, when he was appointed a Lord of the Admiralty.[44]

When Grenville moved to the Home Department, he brought with him his friend from Oxford days, Scrope Bernard, third son of Sir Francis Bernard, Governor of Massachusetts from 1760 to 1771. Scrope Bernard served as Lord Temple's private secretary while Temple was Lord Lieutenant of Ireland from 1782 to 1783; became

37. Samuel Flagg Bemis, *The Diplomacy of the American Revolution* (rev. ed.; Edinburgh and London, 1957), p. 232.

38. *The Adams Papers: Diary and Autobiography of John Adams,* L. H. Butterfield, editor in chief (4 vols.; Cambridge, Mass., 1961), III, 81–85.

39. Diary entry for Nov. 4, 1782, *ibid.,* p. 46.

40. The appointment was gazetted April 12, 1783. *Gentleman's Magazine,* LIII (April, 1783), 367.

For his later life see *DNB,* XXII, 1236–37; Charles Richard Sanders, *The Strachey Family 1588–1932* (Durham, N. C., 1953), pp. 65–81; H.M.C., "Manuscripts in the possession of Sir Edward Strachey, Bart., &c &c, Sutton Court, Somersetshire," *Sixth Report,* Part I, pp. 395–404. The National Register of Archives has a report on the Strachey MSS.

41. Young North succeeded his father as third Earl of Guilford on August 5, 1792, and died in 1802 (*History of Parliament,* III, 212; *DNB,* XIV, 608–609). I could not locate any of his papers. Those of his father in the Bodleian Library at Oxford pertain to the period before 1783. The North MSS in the Kent County Archives are mostly the papers of the first and fifth Earls of Guilford.

42. *First Reports, 1786,* Appendix 1, p. 19.

43. *Ibid.*; J. T. Townshend to Sir Robert Murray Keith, British ambassador in Vienna, March 12, 1787, Keith Papers, Add. MS 35,538, ff. 60–61.

44. *History of Parliament,* III, 553–54; G[eorge] E[dward] C[okayne], *The Complete Peerage of England, Scotland, Ireland, Great Britain and the United Kingdom,* new edition revised by Vicary Gibbs and others (12 vols. in 13; London, 1910–59), XII, Pt. I, 592; Venn and Venn, *Alumni Cantabrigienses,* Pt. II, VI, 219.

secretary to the commission for investigating fees and gratuities in public offices from 1785 to 1786; and then again went as private secretary to Lord Buckingham during his second term as Lord Lieutenant from 1787 to 1789.[45] He set forth his reasons for accepting the post in the Home Office in a letter to his father-in-law:

> . . . In order to set myself right with the world after my late expenses and enable Harriet [his wife] and my self to settle quietly on this side of the water, I intended taking a permanent office here, superior in emolument, but less pleasant in point of labour and confinement in London, in lieu of the temporary office held in Ireland on much easier and more comfortable terms. . . . I had originally determined never to take an office in London, which would confine me so much to London as the Under Secretaryship of State. . . . However little I might like the office, I should not get one of equal emolument and advantage if this opportunity was suffered to pass by.[46]

The historian of the Bernard family observed of Scrope that "all through life the routine of office work was most distasteful to . . . [Scrope's] nervous, excitable nature. . . ."[47]

Bernard, aged thirty in June 1789, may not have liked office life, but he was the only nonpermanent Undersecretary, with the exception of William Wickham, to do any significant amount of work. The many memoranda and letters among his private papers[48] and the frequent appearance of his name in the Home Office papers leave no doubt of this. Though particularly active during the illness of Nepean, Bernard ordinarily confined his attention to colonial affairs.

After Nepean's return from the West Indies in June 1792, Bernard's name does not often appear in the official papers, nor are his private papers full for this period.[49] The payment of a regular salary to his successor, John King, began on August 23, 1792, which was probably Bernard's last day as Undersecretary.[50] Upon his retirement, his father-in-law, in trust for Bernard's wife, received a pension of £554 for the life of Harriet Bernard.[51] He was admitted an

45. *History of Parliament,* II, 87.
46. To William Morland, June 7, 1789, Higgins, *The Bernards of Abingdon and Nether Winchendon,* III, 126–27. 47. *Ibid.,* p. 93. 48. Spencer Bernard MSS.
49. The last letter was to Philip Deare, July 5, 1792, H.O. 43/4.
50. Bernard referred to his having resigned in the autumn of 1792 in a letter to Grenville, July 1794, Doctors' Commons, P.R.O. 30/8/113 (Chatham Papers).
51. The date of the pension is October 2, 1792. *Annual Register,* LX (1798), Appendix to Chronicle, p. 176.

advocate at Doctors' Commons on November 3, 1789;[52] thereafter he did not take part in public affairs.

John King, who was eventually to replace Nepean as permanent Undersecretary, entered the Home Office in 1791, probably because of the illness of Nepean. Born in Clitheroe, Lancashire, in 1760, King was the fifth son of James King, chaplain to the House of Commons and dean of Raphoe in Ireland. John King attended Oxford, where he received his B.A. in 1781 and his M.A. in 1784. In 1781 he entered Lincoln's Inn, but migrated to Gray's Inn on June 4, 1790, and was called to the bar as barrister five days later.[53] On April 9, 1792, King married Harriet Moss, daughter of the Right Reverend Charles Moss, Bishop of Bath and Wells, by whom he had four sons and one daughter.[54]

King's political connections had always been with the Burkes. His brother Walker, who served as private secretary to the Marquis of Rockingham, was one of Edmund Burke's closest friends. There are, indeed, numerous extant letters between John King and Edmund Burke himself, his brother Richard, and his son Richard.[55] It is possible that the ministers employed King as a means of conciliating Burke, who had separated from Fox in May 1791 over the issue of the French Revolution. In early August 1791, probably shortly after King came to the office, he wrote to Burke, at Lord Grenville's behest, to attempt to arrange an occasion when the Duke of Portland might signify his approval of certain resolutions defending the constitution.[56] King may, however, have been known both to Grenville and to Scrope Bernard, since they all attended Christ Church, Oxford, at the same time.[57]

King acted as third Undersecretary from December 3, 1791, to August 23, 1792, the only occasion when three Undersecretaries simultaneously appeared on the Office payroll. Although Nepean's absence probably explains his appointment, King continued as Un-

52. Ernest Nys, *Le Droit Roman, le Droit des Gens et le Collège des Docteurs en Droit Civil* (Brussels, 1910), p. 154.

53. John Foster (ed.), *Alumni Oxonienses, the Members of the University of Oxford 1715–1886* (4 vols.; London, 1888), II, 795.

54. *Burke's Genealogical and Heraldic History of the Landed Gentry Including American Families with British Ancestry* (16th ed.; London, 1939), pp. 1294–95.

55. Thomas Copeland and Milton Shumway Smith, *A Check-List of the Correspondence of Edmund Burke* (Cambridge, 1955), pp. 271–72.

56. August 4, 1791, Fitzwilliam MSS, Sheffield Public Library; see also Edmund Burke to Grenville, Sept. 19, 1792, in which Burke refers to King as their mutual friend (H.M.C., *Dropmore Papers*, III, 466).

57. Foster, *Alumni Oxonienses*, II, 563, 795; III, 984.

dersecretary after Nepean's return and, later, Bernard's resignation. In effect, there were two permanent Undersecretaries from August 1792 to July 1794. After Nepean resigned in July, King remained as permanent Undersecretary for the next twelve years.

King seems to have been an able and competent man. He often did all the work of both Undersecretaries; but while he had an efficient colleague, he concentrated on colonial affairs. Unfortunately, he tended to be a trifle self-important. William Morton Pitt, M.P. for Dorset, came to the Home Office to secure a passport to go abroad, but had to write to Nepean, as "I found so much difficulty in procuring even a *short off-hand* and apparently doubtful answer, from the *great man* in your *outer room* yesterday, that I am Obliged to trouble *you*. . . ."[58] The reference could only have been to King. Canning, explaining a mistake in conveying some foreign dispatches, wrote that "as soon as Lord Grenville had read the despatches to-day, they were given to a messenger to be carried immediately to the king. The messenger, who knew no king so great as *John* King, carried them forthwith to *him*. . . ."[59] King must also have run afoul of *The Times*, for, in referring to the appointment of his colleague, Charles Greville, *The Times* remarked that "the public in general, and the West Indian merchants in particular will . . . now, at least, have a gentleman of polished manners and clear understanding with whom they can converse upon business."[60]

But King had his complaints, too. He wrote to his friend William Osgoode, Chief Justice of Lower Canada, that he had to spend his leisure time waiting upon half a dozen great men, and in return got kicked in the seat of the pants two or three times a week. Furthermore, he was glad to have his way one time in ten, even when he knew he was right.[61]

King resigned as Undersecretary in February 1806 to become secretary to the Treasury at the same time that Lord Grenville became First Lord. He remained a friend of Grenville for many years.[62] King sat as M.P. for Enniskillen from March 14 to October 24, 1806, when Parliament was dissolved.[63] He left his post at the

58. May 25, 1794, H.O. 1/2.
59. To Lord Morpeth, July 27, 1797, quoted in Arthur Aspinall, *Politics and the Press, c. 1780–1850* (London, 1949), p. 193.
60. *The Times*, May 17, 1796.
61. August 21, 1800, copy, H.O. 42/50.
62. Buckingham to Grenville, Feb. 10, 1806, H.M.C., *Dropmore Papers*, VIII, 21; Thomas Grenville to Lord Grenville, Sept. 21, 1817, *ibid.*, X, 431.
63. *Official Returns of Members of Parliament*, II, 228.

Treasury in 1806 to become Comptroller of Army Accounts, which he remained till he died in his sleep in February 1830, aged sixty-nine.[64]

While the Duke of Portland held the seals of the Home Office, King had four different men as colleagues. Thomas Brodrick, born April 17, 1756, was the second son of the third Viscount Midleton by his wife Albinia, sister of Lord Sydney.[65] After attending Cambridge and Lincoln's Inn, he was called to the bar in 1779. He served as an Irish M.P. in 1776, became King's Counsel for the Duchy of Lancaster in 1786, and was a counsel for the Admiralty from 1792 to 1794.[66] Lord Sydney unsuccessfully recommended him for a Welsh judgeship in 1788. At that time the Lord Chancellor informed the King that Brodrick

> has been represented to him as a man of general learning and of good proficiency in the knowledge of the Law, and moreover as a man of worth and much esteemed. But he is not of long standing at the Bar: nor is he yet in business. This is imputed, partly to the excessive modesty of his temper, and partly to some slight defect in his speech.[67]

His precise connection with Portland is unknown, but the Duke brought him into office with him on July 11, 1794. Brodrick began to take part in business and would have directed the Alien Office,[68] had he not fallen ill within a month of becoming Undersecretary. By September 5 he lost the power of speech.[69] He probably never attended the Office thereafter, and died January 13, 1795, aged thirty-eight.

King acted as sole Undersecretary till March 14, 1796, when Charles Greville succeeded Brodrick. Greville, born on November 2, 1782, was the fourth son of Fulke Greville, grandson of the fifth Lord Brooke. After attending Westminster School from 1773 to 1775, he entered the Army, but had risen only to the rank of captain when he retired in 1796. His good fortune in being appointed

64. *Gentleman's Magazine,* C (March, 1830) , 282.
65. *Burke's Peerage,* 99th ed., p. 1545.
66. Venn and Venn, *Alumni Cantabrigienses,* I, 390.
67. July 29, 1788, *Later Correspondence of George III,* I, 386–87.
68. William Wickham to Brodrick, Sept. 5, 1794, H.O. 1/2.
69. Brodrick to Portland, Sept. 6, 1794, PwF 1,635 Portland MSS. The catalog of Midleton MSS in the National Register of Archives in London does not list any letters of this Brodrick. It was not possible to examine the manuscripts. The Portland MSS are in the University of Nottingham. The National Register of Archives also has a report on them.

Undersecretary rested with his marriage in 1793 to Lady Charlotte Bentinck, eldest daughter of the Duke of Portland; his historical importance rests with his having sired the famous diarist, Charles Cavendish Fulke Greville.[70] Greville sat for Petersfield Borough from January 12, 1795, to the dissolution May 20, 1796, but was never again in Parliament.[71] His son, the diarist, observed that his father

> had some faults and many foibles, but he was exposed to great disadvantages in early youth; his education was neglected, and his disposition was spoilt. He was a man of a kind, amiable, and liberal disposition, and what is remarkable as he advanced in years his temper grew less irritable and more indulgent; he was cheerful, hospitable, and unselfish. He had at all times been a lively companion, and without much instruction, extensive information, or a vigorous understanding, his knowledge of the world in the midst of which he had passed his life, his taste and turn for humour, and his good-nature made him a very agreeable man.[72]

Others were less charitable. George Canning directed his friend the Reverend John Sneyd to go to Welbeck Abbey, Portland's country seat, as "you must fight for me against Ch. Greville who will be there, and who I understand has the audacity to abuse me—alleging that I abuse him (which is false) and that I have a great contempt for him (which is nearly true)."[73] Lord Minto described Lady Charlotte Greville as "an excellent woman, excessively attached to an object very unworthy of her."[74]

Greville became Undersecretary on March 14, 1796. In effect he served as *locum tenens* for William Wickham, who would have become Undersecretary had he not been in Switzerland.[75] Greville's name does not appear frequently in the Home Office papers, although it is in a number of letters between August 1796 and January 1797, probably while King was ill. Upon Wickham's return from Europe, Greville vacated the office, on February 28, 1798. He did

70. G. F. Russell Barker and Alan H. Stenning (eds.), *The Record of Old Westminsters* (2 vols.; London, 1928), I, 400.

71. Great Britain, *Members of Parliament,* II, 193.

72. *The Greville Memoirs, 1814–1860,* edited by Lytton Strachey and Roger Fulford (8 vols.; London, 1938), II, 317–19.

73. Josceline Bagot (ed.), *George Canning and His Friends* (2 vols.; London, 1909), I, 155.

74. [George, Prince of Wales] *Correspondence of George, Prince of Wales, 1770–1812,* edited by Arthur Aspinall (3 vols. to date; Oxford, since 1965), III, 237, n. 2.

75. Wickham to Henry Louis Wickham, March 27, 1831, *Correspondence of the Right Honourable William Wickham from the Year 1794,* edited by William Wickham (2 vols.; London, 1870), I, 4–8.

not again hold office (except for sinecures), and died on September 26, 1832.[76]

William Wickham, born in 1761, took his B.A. at Oxford in 1782 and subsequently studied civil law at Geneva. Several of his friends were powerful men—Grenville, Portland, and Charles Abbot.[77] In August 1792 he became a magistrate at the new police office in Whitechapel in East London.[78] From July 11 to December 9, 1794, he served as superintendent of the Alien Office,[79] but resigned to become chargé d'affaires in the Swiss cantons, whence he conducted espionage operations against France.[80]

Upon returning from Europe, Wickham replaced Greville on March 1, 1798. He immediately assumed all duties not connected with the colonies, which were King's responsibility. The official records clearly betoken his great energy and efficiency. But in June 1799 Wickham returned to Europe to begin his second espionage mission,[81] and evidently resigned with Portland's permission by January 4, 1801, the last date for which he received pay.[82] He remained in public life till the dismissal of the ministry of his friend Lord Grenville in 1807; thereafter he lived on his estates until his death in 1840.

The last Undersecretary for this period was (John Emilius Daniel) Edward Finch Hatton. Born on May 19, 1755, he was the second son of Edward Finch (who took the additional surname Hatton), a younger son of the Earl of Winchilsea and Nottingham. After attending Cambridge, Hatton was admitted to the Inner Temple in 1776 and was called to the bar in 1781.[83] His connection with Portland is unknown; he seems to have been offered the position of Undersecretary without solicitation. Hatton expressed hesitation at accepting it because of the importance and complicated nature of the work, but took office on the assurance that he would have Portland's indulgence and King's assistance.[84] He was Undersecre-

76. For the dates of his service see Account Book, 1795–1812, H.O. 82/16; for some of the letters he signed see H.O. 5/2. 77. *DNB*, XXI, 177–78.

78. Warrant, H.O. 38/5. 79. Portland to the Treasury, Sept. 26, 1795, H.O. 36/9.

80. Harvey Mitchell, *The Underground War Against Revolutionary France: The Missions of William Wickham 1794–1800* (Oxford, 1965), *passim*. 81. *Ibid.*, p. 229.

82. Account Book 1795–1811, H.O. 82/16; Wickham to Grenville, March 7, 1801, H.M.C., *Dropmore Papers*, VI, 465–67.

83. Venn and Venn, *Alumni Cantabrigienses*, Pt. II, II, 496; *Burke's Peerage*, 99th ed., p. 2156.

84. Edward F. Hatton to Portland, [Feb.]13, 1801, Lincoln's Inn, H.O. 42/56.

tary only from February 19 to August 17, 1801.[85] While in office he signed most of the correspondence with the Treasury.[86] Hatton apparently practiced law for most of the rest of his life; he was treasurer of the Inner Temple in 1823. He died unmarried, on January 10, 1841.[87]

The duty of the Undersecretary of State in the Home Office, Nepean told the commissioners in 1785, consisted of following "all such directions as he received from the Principal Secretary of State, to prepare drafts of all letters to persons of all descriptions in correspondence with the Office, whether of the most secret and confidential nature, or otherwise; he has the entire superintendence of the business of the Office."[88]

Whenever the Secretary directed that a letter be sent, the Undersecretary made a draft either from what the Secretary orally told him or from a draft that the Secretary himself had written. Portland, as we have seen, usually indicated the substance of a reply on the back of a letter, from which the Undersecretary drew up a more formal draft.[89] The Undersecretary, when he completed the approved draft, gave it to one of the clerks, who made the fair copy that went to the recipient and also transcribed the letter into the book containing copies of outgoing correspondence.[90]

Some understanding of the procedure may be gleaned from a note from King to Nepean in 1794:

> Mr. Dundas desired me to prepare a draft for Sir Ch[arles] Grey this Evening & be with him tomorrow by breakfast with it at Wimbledon. But my boy you have not acquainted me with what was settled . . . in regard to Sir Chs. & for which Mr. Dundas referred me to you. I was up this morning before 5 & must now go to sleep. But I shall be here tomorrow morning by seven & if you will put down on paper the points agreed upon & send them here I shall be obliged to you.[91]

85. Account Book 1795–1811, H.O. 82/16. 86. H.O. 36/11.
87. Venn and Venn, Pt. II, II, 496. His will (1841, f. 41 in Somerset House, dated Oct. 24, 1840, and proved Jan. 30, 1841) made his nephew, the tenth Earl of Winchilsea, residuary legatee. The present Lord Winchilsea has informed me that he has none of Hatton's papers. 88. *First Report, 1786,* Appendix 1, p. 19.
89. The correspondence between Bernard and Grenville and later Dundas makes the procedure pretty clear (Spencer Bernard MSS, O.E. 10 and O.E. 3); the correspondence between Wickham and Portland confirms it. Wickham MSS, Hampshire Record Office.
90. The Public Record Office, at some point in the past, culled all the drafts from the Home Office papers if copies existed in the ledger books; consequently, it is impossible to know for certain who wrote many of the letters. Note attached to an unsigned draft to the Hon. George Walpole, June 1801, H.O. 42/61.
91. [April 21, 1794] 11 P.M., H.O. 44/42.

Nepean also kept all accounts relating to Secret Service payments and made copies of all Secret Service letters in his own hand.[92] Perhaps King later did the same.

Besides the preparation of drafts and the supervision of the clerks, the Undersecretaries regularly had appointments in the office where interested persons consulted them on public business. Portland, for instance, directed King to see a Vincenzo Baretta about a shipment of grain which the merchant offered to bring from Naples.[93] The diary of William Smith reveals much about the Undersecretary's duties regarding such appointments. By July 5, 1786, Smith had reached the limit of his patience with the delays over his appointment as Chief Justice of Quebec. He recorded the following outburst of frustration:

> A verbal Answer [from Nepean] that he was dressing to go abroad & I should hear from him in the Course of the Day. As little probably to be depended upon as his Promise on Thursday to see me on Monday & then to call yesterday. Such a Conduct in private Life would instantly ruin any Man! Nepean is shameless! What a sure Wreck of Vertue to be hunted into Promises which he has not Power to fulfill & yet to be obliged to keep People in good Humour by Lying or lose the Favor of the Responsible Superior who by these Lies is to escape Censure!

But by afternoon Smith had mellowed a little as he wrote: "Poor Nepean! He knows not what to say & is willing to conceal Mr. Pitt's Contempt of the Secretary of State."[94]

The Undersecretaries received payment for their services from the public. From 1782 through 1794 the civil list granted each Undersecretary a salary of £500 (£452 after taxes). The Irish Concordatum Fund, as voted by the Irish Parliament, paid each man £50 per annum. Of the fees collected by the Home Office, 25 per cent belonged to the Undersecretaries; they divided the fees equally. Each Undersecretary received a share (about 25 per cent) of certain gratuities arising from the fees paid by persons appointed ambassadors and consuls. The returns from fees and gratuities varied slightly each year,[95] but the average between 1784 and 1791 was about

92. Nepean's Secret Service Account Book, 1782–1791, Sydney Papers, Clements Library.

93. Baretta to Portland, Oct. 28, 1800, No. 7 Cannon St., H.O. 42/52. The orders and date of appointment are on the back of the letter.

94. *Diary of William Smith,* II, 123–24.

95. *First Report, 1786,* p. 6; Appendixes 1 and 2, pp. 19–20.

£575.[96] From his official salary and fees, an Undersecretary averaged about £1,077 annually from 1784 to 1794. This figure conforms pretty well to what all but the permanent Undersecretaries received, at least as far as income from the Home Office is concerned.

The permanent Undersecretaries always received more than their annual, average income. When Nepean was sole Undersecretary from December 19, 1783, to February 19, 1784, the custom of the office allowed him to receive the salary and fees of the vacant post—in all £200. He had two windfalls during 1784. When the King put the Privy Seal into commission between March 8 and November 24, 1784, he received £318 for being one of the three commissioners. He also received £500, which was a 1.5 per cent commission for acting as agent for the government in purchasing presents for the Canadian Indians. Although Nepean informed the Commission in 1785 that he considered this commission a favor from the government rather than a perquisite of office,[97] he wrote to (probably) Lord Sydney in January 1784 that he wanted the commission, as it was the "only Doucer annexed to the office of Under Secretary. . . ."[98] There is no record of the commission's being granted after 1784, probably because Pitt objected to Nepean's having it, as he thought it not in keeping with the dignity of the office of Undersecretary.[99]

Nepean always held one permanent sinecure—that of Naval Officer of Grenada, Dominica, and St. Vincent, to which he had been appointed on March 3, 1783.[100] This office, which he executed by deputy, brought him £450 in 1784. It is not clear whether the post of Naval Officer continued to bring about £450 per year. If so, his income averaged about £1,500 each year, except in 1784, when he realized £2,547.[101] In June 1791 he received a grant in reversion of the offices of clerk of the peace and chief clerk of the Supreme Court in Jamaica.[102] He resigned the naval office in July 1792, probably when he succeeded to the Jamaican offices.[103] In 1820 the

96. *Sixteenth Report, 1797,* Appendix C.4, p. 32. I have divided the total of the second column by 4. The figure in this column evidently includes the receipt of £50 from the Irish Concordatum Fund, in which case the fees and gratuities for 1784 were £50 above those for the succeeding years.

97. *First Report, 1786,* Appendix 1, p. 19.

98. Dated Wed. Jan. 27 [1784]. The year is certainly correct, but Wednesday fell on the 28th, not the 27th. P.R.O. 30/8/163 (Chatham Papers).

99. Nepean to Sydney, Jan. 27 [1784], P.R.O. 30/8/163 (Chatham Papers).

100. Patent Rolls 19–43 George III, p. 169, C. 66.

101. *First Report, 1786,* Appendix 1, p. 19.

102. June 13, 1791. Patent Rolls 19–43 George III, p. 202, C. 66.

103. Warrant Book, C.O. 324/45.

two sinecures brought him £2,620.[104] As an additional security, Nepean's wife was granted a pension of £643 in 1792 to become effective upon the death of her husband or when he ceased to hold employment under government;[105] and in 1793 Nepean's eldest son was granted the reversion of his father's Jamaican offices.[106]

Nor was John King neglected. He always received £300 as law clerk of the Home Office.[107] The patent granting him the reversion of the post of Naval Officer in Jamaica passed the great seal in 1796.[108] He succeeded to the post shortly thereafter, and on January 27, 1798, his eldest son received the office in reversion to his father.[109] In 1820 the sinecure brought King £1,500 per annum.[110] Like Nepean's wife, King's also had a pension to begin at his death or whenever he should cease to hold office under the government. The pension amounted to £554.[111] In 1796 King's income was about £2,000, without the return from the naval office.

No other Undersecretary held a sinecure or pension while in the Home Office. As we have just seen, however, when Bernard retired, his wife received a pension of £554. His brother, Sir John Bernard, accepted a vacant office in the Barbados, but he had to live there, at least for a time.[112] Shortly after his retirement Charles Greville was appointed Naval Officer of Berbice, Demerara, and Essequibo in Guiana,[113] and in 1801 got the posts of secretary, registrar, and clerk of the council of Tobago.[114] Greville's eldest son, the diarist, received the offices of secretary to the council, steward general, and clerk of emoluments in Jamaica.[115] All the offices were sinecures.

An alteration in the mode of paying the Undersecretaries occurred in February 1795. The Order in Council directed the Undersecretaries to relinquish all former salaries, fees, and gratuities effective January 5, 1795, in return for a salary of £1,500 clear of all deductions. When one Undersecretary acted alone in the office, he might, at the discretion of the Secretary of State, receive one-third of

104. John Wade, *The Black Book; or Corruption Unmasked* (2 vols.; London, 1820), I, 67. 105. *Annual Register,* XL (1798), Appendix to Chronicle, pp. 179–80.
106. August 15, 1793. Patent Rolls 19–43 George III, p. 252, C. 66.
107. See Chapter III.
108. March 8, 1796. Patent Rolls 19–43 George III, p. 294, C. 66.
109. *Ibid.,* p. 331. 110. Wade, I, 56.
111. June 5, 1792. *Annual Register,* XL (1798), Appendix to Chronicle, p. 179.
112. June 3, 1791. Patent Rolls 19–43 George III, p. 210, C. 66; Grenville to Buckingham, Feb. 4, 1791, Buckingham, *Court and Cabinets of George III,* II, 188.
113. Oct. 10, 1798, C.O. 324/46. 114. July 13, 1801, *ibid.* 115. *Ibid.*

the salary of the vacant Undersecretaryship.[116] King, while sole Undersecretary, always received the additional increment.[117] Another order in council on January 23, 1799, at the request of the Secretaries of State, raised the salary of any Undersecretary who had served over three years by £500.[118]

In making any generalizations about the Undersecretaries, it is necessary to distinguish between those who were seeking careers in government service and those who served for other reasons.[119] The status of the permanent Undersecretary did not alter significantly. Both Nepean and King were young men (about thirty) when they entered office, and for each the Home Office was the first step in a long public career. Necessity demanded a permanent official who could advise the new Secretaries (six in twenty years) on the procedure of the Office and perhaps suggest lines of policy. A second Undersecretary might assume some of his duties, but the permanent official was always present to take all responsibility when his colleague departed.

These permanent Undersecretaries were not civil servants in the modern sense. No law guaranteed their rights, although when the one major political upheaval occurred—the Fox-North coalition—Nepean placidly remained in office. Probably only a direct personality clash with a superior would have resulted in their removal. King had a more open political connection—with Grenville—than might be usual today, but Nepean, it appears, did not. The Undersecretaries differed from a modern civil servant in that they did not rise through lesser posts to become Undersecretaries. Nepean came directly to the Home Office from the post of secretary to an admiral. King had no administrative experience at all. They needed influence to obtain their positions, but not necessarily to retain them. Professor Wickwire has labeled these men "subministers," which seems to capture the meaning of their position quite well.[120]

116. *Sixteenth Report, 1797*, Appendix A.1, pp. 309–11.

117. Account Book, 1795–1811, H.O. 82/16.

118. Privy Council Register, P.C. 2/152.

119. The three following useful studies by Franklin B. Wickwire should be consulted for information on the status of men in undersecretarial positions: "Admiralty Secretaries and the British Civil Service," *Huntington Library Quarterly*, XXVIII (May, 1965), 235–54; *British Subministers and Colonial America, 1763–1783* (Princeton, 1966); "King's Friends, Civil Servants, or Politicians," *American Historical Review*, LXXI (Oct., 1965), 18–42.

120. Wickwire, *British Subministers, passim.* The term does not apply to the many lesser public servants.

If King and Nepean did well professionally to begin their careers in the Home Office, they also did well financially, although they had to maintain themselves in a fashion suitable to entertain persons of quality.[121] Nepean resided in three different homes between 1785 and 1795. All were of modest size and had plain exteriors; each, however, had an interior of distinction. No. 13, Great George Street, where he lived from 1785 to 1788 and where Wilkes had lived from 1757 to 1763, was at the very foot of Whitehall. No. 13, St. James's Place, where Nepean lived from 1789 till 1792, was a good walk from the Home Office, but he no doubt cut through St. James's Park. Perhaps he went on horseback. His residence from 1792 to 1795—Cadogan House, No. 2, Whitehall Place—was little more than across the street from the Home Office.[122] (The two last-mentioned houses are still standing.) Nepean was able to acquire an estate in Dorset, and King purchased one in Hampshire.

The status of the second Undersecretary did alter somewhat in these twenty years. The first two Undersecretaries, Orde and Strachey, were men of experience in politics and administration. Strachey took an active role in the peace negotiations, and both would probably have been efficient members of the office had they remained longer than a few months. Shelburne obviously intended to make the second Undersecretaryship functional, just as both Porten and Bell had been active in the Southern Department. North (briefly) and Sydney appointed their sons as Undersecretaries. Neither son was active. The position revived in the person of Scrope Bernard from 1789 to 1791. From 1791 to 1794 there were two permanent Undersecretaries. Portland's first two appointees, Brodrick and Greville, were inactive, although Brodrick might have acted had his health not failed. And Portland may be excused for appointing Greville in that no career man would have taken the post merely to await Wickham's return. The flexibility of the position may be seen by its importance when Wickham occupied it. It is likely that Hatton would also have been effective.

Perhaps the post could have been eliminated, as the commission-

121. William Smith's *Diary* is valuable for its information on Nepean's life.

122. For Great George Street, see London County Council, *The Parish of St. Margaret, Westminster, Part One* (Survey of London, X; London, 1926), p. 35; for St. James's Place, see L.C.C., *Parish of St. James, Part One,* pp. 515–16 and Plate 246d; for Cadogan House, see L.C.C., *The Parish of St. Margaret, Westminster, Part Two: Neighborhood of Whitehall,* Vol. I (Survey of London, XIII; London, 1930), p. 149.

ers recommended in 1786, but Bernard's activity during the illness of Nepean demonstrated the desirability of a standby, and it was probably during King's illness that Greville acted. Had the Secretaries consistently employed efficient men, colonial affairs might have received the strict attention they deserved. Whenever there were two active Undersecretaries, one generally concentrated on colonial business. It may be, however, that these Undersecretaries with close personal relations with their superiors performed certain private functions for the Secretary—perhaps meeting persons of importance on various matters on a more even social footing than the permanent Undersecretary could do. There is a direct correlation between a fairly inactive Undersecretary and the absence of a private secretary. Sydney had no private secretary, and Portland had none during the entire period that Greville was in office. In that sense, the second or private Undersecretary served a purpose even if he did not spend much time in the office. We have already seen that the position was not that of a parliamentary Undersecretary.

Chapter Three

CLERKS AND OTHER OFFICERS

Besides the Secretary of State and the two Undersecretaries, one would have found fourteen other persons in the Home Office on any given working day between 1784 and 1789: a chief clerk, ten other clerks, two chamber keepers (only one of whom attended), an office porter, a housekeeper, and an interpreter and translator of Oriental languages completed the establishment, exclusive of the Plantation Office (a subdepartment) with an Undersecretary and three clerks.[1] The translator of Oriental languages did not, however, regularly attend, as his work could be done at his home as well as at the office.

By 1789 changes began to alter the composition of the Office. The Plantation Office ceased to be in 1789, but an additional clerk from that office joined the Home Office.[2] In 1791 the position of law clerk was revived for John King during the time he served at the Home Office before becoming Undersecretary. He continued, however, to hold the office of law clerk thereafter. Between 1789 and 1793 a private secretary to the Secretary of State, a précis writer, a librarian, a keeper of criminal registers, and several temporary or extra clerks appeared. The creation of the Alien Office in 1793 added a superintendent and two clerks plus three agents serving at coastal ports.[3]

In the eighteenth century a modern civil service had not yet come into being, and how men entered office and the status they enjoyed thereafter reveal the nature of public service of that time. Nor should the identification of the men themselves, their duties, and

1. There is a description of the Plantation Office in Chapter X.

2. All three clerks actually came into the Home Office from the Plantation Office, but two filled existing vacancies. The three were Bradbury, Jessep, and Robert Chapman.

3. For the Alien Office, see Chapter IX.

their incomes be ignored.[4] Perhaps the most significant difference in actual practice between modern civil servants and those employed in eighteenth- and early nineteenth-century public offices is in the manner of recruitment. Whereas today examinations indicate to prospective employers suitable persons to fill a vacant office, in the eighteenth and early nineteenth century, politicians and administrators relied upon personal contacts and upon recommendations from influential persons. In most cases the employers had little difficulty, for there were probably numerous applicants hungering for an opening. Yet, a conscientious man had to exercise some discretion in employing persons in positions that required some measure of efficiency and competence and that certainly demanded regular attendance. Dundas, while Secretary of State, could not tolerate the inefficiency of four of his clerks during the great press of business brought on by the war. All four shortly retired.[5] The clerkships in the Home Office were far from being sinecures.

To be sure, the Secretaries looked upon the clerkships as legitimate objects of patronage either to serve their personal or political ends or to assist old acquaintances by placing their dependents in office. Lord Grenville, for example, wrote to his brother Lord Buckingham: "I have a clerkship vacant in my office: can it be made useful to any object of yours?"[6] Portland, in particular, exerted himself to accommodate old friends. He wrote to one such friend, who had solicited an office for his son, that "the two next vacancies in my office are positively promised, & though to sons of gentlemen, very old & sincere friends of mine, yet differing from you in . . . that the emoluments of the situation are as valuable to them as they are insignificant and indifferent to you."[7] While the numbers employed by the government remained small, it would be unwarrantably presumptuous to assert that the public suffered materially by this means of staffing offices. When bureaucracies grow large, it becomes,

4. In general for the civil service, see Emmeline W. Cohen, *The Growth of the British Civil Service, 1780–1939* (London, 1941). For the seventeenth century, see the excellent study by G. E. Aylmer, *The King's Servants: The Civil Service of Charles I, 1625–1642* (New York, 1961).

5. The four were Charles Brietzcke, George William Carrington, James Nassau Colleton, and George Lewis Palman.

6. Feb. 4, 1791, Buckingham, *Court and Cabinets of George III*, II, 188.

7. To John Bacon (1738–1816), April 2, 1796, copy, H.O. 42/37. Bacon had been first clerk of the First Fruits Office since December 17, 1776, and receiver of that office since March 16, 1782. *DNB*, I, 834.

of course, impossible for the chief administrators to be familiar with all persons serving under them. The great size of modern bureaucracies would mean, were it not for modern civil service examinations, that total strangers would be hired without any means of judging them. In the small public offices of the eighteenth century this problem did not arise. It is doubtful whether the chief administrators of the modern civil service have any advantage over their eighteenth-century predecessors when it comes to insuring maximum or at least reasonable efficiency among the personnel of offices.[8]

Once the clerk received his position, however, the differences between him and his modern counterpart ceased to be very clear. Tenure was virtually permanent. Only grave misbehavior brought outright dismissal: this occurred but once among the thirty-four men who served as clerks.[9] When the clerks grew too old to work they received a pension, which, in the late eighteenth century, consisted of the full salary they were receiving at the time of retirement, but without perquisites.[10] If the clerk predeceased his wife, the widow received a pension—usually one-half of that given to her husband.[11] When ill health forced retirement, the pension system was identical to that practiced for those retiring because of age. Sometimes, however, the clerk remained on the regular payroll although he could not attend the office.[12] The Secretaries granted leaves of absence with full pay for good cause, although this hap-

8. It has been difficult to discover the exact relationship between a clerk or his relations and the Secretary who hired him. Dundas' influence certainly got Hepburn a place, as Grenville's secured a position for Goddard. Noble and Norris were certainly sons of friends of the Duke of Portland. Charles Brietzcke secured a clerkship for his own son.

9. Robert Douglas had been absent for months without explanation, and then had the audacity to request more leave, as he had incautiously taken a house in Bury St. Edmunds, seventy-five miles from London, and needed additional time to settle his affairs. Lord Pelham, who succeeded Portland, discharged him at once. Sir George Shee, the Undersecretary, to Douglas, Nov. 11, 1802, H.O. 43/13. Dundas had earlier warned Douglas that he would dismiss him if he continued to be inattentive to his duty. June 2, 1794, H.O. 43/5.

10. Pensions were placed on the contingent account of the office and were paid by the Treasury, not by the Secretary of State, even under the system existing before the reform in 1795. H.O. 82/3.

11. *Ibid.* The widows of Thomas Daw and G. L. Palman received irregular payments. They may have died very shortly after their husbands, which would account for the absence of extended records. Mrs. Palman's payment is in the Contingent Account Book, 1822–38, H.O. 82/3.

12. This was the case with George Randall, who could not attend the office in March 1797 and yet remained on the payroll till his death on January 16, 1798. Portland to the Treasury, March 22, 1797, H.O. 43/9.

pened only three times in twenty years.[13] Hours seem to have been from 10 A.M. till 3 P.M. five days a week. At the time of the parliamentary commission in 1786, the amount of work was insufficient to require the constant attention of all the clerks. The clerks certainly had some holidays, but not a great many; it is uncertain whether they had vacations. Perhaps the major distinction between the status of the eighteenth-century minor officeholders and their modern counterparts is the former's dependence upon custom for their rights and the latter's dependence upon law for theirs.

Thirty-four permanent clerks worked in the Home Office from 1782 through July 1801, including clerks in the Plantation section. The average age at which a clerk first entered public office was nineteen and one-half, but four were sixteen or under.[14] Of the thirty-four, six died while employed in the office; fourteen retired on pensions; and thirteen resigned. Only one was dismissed. The average life span was sixty-eight years, but, if we omit Lefroy, who died at about twenty, and Edward Wood, who died of cholera at forty-six, the average rises to seventy-one and one-half. Life, in years at least, was generous to clerks.[15]

Although the information is incomplete, a sketch of the family backgrounds and education of the clerks provides an understanding of the kind of men who held office. In the twenty cases where patronage is known, the fathers of seven held court or government offices;[16] the grandfather of the two Woods brothers had been treasurer of the Inner Temple and the largest landowner in Middlesex. Three came from the landed gentry (Adams, Chapman, and Shadwell). The fathers of two others were army officers (Colleton and Lefroy), and the fathers of another two were clergymen (Carrington and Mills). Two came from merchant families (Gordon and Noble). Chetwynd was the son of an impoverished peer, Norris the

13. Colleton left in March 1782 to try to recover his property in South Carolina; Higden served as secretary to a British envoy abroad; Lefroy was absent for an unknown reason from January 1795 or before, to July 1799.

14. I have found the ages at entry of twenty-two, but excluded Shadwell and Porter because of uncertainty when they first entered public office.

15. The data are based on but twenty-two men. William Dacres Adams held the record with eighty-seven years, but Mathias may have been as old.

16. Chief Justice of the King's Bench (Wilmot); subtreasurer to the Queen's household (Mathias); Undersecretary in the Southern Department (Morin); page to George III (Palman); king's messenger (Pollock); Home Office clerk (Brietzcke); commissioner of the Customs in Scotland (Hepburn).

son of a bankrupt M.P., and the elder Brietzcke the son of the valet to the second Duke of Grafton.

All the clerks obviously had some education, or they could never have held their jobs. Shadwell, the chief clerk, attended Oxford and had been called to the bar at the Inner Temple. Goddard, Grenville's private secretary, also attended Oxford. Hepburn may have attended St. Andrews University. Chapman attended the Merchant Taylors School for four years, and Mathias was at Eton for the same length of time. Palman entered Westminster School, Wilmot entered Derby, and Mills attended Harrow, but none was graduated. Many, such as Adam Gordon, must have gone to schools without printed registers or had private tutors.[17]

The duties and responsibilities of the clerks do not appear to have been onerous. Many of them must have passed the greater part of their time in the Home Office in copying. The clerks probably made almost all the fair copies of letters sent from the Home Office, and they certainly made all those found in the letter books, invariably in a neat and clear hand. They often copied long reports on colonial affairs for distribution to various departments of state. When part of the contents of a letter received by the Home Office had direct bearing on the responsibility of another office, the clerks made extracts from the original letter to be sent to the other offices. Robert Hepburn, upon first entering the office in 1785, took his seat at a long table in the Board Room.[18] Nepean frequently kept him not only late in the day but also into the night copying letters.[19] The younger clerks probably sat at one long table, where they copied whatever the chief clerk put into their hands.

The clerks, at least in 1785, did not have any particular branch of business for which they had responsibility.[20] Throughout the period the hands of different clerks made the entries into the several letter books, which would tend to confirm the absence of fixed duties. The senior clerks may, however, have had some specific areas of responsibility. In 1789, for example, Nepean placed the correspondence and

17. These data come from an examination of all the university and school registers in print. Phyllis M. Jacobs, *Registers of the Universities, Colleges and Schools of Great Britain and Ireland* (London, 1964).

18. To James Chapman, Edinburgh, October 23, 1827, Chapman MSS, U. 619, c.14, Kent County Archives Office, Maidstone, Kent.

19. Hepburn to [Sir] Coutts Trotter, his brother-in-law, n.d., but 1827, copy, *ibid.*, U. 619, c.13. Trotter (1767–1837), a partner in Coutts and Co., was created a baronet in 1821. *Gentleman's Magazine*, n.s. VIII, 422–23.

20. *First Report, 1786,* p. 4.

dispatches to and from New South Wales in the hands of George Randall, who made certain that every point of business had received the proper attention.[21] Since 1770 Randall had prepared fair copies of all speeches that the King read to Parliament.[22] Another senior clerk, Charles Brietzcke, kept all the papers relating to the Barbary states.[23] There is an extant plan, prepared about 1792, to divide the business of the office among the personnel, but it apparently was never put into effect.[24]

Before 1795 the official income of the clerks came from a salary paid by the Secretary of State, from certain allowances out of the Post Office revenue, and from profits from franking newspapers in Great Britain. The income of the chief clerk was entirely different and is dealt with separately. The four senior clerks[25] also received five guineas each from the East India Company once a year.[26] Salaries were paid according to length of service; £175 was the highest and £45 the lowest. The Post Office revenue payment consisted of an annual grant by Parliament of £1,500 in lieu of the right of the clerks to frank letters, taken away by Act of Parliament in 1769, and a second grant of £1,000, beginning in 1784, to compensate the clerks for the loss of their privileges in franking newspapers to Ireland.[27] The clerks divided these grants according to seniority; the one longest in office received £280 and the one with least seniority got only £20. All clerks had the right to frank newspapers, votes and proceedings of Parliament, and *London Gazettes* within Great Britain, which they could do according to their inclination. One clerk made £100 by this means in 1784, while two did not make use of the privilege. The others earned varying amounts.[28] One clerk received an additional £20 per annum for his work with Irish military commissions.[29] All clerks had stationery for their own use.[30]

21. Nepean to Scrope Bernard, Nov. 3, 1789, Bath, Spencer Bernard MSS, O.E. 7/3. Randall also had charge of the correspondence relating to Cape Breton. Richard Spiller, agent for Cape Breton, to Bernard, July 15, 1790, No. 26 South Audley St., same MSS, O.E. 1/73.

22. Randall to Grenville, Nov. 24, 1790, P.R.O. 30/8/170 (Chatham Papers).

23. Nepean to Bernard, Nov. 8, 1789, Bath, Spencer Bernard MSS, O.E. 7/3.

24. H.O. 42/10.

25. Home Office clerks were always distinguished by the application of the term "senior" to the four with the longest service and "junior" to all others. Except in financial receipts the distinction presumably had little importance.

26. *First Report, 1786,* p. 6. 27. *Ibid.,* p. 5.

28. Appendix 2 contains a list of the clerks in 1784 with their earnings. Appendix 3 lists the clerks and their income in 1796.

29. *First Report, 1786,* Appendix 6, p. 22. 30. *Ibid.,* pp. 22–24.

In addition to their official incomes some clerks had other sources of revenue. Charles Brietzcke had served as engrossing clerk in the Alienation Office since 1766, a function which he executed by deputy. He received about £80 per annum.[31] He was deputy to one of the clerks of the Signet, for which he netted about £227 in 1784, but the average was about £104 per annum.[32] The civil list records a payment of £27 per annum to him throughout this period, and after his death, to his widow.[33] Brietzcke also had a few other minor emoluments.[34] In 1791 he and Goddard divided £110 for their extra work in summoning peers to the House of Lords.[35]

Several other clerks during the twenty years also received appreciable sums from other sources. Randall derived a small emolument from acting as an agent to one of the consuls in the Barbary states.[36] Chetwynd, who was clerk extraordinary to the Privy Council, received a gratuity of £250 in 1784 for his voluntary attendance at the Council on business relating to the management of colonial affairs.[37] Eardley Wilmot had been appointed Clerk of the Signet in reversion in 1782,[38] but did not receive any profit until October 10, 1797.[39] In 1800 Richard Hatt Noble, whose father was Portland's friend, was appointed Naval Officer at St. John's, Newfoundland;[40] in 1827 he received about £380 a year in compensation for the abolition of his office.[41]

An alteration in the manner of paying the clerks occurred in 1795 in keeping with the recommendation of the commissioners of 1786. The Secretaries agreed to the Order in Council in February 1795 that declared that effective January 5, 1795, the clerks would receive their salaries not from the Secretary of State, but from a consolidated fee fund consisting of the fees and gratuities collected in the Office and of the Post Office revenue payments. The reform actually worked to the financial advantage of the clerks, as two senior clerks gained about £150 each, and the others gained lesser amounts. The gift of five guineas to the senior clerks continued, as did their rights

31. *Ibid.*, Appendix 3, p. 21; Deputy Receiver's Cash Accounts, Alienation Office, A. 1/4.
32. *First Report, 1786*, Appendix 3, p. 21.
33. T. 38/212–219.
34. *First Report, 1786*, Appendix 3, p. 21.
35. July 5, 1791, Contingent Account, H.O. 82/3.
36. *First Report, 1786*, Appendix 4, p. 22.
37. *Ibid.*, Appendix 10, pp. 23–24.
38. July 15, 1782, Patent Rolls 19–43 George III, C. 66, p. 67.
39. Signet Board Wages, H.O. 82/19. Wilmot had been retired because of ill health in 1788.
40. April 1, 1800, Warrant Books, C.O. 324/46.
41. *An Account in Detail of All Pensions Granted under the Head of Compensation or Otherwise, on the Abolition of or for Sinecure Offices in the Different Branches of the Revenue, and in Other Departments of the State: etc.*, H. of C. 494, p. 452; *PP 1834*, XLI.

to frank newspapers, votes and proceedings, and *Gazettes* in Great Britain. But the earnings from these franking privileges were not great. Eight clerks received less than £22 each from this activity; three received respectively £40, £50, and £60.[42] Effective July 18, 1798, the clerks received £4.9.8 each in lieu of the privilege of franking votes and proceedings of the House of Commons.[43] Effective July 24, 1798, each clerk received a little over £75 per annum in lieu of the right to frank and receive free copies of the *London Gazette*.[44] These changes reflect the tendency to regularize the salaries of the clerks and to remove the old system that relied upon fees and perquisites.

The chief clerk of the Office had a special status and importance. Only two men served in this position during the twenty years. Richard Shadwell, an Oxford graduate and a barrister, had been chief clerk in the Northern Department since 1772 and thereafter in the Southern Department. But he was sixty-four years old in 1782, and retired on May 31 of that year. His successor, William Pollock, had been chief clerk in the Colonial Office since 1768 and on its abolition joined the Home Office. He became chief clerk at age forty-one on June 1, 1782, and remained in that position until 1816, when he retired. His father was a king's messenger. He does not appear to have been so well-educated as his predecessor, but by all accounts he was the model of a dedicated and efficient servant of the public. An associate of Shelburne in 1766 remarked that he had always had a good account of Pollock as a sober, diligent young man who minded his own business.[45] In 1782 William Knox, Undersecretary in the Colonial Office, told the King that in the twelve years he had been in office Pollock had had the responsibility for making up the dispatches, and "was so extremely diligent, that . . . I never knew him [to] leave out a single inclosure but in one instance. . . ."[46]

Pollock described his duties as chief clerk to the commissioners in 1786:

> to prepare all warrants and commissions for the Royal Signature, to distribute the official business to the Clerks, to examine it when done, to take care that the public dispatches are properly entered in the books of

42. *Sixteenth Report, 1797,* p. 303; Appendix B.1, pp. 316–17.
43. Memo on the flyleaves of the Contingent Account 1798–1811, H.O. 82/3.
44. *Ibid.*
45. "Memo on clerks," Shelburne MSS, Vol. 134; printed in Thomson, *Secretaries of State,* pp. 179–80.
46. [Knox], *Extra Official State Papers,* p. 28.

the Office, and punctually transmitted, to receive the Secretary of State's salary, all the fees, and to pay all the Under Clerks salaries, and contingencies of Office. . . .[47]

He also corresponded with various people, but usually in regard to financial matters connected with the office.[48]

Prior to 1795 the chief clerk had no salary whatever. His income arose from his share (about 15 per cent) of fees, one-half of the gratuities received from certain warrants signed by the king, a perquisite of £25 from the Irish Concordatum Fund, five guineas a year from the East India Company, one guinea a quarter upon paying the bill for stationery, and £100 in lieu of the privilege formerly enjoyed by all clerks of franking letters and of franking newspapers to Ireland. He also received ten shillings per sheet when he copied papers required by someone outside the Home Office. Like the other clerks, he had stationery for his own use. When a new consul to any of the Barbary states was appointed, it was customary to send a present worth £500 with him to be given to the ruler of the country. Pollock bought the gifts, for which he could receive a commission of 5 per cent. He did not take the 5 per cent, but only the discount that merchants often allowed for cash-in-hand purchases. By these sources of income Pollock netted about £850 in 1874. This sum is probably what he received on an average for any given year before 1795.[49] In addition, Pollock received £250 per annum from the sinecure office of Clerk of the Crown in Quebec,[50] to which he had been appointed March 16, 1781.[51] Pollock also served as deputy Clerk of the Signet to James Rivers, and estimated that he would net about £70 in 1784;[52] but in 1796 this position brought him £180.[53] In all, Pollock probably averaged £1,200 per year, taking the annual receipts from the Signet Office at £100.

The Order in Council in 1795 granted the chief clerk a salary of £1,000 in lieu of the above fees and perquisites. But he also received £3 from the Signet Office (apparently a gratuity for a special warrant passed), £50 from Ireland (evidently for extra work done by

47. *First Report, 1786,* Appendix 2, p. 20.

48. For example, Pollock to Jeremiah Hatton, keeper of St. Dunstan's Gaol near Canterbury, April 25, 1799, H.O. 43/11; William Wilberforce to Scrope Bernard, Nov. 26, 1791, Yoxall Lodge near Lichfield [Staffordshire, seat of the Reverend Thomas Gisborne who died in 1846], Spencer Bernard MSS, O.E. 5/2 and other notes in the same packet.

49. *First Report, 1786,* Appendix 2, p. 20.

50. *Ibid.*

51. Warrant Book, C.O. 324/44.

52. *First Report, 1786,* Appendix 2, pp. 20–21.

53. *Sixteenth Report, 1797,* Appendix B.1, p. 317.

him personally in preparing Irish bills to be passed through the Privy Council), and the customary five guineas from the East India Company. The receipts from his two other offices also continued. In 1796 he cleared almost £1,500—£300 more than in 1784.[54] An Order in Council in February 1801 added £250 per annum to the basic salary of all chief clerks who had held the positions for over five years.[55]

Four menial offices completed the establishment of the Home Office proper: two chamber keepers, a housekeeper or necessary woman, and an office porter. From 1782 to 1787, only one chamber keeper performed the duties of that office, but two were on the establishment.[56] William Kirby, the active chamber keeper, described his duties as taking care of the apartments, attending the Secretary, Undersecretaries, and clerks, and issuing stationery and other necessary articles.[57] He also inspected, if he did not actually keep, the ledgers containing an account of all fees received in the office.[58]

Each chamber keeper received a salary of £20.16.0 and about 2.5 per cent of the fees and gratuities collected by the office (£134 in 1784). Kirby, who acted as sole chamber keeper after 1770, paid his brother-in-law, from whom he had evidently got his position, one-half of his share of fees and gratuities and salary—£77. But he also collected the salary and share of fees and gratuities of his absentee colleague—John Doudiet, who had never been active. He paid Doudiet fifty-five guineas per year, and retained the residue for himself.[59] Doudiet, a connection of Lord Weymouth, later Marquess of Bath, with whom he had lived since 1737, was a page in the bedchamber of the King.[60] Kirby had some perquisites that were entirely his. Gifts at Christmas from the Secretary, Undersecretaries, and certain British and foreign ambassadors amounted to £17; franking *Gazettes*, votes, and newspapers brought him £5; and the stationer paid him £5 for old inkbottles and sandbags and two guineas in lieu of a

54. *Ibid.*; and Appendix A.1, p. 311.
55. Privy Council Register, Feb. 18, 1801, P.C. 2/157.
56. *The Royal Kalender* for 1783 and 1784 lists Nathan Crowder as deputy chamber keeper. He had formerly filled that position in the old Colonial Office, but he died in early 1784. "List of the American Office, 1782," H.O. 42/1; entry in the civil list for quarter ending July 5, 1784, T. 38/212, p. 58.
57. *First Report, 1786,* Appendix 13, pp. 24–25.
58. Fee Fund Books, H.O. 88/1–3.
59. *First Report, 1786,* Appendix 13, pp. 24–25.
60. He died on June 4, 1787. *Gentleman's Magazine,* LVII (June, 1787), 548.

Christmas dinner. In all, his net earnings for 1784 reached £225.[61] He had a rent-free apartment adjoining or near the Home Office as well as coal, candles, and stationery for his own use.

The commissioners in 1786 recommended that the office of second chamber keeper be abolished, but Dundas objected on the grounds that two were necessary. The Cabinet, although it usually met in the Foreign Office, sometimes had meetings in the Home Office, occasions which required at least two chamber keepers. By 1789 the new chamber keepers, Anthony Gander and John Hancock, both regularly attended the office. Dundas, however, did accept the recommendation that a salary of £100 to each chamber keeper be substituted for the receipt of fees and gratuities.[62] Although after 1795 the chamber keepers got their salary, they continued to receive some perquisites and also to frank the *London Gazette*. Each received about £12 in New Year's gifts, and over £166 in perquisites, for a total of about £280 each.[63] The large amount in perquisites arose from a voluntary donation by military agents for each military commission taken out. There were, of course, a great number of such commissions during the war.[64]

Until 1795 Mrs. Elizabeth Emmitt held the office of housekeeper, but she never attended. She paid Mrs. Catherine Drinkwater to do the actual work.[65] Her duties consisted of cleaning the rooms, lighting the fires, and finding towels, soap, sand, and other items for the office. She employed two women to assist her, as she was also housekeeper in the Plantation Office from 1783 to 1789. Mrs. Emmitt received a salary of £48 from the Secretary of State, of which she paid Mrs. Drinkwater about £30. Mrs. Drinkwater got £5 or £6 in Christmas gifts from the office staff and one-half guinea from the coal merchant and about £30 or £40 from the sale of the candle

61. *First Report, 1786,* Appendix 13, pp. 24–25.

62. *Sixteenth Report, 1797,* Appendix A.1, p. 309. Anthony Gander died on November 28, 1810. *Gentleman's Magazine,* LXXX (December, 1810), 594. Hancock retired on January 4, 1806, because of ill health. Contingent Account, 1798–1811, entries for Jan. 5, 1806, and Feb. 3, 1809, H.O. 82/3.

63. *Sixteenth Report, 1797,* Appendix B.1, pp. 316–17. Gander succeeded Kirby about 1785, when he either died or retired. Hancock replaced Doudiet.

64. *Sixteenth Report, 1797,* Appendix B.1, p. 303.

65. Mrs. Drinkwater had been deputy housekeeper since 1753. She had been a nurse to Elizabeth Harriet Warren, daughter of Sir George Warren of Stockport and Poynton, Cheshire. Miss Warren married in 1777 Thomas James (Bulkeley), seventh Viscount Bulkeley (Lord Bulkeley to Lord Sydney, July 20, 1786, Stowe, H.O. 42/9; *History of Parliament,* II, 128; III, 607). Mrs. Drinkwater died May 10, 1797 (Account Book, 1795–1811, H.O. 82/6). Mrs. Anne Moss succeeded her on May 11, 1797, and continued to January 4, 1822 (*ibid.*).

ends, old pens, and loose paper. She also had apartments, coals, and candles for her own use.[66] The commissioners in 1786 recommended that Mrs. Emmitt be pensioned at £20 per annum and that Mrs. Drinkwater receive a salary of £70 in lieu of her former income.[67] The Order in Council in 1795 followed both recommendations, but raised the salary to £100.[68] The housekeeper may have continued to receive her little perquisites as well.

The last menial officer was the office porter. Throughout the twenty years, Charles Henry filled this post, although he employed an assistant with whom he shared all his profits. His duty obviously consisted of carrying messages between government departments, much as is done today. He received no salary but was paid a certain sum for each message that he carried. In 1784 his receipts were about £194,[69] but by 1795 they had risen to £300.[70] The office porter or messenger also had some perquisites, but they amounted to less than £10 per annum.[71] His income seems high for such a menial position, and there was no explanation for it that could be found.

Another Home Office position passed under the rather imposing title of "interpreter and translator of Oriental languages." During twenty years, three different men filled the post. Isaac Cardozo Nuñes, a Jew, served from March 2, 1782,[72] to February 1784, when he was dismissed.[73] He had been obliged to abscond from England for "improper transactions—some of a capital nature" (to use Lord Sydney's phrase).[74] The office of translator next passed to Simon Lucas (February 24, 1784). Lucas, a former British vice-consul at Tangiers, served till December 24, 1792, when he departed for

66. *First Report, 1786,* p. 7; Appendix 14, p. 25.
67. *Ibid.,* p. 15.
68. *Sixteenth Report, 1797,* Appendix A.1, pp. 309, 311.
69. *First Report, 1786,* Appendix 2, p. 21.
70. *Sixteenth Report, 1797,* Appendix F.1, p. 322.
71. *First Report, 1786,* Appendix 45, p. 41.
72. Cardozo to Sydney, Nov. 3, 1784, H.O. 42/5.
73. Simon Lucas to Grenville, Aug. 22, 1790, H.O. 42/16.
74. Sydney to Sir George Augustus Eliott, governor of Gibraltar, March 12, 1787, C.O. 91/34. Cardozo certainly had the most interesting end of any person employed by the Home Office. After leaving England he went to Morocco; there he insinuated himself into influence with the Emperor, whom he tried to turn against the British. But on September 22, 1786, he ran afoul of the Emperor, who directed Cardozo to appear before him at the *musjcar* (great place of audience). Without saying a word to Cardozo the Emperor had him choked until he fell to the ground. Servants then administered two hundred blows with rods, fired ten bullets into him (proceeding from the extremities inward no doubt), cut his body in half with an axe, and burned his remains on the spot. The Emperor said that *"this Infidel has had the Impudence to endeavour to make me and the King of England upon bad terms together."* Enclosure dated October 8, 1786, from Tangier, in Eliott to Sydney, Oct. 13, 1786, C.O. 91/33.

Tripoli to become British consul.[75] Richard Tully, Lucas' predecessor in the consulship in Tripoli, succeeded him as translator on January 5, 1794,[76] and continued until his death sometime in 1802.[77]

It was the duty of the translator, Lucas told the committee in 1786, to translate all official papers from French, Spanish, Italian, and Portuguese. He could speak Arabic fluently, but could not read it. His duty also entailed attending the ambassadors from the Barbary states.[78] Very few letters from the Barbary states came to England in the original Arabic, but when the occasion arose the Home Office employed various persons who had a command of the language to translate letters and also to write letters to the reigning chiefs of state when that became necessary.[79]

75. Lucas appears in the *DNB,* XII, 242–43, under the name William Lucas, which is in error. Since the article is incomplete, I have added the following information: Lucas served as vice-consul to Joseph Popham, consul-general in Morocco from 1768 to 1770, as chargé d'affaires at Tetuan from 1770 to 1772, and as vice-consul at Tangiers from August 2, 1772 to 1780. He was ordered to withdraw from Morocco along with the British consul, Charles Logie, in December 1780 and arrived in London on March 10, 1781. Lucas to Grenville, Aug. 22, 1790, H.O. 42/16; F.O. 52/6. He was interpreter and translator of Oriental languages from February 24, 1784, to December 24, 1792. Sydney to Treasury, May 12, 1784, H.O. 36/4; entry for January 4, 1793, Contingent Accounts, H.O. 82/3. His pay as consul at Tripoli began on April 5, 1792 (T. 38/2/6), but the appointment was not gazetted till December. *Gentleman's Magazine,* LXII (Dec., 1792), 1158. He arrived in Tripoli on July 26, 1793, while the city was besieged, and lived in danger until the Tunisian army restored the family of the old Bashau on January 19, 1795. Lucas died in Tripoli on May 4, 1801, leaving an adopted son—his physician, Bryan McDonough (F.O. 76/5). He married on January 12, 1791, Mrs. Eliza Griffith. *Gentleman's Magazine,* LXI (Jan., 1791), 88. She died on January 11, 1798. He married again in January 1800 a "woman of easy virtue" whom he divorced shortly thereafter. F.O. 76/5.

He secured leave as translator in order to make an expedition for the African Association. He left London in August 1788 and arrived in Tripoli by October 25. He returned to Tripoli from his journey to Mesurata by March 26, 1789. F.O. 76/4. Robin Hallett (ed.), *Records of the African Association, 1788–1831* (London, 1964), supersedes the edition cited in the *DNB* and contains considerable information about Lucas.

76. Entry for May 13, 1794, Contingent Accounts, H.O. 82/3.

77. Richard Tully had been acting consul at Tripoli since April 1778, but had acted as secretary to some of the consuls at least since 1772. Tully to Hillsborough, April 24, 1784, Tripoli, F.O. 76/4. He left Tripoli on December 13, 1781, but returned by July 5, 1783. Tully to Shelburne, n.d., but probably May 2, 1782; same to same, June 17, 1782, London; same to North, July 5, 1783, Tripoli, F.O. 76/4. He left Tripoli, where he was always burdened by debts, in early 1793 and returned to London. Tully was married and had two daughters. Louisa Maria married on March 19, 1795, at Gibraltar, Alexander Simpson of Aberdeen. *Gentleman's Magazine,* LXV (May, 1795), 437. Tully evidently died on July 5, 1802, when the pension of £80 to his widow begins. Entries for July 6, 1802, and Oct. 8, 1803, Contingent Accounts, 1798–1811, H.O. 82/3. Mrs. Catherine Tully died on December 12, 1828. Entry for Jan. 5, 1830, Contingent Account, 1822–28, *ibid.* The letters written by Tully's sister during his consulship in Tripoli form one of the most important sources for the history of that area. They were first published in 1816. The most recent edition is *Letters Written during a Ten Year's Residence at the Court of Tripoli,* edited by Seton Dearden (London, 1957).

78. *First Report, 1786,* Appendix 44, p. 41.

79. Contingent Accounts, H.O. 82/3; and the Contingent Accounts for Dec. 1, 1785–April 4, 1786, enclosed in a letter from Sydney to the Treasury, May 2, 1786, T. 1/630.

The translator's regular salary was always £80 per annum, but attendance upon visiting ambassadors from the Barbary (which the government always did its best to avoid because of the expense involved) brought additional income to the translators. Lucas received £203 for attending the ambassador from Tripoli for fifteen months.[80] Tully, however, only once attended some Moors, for which he received £20.[81] Charles Logie, former consul in Morocco and Algiers, served as the regular interpreter for the Tunisian ambassador in 1793, for which he received £150, and for the Algerian ambassador in 1801, for which he was paid £300.[82]

The office of law clerk had been vacant since 1774, but it was revived January 1, 1791, in the person of John King.[83] It was the duty of the law clerk to "prepare Drafts of Warrants issuing from the Office and of Letters of Reference to the Judges and His Majesty's Law Servants, on such points of Law as the Secretary of State shall require their opinion upon for His Majesty's information."[84] Since most of the warrants were already in a standard form that any clerk, substituting the proper names and dates, could copy, letters to the law officers must have constituted the sole duty of the law clerk. The salary, £300 per annum, ought to be considered as a means of providing for King before he became Undersecretary and thereafter as a means of supplementing his income.

Although the office of précis writer is first mentioned officially on June 8, 1791, Charles Goddard acted in that capacity for Grenville in 1789. James Chapman, a clerk in the office, served as Dundas' précis writer, and followed him to the new War Department on July 11, 1794. On September 29, 1794, Robert Moss, second son of the Bishop of Bath and Wells and brother-in-law of John King, succeeded. He remained till his death on June 17, 1801.[85] The duty of the précis writer consisted of abridging important correspondence in order to facilitate references to it in case the originals were temporarily removed from the office, and, of course, to eliminate the

80. Sydney to the Treasury, July 31, 1787, H.O. 36/5.
81. Dec. 26, 1796, Contingent Accounts, H.O. 82/3.
82. Dec. 12, 1796, and Dec. 5, 1800–June 20, 1801, Contingent Accounts, H.O. 82/3.
83. Jan. 2, 1792, *ibid.* 84. *Sixteenth Report, 1797,* Appendix L, p. 325.
85. *Sixteenth Report, 1797,* Appendix M, p. 325. Robert Moss, born about 1772 in Salisbury, attended Eton and Cambridge, where he received his B.A. in 1793 and his M.A. in 1796. He was admitted to the Middle Temple on April 18, 1793. He married on August 30, 1798, Sophia, daughter of John Weyland of Woodeaton, Oxford. Moss died at Grosvenor Place, aged thirty. Venn and Venn, *Alumni Cantabrigienses,* Pt. II, IV, 482.

necessity for ministers to consult the voluminous correspondence in the original.[86] Before 1794 the stipend was £200,[87] but thereafter it increased to £300.

There is no indication that Lord Sydney had a private secretary, but Grenville employed his protégé Charles Goddard, for that purpose. Dundas used Robert Hepburn in that capacity from June 8, 1791, to December 31, 1793, and thereafter James Chapman, till both Dundas and Chapman migrated to the War Department.[88] Thomas Carter served Portland as private secretary, probably from the time the Duke entered office to April 5, 1796, when he resigned to stand for Parliament.[89] Apparently no one filled the post till August 6, 1798, when William Frankland became Portland's secretary. He resigned on July 30, 1801, presumably to stand for Parliament.[90] The duties of the private secretaries may be imagined —handling the personal correspondence of the Secretary, keeping his personal accounts, etc. The salary was always £300 per annum. The post obviously carried considerable prestige with it. The secretaries were both men of some importance.

In 1792 Dundas added a librarian to the Home Office. Charles Peace, former clerk in the Colonial Office, served in this capacity from October 13, 1792, to July 4, 1806, when a stroke deprived him

86. *Sixteenth Report, 1797,* Appendixes M, O, 325.

87. Aug. 23, 1792, Contingent Accounts, H.O. 82/3.

88. Information on Goddard, Hepburn, and Chapman is in Appendix I.

89. *Sixteenth Report, 1797,* Appendix B.1, p. 316. Thomas Carter, born about 1761, was the son of Thomas Richard Carter (c.1724–1795) by Anna Tobina, daughter of Toby Chauncy of Edgcott, Northamptonshire. He entered Westminster School in 1774 and Oxford in 1779; he received his B.A. in 1783 and his M.A. in 1786. He married in November 1791, Glencairn, daughter of Walter Campbell of Shawfield, New Brunswick. He sat as M.P. for Tamworth 1796–1802 and for Callington 1807–1810, and served as high sheriff of Northants in 1806. He died on June 10, 1835 (Barker and Stenning, *Old Westminsters,* I, 167) . He received the reversion to the office of provost marshal general of the Barbados on August 28, 1801 (Patent Rolls 19–43 George III, p. 391, C. 66) . He was superintendent of the Alien Office from December 10, 1794, till early in 1798. The *Gentleman's Magazine,* n.s. IV (Aug., 1835) , 205, contains a lengthy and laudatory obituary.

90. Frankland, born about 1792, was the second son of Sir Thomas Frankland, Bt., Admiral of the White. He received his B.A. from All Souls in 1783 and his M.A. in 1794. He entered Lincoln's Inn in 1787 and became a barrister. He represented Thrisk 1801–1806, 1807–1815; and Queensborough 1806–1807. He died unmarried on June 10, 1816 (Foster, *Alumni Oxonienses,* II, 490; *Burke's Peerage,* 99th ed., p. 791) . He was attorney general of the Isle of Man and a lieutenant colonel in the Yorkshire militia. In 1806 he served as a lord of the Admiralty. "At the University, at the bar, in the House of Commons, and among military men, his brilliant talents and extensive attainments made him equally conspicuous and acceptable. Few men have been more generally beloved, or will be more deeply regretted." *Gentleman's Magazine,* LXXXVI (June, 1816) , 571. Records of his payments as private secretary are in the Salary Book, 1795–1811, H.O. 82/16.

of his mental faculties.[91] Pollock, the chief clerk, told the committee in 1797 that a great accumulation and consequent confusion of papers, which could not conveniently be transferred to the State Paper Office, made the addition of a librarian necessary.[92] Having one person familiar with all the papers of the Office must have greatly facilitated referring to them, and certainly justified this additional officer. Peace received a salary of £200 per annum in addition to the £90 pension that he had for his services in the old Colonial Office. He also had the privilege of franking newspapers, votes and proceedings of Parliament, and *Gazettes,* which brought him £34 in 1796.[93] In 1797 he received £50 for his care and diligence as librarian and as clerk. Both in 1797 and in 1798 he received payments of £100 for his care and trouble in the correspondence relating to the Volunteer Corps.[94]

The title of the last officer to be considered was the keeper of the criminal register of the felons in Newgate. Edward Raven maintained the register for the sheriff of London till September 28, 1793, when the sheriff discontinued it; thereafter Dundas ordered Raven to continue to keep it in the Home Office.[95] Raven, an extra clerk in the office since February 1793, kept the register (always in the most splendid hand printing) until August 2, 1800, when Portland dismissed him for negligence.[96] William Day succeeded him on August 3, 1800, and continued in that position till he retired in 1841.[97] The purpose of the keeper of the criminal register was "to note each Committment and Conviction, for the purpose of distinguishing

91. Peace had been a clerk in the Colonial Office from 1772 to 1782, when he was pensioned. Upon retiring from the Home Office in 1806 he received a pension of £300. He died on February 9, 1820. His widow, Elizabeth Peace, aged seventy-five in 1837, had a pension of £150. Salary Books 1796–1811, 1820–1822; *Sixteenth Report, 1797,* Appendix M., p. 325; *Abstract of Papers and Documents Relative to Pensions Granted for Various Services,* H. of C. 621, p. 151, *PP 1837–38,* XXIII.

92. *Sixteenth Report, 1797,* Appendix M, p. 325; p. 301.

93. *Ibid.,* Appendix B.1, pp. 316–17.

94. Contingent Account, H.O. 82/3.

95. Raven to Nepean, March 12, 1794, H.O. 42/29.

96. Contingent Account, 1798–1811, H.O. 82/3; Raven to Portland, Sept. 2, 1800, H.O. 42/51.

97. Contingent Account, 1798–1811, H.O. 82/3. Day retired on a pension of £390 in 1841, aged sixty-nine. *Account of Allowances or Compensations granted as Retired Allowances or Superannuations in Public Offices or Departments which Remained Payable on the 1st January; the Annual Amount granted, the Annual Amount which Ceased, and the Amount Remaining Payable,* H. of C. 137, p. 698; *PP 1842,* XXVI; hereafter reports on superannuations are cited as *Superannuations.* Day died on August 29, 1841. Salary Book, 1822–41, H.O. 82/16.

John Henry Capper was paid for "executing the Criminal Branch" at £100 p. a. from August 3, 1800, to January 5, 1801. At least as early as 1797 he had served as an extra clerk (H.O. 82/1; H.O. 82/3). He retired, aged seventy-three, in 1847. *Superannuations,* H. of C. 203, p. 581; *PP 1847–48,* XXXIX.

between the old and new Offenders; to shew the increase or decrease of the several descriptions of Felons; to make entry of all References to Judges upon solicitation for Pardons," and likewise the entry of all pardons. The practice of soliciting mercy for criminals, which had greatly increased, necessitated more extensive records.[98] Raven always received £120 for keeping the register and £80 for serving as an extra clerk, but Day received only £50.[99]

Although the information is slender, the official, social, and economic status of the clerks provides an understanding of the sort of men who held minor public offices. Were it at all possible, one would like to know their opinions on politics and the workings of the office. Some of the senior clerks must have had influence, if not on policy at least on Office procedure. Did any of them encourage a particular course of action by embellishment or deletion of facts? Did any try to sabotage a policy? Edward Raven apparently attempted the last-mentioned course, and it cost him his job. As keeper of criminal registers in 1795 he protested against granting pardons to criminals who consented to enter military service.[100] In 1800 Portland fired him for failing to prepare pardons for some mutineers.[101] Did Raven have a fixation about the necessity for disciplined men in the military? Official records seldom reveal the opinions of small men.

Most clerks probably lived quite near the office.[102] After 1780 Charles Brietzcke resided at St. James's Place—a few steps from the Southern Department on Cleveland Row—and about half a mile from the Home Office on Whitehall. Brietzcke had formerly occupied No. 8 Buckingham Street, off the Strand. William Francis Johnston died in his house on that street in 1799. It was about a quarter of a mile from the Home Office. George Mathias and (at least in later life) Richard Hatt Noble lived in Middle Scotland Yard—practically across the street from the Office. John Bradbury resided on Millbank Street—except by name and a few jogs an extension of Whitehall. William Henry Higden, George Randall, William Pollock, and (later) George Brietzcke lived across the

98. *Sixteenth Report, 1797,* Appendix M., p. 325.

99. H.O. 82/3.

100. Raven to Portland, July 21, 1795, H.O. 42/35.

101. Same to same, Sept. 2, 1800, H.O. 42/51.

102. A diligent person with much time could search the London tax rolls to find the location and ownership of the clerks' dwellings. The residences of several others are known, but generally from wills made well into the nineteenth century. It has been deemed best not to impose later circumstances on the late eighteenth century. Information about the residences of ten of the clerks provides the basis for this paragraph.

Thames in Lambeth. Using Westminster Bridge, they had perhaps under a mile to travel. Thomas Daw lived on the ground floor of the Home Office till late in 1783, when the rooms were needed. The housekeeper and chamber keeper had apartments in or near Whitehall. Eardley Wilmot, at least after he retired, lived near the more fashionable Bedford Square, and Robert Moss, the précis writer, resided at Grosvenor Place, adjoining the grounds of Buckingham Palace.[103] Distances were important, since living too far from work entailed either riding a horse, and paying for its stabling, or depending on the vagaries of London transportation; furthermore, after dark the streets could be dangerous.

The social life of the clerks is totally blank. Did they and their wives attend parties regularly? Who were the other guests? Were they people employed by government? They certainly traveled in circles outside the world of high fashion; the society memoirs mention none of them.

The family life of the clerks is a little better known. Of the twenty-five clerks on whom there is definite information, twenty-one married at some point in their lives. William Adams married into a landed family in Kent. The younger Brietzcke married the daughter of a baronet. Robert Hepburn, after he left the Home Office, married the daughter of a Scottish lord of session (and the granddaughter of the Earl of Aberdeen). At least thirteen of the clerks had children. Often the children acquired social and economic positions higher than those of their parents. Of Adams' four sons, one became consul-general to Peru, two became clergymen, and one succeeded to his mother's estates. One of Brietzcke's sons attended Oxford and eventually became chairman of the Board of Customs. Chapman's eldest son succeeded to the estates in Kent, and the second appears to have been successful. Two of Mills's sons attended Cambridge—one entered holy orders and the other the law. The evidence about others is too fragmentary to be certain. In any case, it would appear that the Home Office provided a position sufficiently comfortable to allow a clerk to give his children breeding and education superior to his own.[104]

103. Appendix I contains most of the references. The wills and obituaries were the principal sources. For Daw, see Sydney to the Treasury, Dec. 27, 1783, H.O. 36/4. Randall's will contains the reference to Bradbury's residence.

104. Morin's children died young. His daughter married well, as did Brietzcke's. Colleton's eldest son had a distinguished military career, and certainly did better in life than his poor father. Goddard's eldest son did well in the church, but I could find no record of his other six children. The eldest sons of Plasket and Shadwell became army officers.

As the Home Office provided a comfortable living for those who remained with it, it also served as a steppingstone to advancement for most of the thirteen who resigned. James Chapman and Adam Gordon eventually became chief clerks (in succession) in the Colonial Office, and Porter became chief clerk of the Board of Trade. Edward Wood rose to the position of chief secretary to the government at Madras. Hepburn became chief commissioner of stamps in Scotland, and Mathias an inspector at the Audit Office. Chetwynd became a clerk at the Board of Trade and clerk to the Privy Council before he succeeded his father to the peerage. Morin left to serve as Lord Shelburne's secretary, and in any case was a person of some means. William Dacres Adams served Pitt and later Portland as private secretary, and held commissionships in the Office of Woods and Forests and in the Lottery Office. Bradbury, who took the name Norton, resigned upon inheriting considerable property in Sussex.

Economically, the clerks occupied a position in what would be called the middle class. A moderately wealthy landed peer, the second Viscount Palmerston, for example, had an annual income of around £12,000.[105] Pollock, the chief clerk, netted £1,500 in 1796. A London printer, one of the better-paid journeymen, earned about £70 a year.[106] Like all people with fixed incomes, the clerks probably suffered from the general inflation that began in 1760 and did not crest until 1815. A year such as 1795, when inflation reached a high point and a crop shortage forced up food prices, must have been particularly severe.[107] Yet, Pollock died a well-to-do man, and Higden's estate was considerably in excess of £6,000. John Tirel-Morin left valuable property in Buckinghamshire to his daughter. When George Brietzcke died, however, he left less than £600.[108] In general, the senior clerks could probably afford at least one servant, eat and dress well, and live in comfortable homes.[109]

105. Brian Connell, *Portrait of a Whig Peer: Compiled from the Papers of the Second Viscount Palmerston 1739–1802* (London, 1956), p. 17.

106. M. Dorothy George, *London Life in the Eighteenth Century* (London, 1925), p. 164.

107. Phyllis Deane, *The First Industrial Revolution* (Cambridge, 1965), pp. 31, 244–45. In 1767 (a year of high prices) a clerk receiving £50 a year lived pretty wretchedly. D. George, *London Life*, pp. 92–93, 166–67, 369–70.

108. The wills cited in Appendix I are the sources of information for the clerks; unfortunately, a will provides little indication of the value of property. Clerks who lived into the middle of the nineteenth century often had considerable wealth, but I have not included that information to avoid distorting the view of the late eighteenth century.

109. Dorothy Marshall, *English People in the Eighteenth Century* (London, 1956), pp. 127–29.

Chapter Four

LOCATION, FINANCE, AND PROCEDURE

Since 1760 the office of the Secretary of State for the Southern Department had been at Nos. 4 and 5, Cleveland Row, opposite St. James's Palace;[1] but following the reorganization in 1782 the Home Office almost immediately moved into the buildings on Whitehall known as the Montagu lodgings, where it remained into the early nineteenth century. The Board of Trade and the old Colonial Office had used those quarters till their abolition in 1782. The engravings of the building reveal an unpretentious two-storied structure occupying the area on which the northern part of the Treasury Building now stands.[2] The Home Office occupied the second floor ("first floor" in English terminology).[3] The office proper had only four rooms, of which one had a remarkably fine decorated oval ceiling.[4] The Secretary and Undersecretaries each had a private office, but the clerks shared a single room.[5] Most of the clerks must have sat with quill pens, ink, and blotting sand at a long table in the "Board Room" where they spent most of their time copying letters and

1. The Plantation Office may have continued in Cleveland Row. As late as 1792 the Home Office had some sort of office there. Home Office to William Ross, Sept. 26, 1792, H.O. 42/2. London County Council, *The Parish of St. James, Westminster, Part One,* pp. 487–89, Plate 277a. The buildings have been demolished, and replaced by Nos. 3 and 7, Cleveland Row.

2. London County Council, *The Parish of St. Margaret, Westminster, Part Three: Neighborhood of Whitehall,* II (Survey of London, XIV; London, 1931), 79–80, Plates 61–64; George S. Dugdale, *Whitehall Through the Centuries* (London, 1950), pp. 134–35, has additional plates.

3. L.C.C., *St. Margaret, Westminster, Part Three,* pp. 78–82, does not clearly explain the location of the Home Office during this period and fails to point out that the Board of Trade (after 1786) occupied only the ground floor of the building on Whitehall. John King informed the inspector of aliens at Dover, Peter Newport, who was coming to London, that the Duke of Portland's office was in the same staircase as, but above, that of Lord Hawkesbury, president of the Board of Trade. May 17, 1796, H.O. 43/7.

4. L.C.C., *St. Margaret, Westminster, Part Three,* Plates 61, 63.

5. John King to John Calvert, Jr. (?1758–1844, an M.P.), secretary to the Lord Chamberlain, Sept. 9, 1797, H.O. 43/10.

papers for their superiors.[6] The chief clerk and perhaps two or three of the senior clerks had separate desks in the same room. Between the windows and elsewhere stood presses with leather-bound volumes of official correspondence as well as bundles of loose letters and papers.[7] All the rooms had fireplaces with screens, and at least the offices of the Secretary and Undersecretaries had carpets and curtains.[8] Although business hours lasted only from ten in the morning to three in the afternoon,[9] candles had to be used a good deal of the time during the dark, overcast, and cold London winters.[10]

The cost of maintaining the Office was not great. In 1784 the total amount came to but £16,000,[11] exclusive of payments out of the Secret Service funds, which totaled almost £6,000 in 1784; but the average from 1784 to 1792 was £2,600 per annum,[12] for an average total cost of £18,600. Expenses remained fairly constant till 1792, when the addition of six officers and increased expenditures brought by the war forced the cost of maintaining the establishment up to about £27,000 per annum, including roughly £10,000 for the Secret Service.[13] (Although Secret Service expenditures did not appear in either of the two reports on the Home Office ordered by the House of Commons, they ought to be considered part of the cost of the Office.)

Three principal sources of income defrayed the expenses of the Office. (Figures are for 1784, when the amount spent was £18,600.) Only £1,150, constituting part of the income of the clerks, came directly from a grant of Parliament. The king's civil list, most of which was granted by Parliament, defrayed approximately £8,730 annually: £6,680 in salaries, £600 for incidental charges, and £1,500 for stationery. Secret Service money always came from the civil list. The public annually defrayed, directly or indirectly, about £12,600 —Secret Service expenses averaging £2,600. Fees collected from private citizens made up the remaining £6,000 of the cost of the Office

6. Robert Hepburne to James Chapman, Feb. 26, Oct. 23, 1827, Edinburgh, Chapman MSS, U. 619, c. 14.
7. Evan Nepean to Scrope Bernard, Nov. 8, 1789, Spencer Bernard MSS, O.E. 7/3.
8. King to Calvert, Sept. 9, 1797, H.O. 43/10.
9. Home Office to William Ross, Sept. 26, 1792, H.O. 42/21.
10. General Account Book, 1791–1815, H.O. 82/1. 11. *First Report, 1786,* p. 8.
12. Alfred Cobban, "British Secret Service in France, 1784–1792," *English Historical Review,* LXIX (April, 1954), 233, 236.
13. *Sixteenth Report, 1797,* Appendix B.1, p. 317; Appendix F.1, p. 322. See the chapter on the Secret Service for those expenditures. These figures are for 1795, but those for 1793 and after were probably similar.

establishment in 1784.[14] Despite the increase in the cost of maintaining the Office, after 1792 public sources (Parliament and the civil list) continued to defray about two-thirds of the cost, and private fees the remaining one-third.[15] The reform in 1795 did not alter significantly the general sources of income, but affected the internal financial organization of the Home department.

The heart of any office is its procedure—precisely how it handles the duties for which it is responsible. Most basic to procedure is the standard routing of incoming and outgoing correspondence. The Undersecretary evidently opened all or nearly all incoming letters and dispatches and docketed them with the name of the sender and the date received. He then decided which letters ought to go to the Secretary. The Undersecretary probably laid all but the most perfunctory letters before his chief, who determined the appropriate course of action. The Secretary sent to the King most important dispatches and letters. On matters not requiring the opinion of other officials the Secretary drafted an answer or conveyed his decision orally to the Undersecretary. The Undersecretary polished the draft before giving it to the clerks, who made a fair copy as well as entered a copy in the office letter books.

Letters requiring the attention of other departments followed a different course. The King received nearly all of them. They then went to the law officers, the Privy Council, or members of the Cabinet. Seldom did the letters circulate to all members of the Cabinet—only to those with an interest in the particular subject. The Cabinet might as a body consider the proper course of action. Once the decision had been made, the outgoing letters followed the same route as any others. Occasionally drafts of outgoing letters might be sent back to the Cabinet for approval.

Within the Home Office itself there were two echelons of letters—those signed by the Secretary and those signed by the Undersecretary. The Secretary nearly always signed letters to the heads of all government departments, to the governors of the colonies, to consuls in the Barbary states, to the Lord Lieutenant of Ireland, to most magistrates, and to most private citizens. The Undersecretary signed all correspondence with subordinate officials in other departments and to the Chief Secretary in Ireland. On matters involving minor

14. *First Report, 1786,* pp. 5–6. A table of the fees collected is in Appendix 50, pp. 45–46.

15. *Sixteenth Report, 1797,* especially Appendix C.1, p. 320.

financial or administrative actions the Undersecretary may not have troubled the Secretary.

It would be advantageous to learn about the decision-making process that took place between the arrival of a letter and the sending of a reply. Unfortunately it has proved nearly impossible to grapple with this problem. In the nineteenth century one can follow the course of a letter through the hands of many men, as they minuted the letter with their names, dates, and often their opinions of the contents. In the Home Office before 1800 this rarely happened. On certain occasions, such as the deliberations about the Canada Act of 1791, it is possible to peer into the minds of some of the statesmen involved, by virtue of their correspondence;[16] but on the intra-office operations this has proved impossible. The absence of the papers of the two permanent Undersecretaries for this period precludes a complete understanding of the decision-making process. One would like to know what factors the officials considered before replying to the request of a colonial governor to remove a member of his council or a request from a magistrate for troops. For such routine matters as the preparation of warrants the process must have been elementary—probably a carry-over from the Southern Department. For other matters, such as much of the militia correspondence, the Home Office simply referred the letters to other departments.[17]

Although the factors the officials considered obviously varied with the category of decision, they consistently relied upon precedent to assist them. On innumerable occasions the Secretary or Undersecretary requested documents from an earlier period that might either shed light on a current problem or serve as a precedent for a particular course of action. The revitalization of the State Paper Office in 1792 was in part intended to facilitate references to the papers of previous statesmen. Use of precedent is of course one of the practices that results in consistency and order in any administrative office. It is perversion of the use of precedent that leads to inflexibility and immutability.

Changes in both organization and procedure occurred during the twenty years of this study. The principal departures from established routine received impetus from outside the office itself. Shel-

16. Many of these papers are in H.M.C., *Dropmore Papers*, Vol. I, and in Adam Shortt and Arthur G. Doughty (eds.), *Documents Relating to the Constitutional History of Canada, 1759–1791* (2nd ed. rev.; 2 vols.; Ottawa, 1918). 17. See Chapter X.

burne and others brought about the greatest reform in 1782 when the Southern Department became the Home Office. All the papers and records relating to domestic affairs came under one roof. One man became responsible for internal problems, which undoubtedly speeded their being noticed and resolved. No longer did the problems go haphazard to one or the other Secretary.

Two other important reforms came through parliamentary action. Pitt and the parliamentary commissions were instrumental in reorganizing the financial structure of the Home Office. The new methods marked a sharp break with the ancient customs of the Office and adumbrated the concept of a modern, rational administration. Parliament was also responsible for the creation of the Alien Office —the sole instance in this period, as far as the Home Office is concerned, of an institutional response to a problem; that is, Parliament planned and enacted legislation that set up an office with definite duties and distinct jurisdiction in order to meet a specific need.

Pragmatic considerations brought about nearly all other procedural and organizational changes within the Home Office. Grenville's use of a private secretary and a précis writer proved successful; hence, each remained on the establishment. When the papers became unmanageable, Dundas added a librarian. When the sheriff of London terminated the employment of the keeper of criminal registers, Dundas placed that officer on the establishment. Both offices eventually became permanent. Registers of circulation came into being to control an increasing flow of dispatches.[18] In 1790 the governing officials of the colonies received strict instructions to number each of their dispatches and otherwise facilitate reference to them.[19] Later, under Portland, the Office adopted the useful practice of noting in the margin of the Office's copy of dispatches to colonial governors the name and date of sailing of the vessels carrying the original and duplicate dispatches.[20] Theories of administration had little part in these changes in the Home Office; common sense combined with an increased interest in efficiency produced most of the alterations and innovations in organization and procedure.

Generally, the Office maintained a fairly high level of efficiency.

18. H.O. 97/1–2; C.O. 324/61.

19. For example, a draft from Bernard to William MacCarmick, lieutenant governor of Cape Breton, Aug. 4, 1790, Spencer Bernard MSS, O.E. 1/79a.

20. For example, C.O. 133–42 (Jamaican letter book).

There are not many complaints, except by colonial officials, about inordinately long delays in replying to dispatches. The fault for delays in writing to the colonial officials often lay with members of the Cabinet rather than the Home Office, since some ministers (particularly Lords Chatham and Camden) kept the papers for long periods. Sixteen dispatches from Lord Dorchester, received on October 22, 1789, did not return from circulating to all the ministers till March 6, 1790.[21] Many times delays may have been deliberate, as when the Duke of Northumberland kept writing to the office to demand that his resignation as Lord Lieutenant of Northumberland be accepted immediately. The Home Office postponed acting, since there was no one else in the county of sufficient weight and importance to take the post.[22] But there were times when papers got lost in the office, or letters followed a minister to his country seat rather than going to the Home Office.[23] Not all letters sent were first copied in the letter books. The indexing system of out-letters was faulty. The chief clerk had the only index (through March, 1792) made at his own expense, and when he retired he removed it as his personal property.[24] Pollock apparently kept at his home all the Office's copy-books of correspondence not currently in use. This arrangement caused inconvenience on at least one occasion.[25] A particularly embarrassing incident occurred before the assembled Parliament in the House of Lords in 1797 when the Home Office sent the King a rough draft instead of a fair copy of the speech from the throne. George III was unable to decipher the scrawl. The result was much confusion until a legible copy arrived.[26] The mortal illness of George Randall, the clerk who had made the fair copy for many years, caused the blunders, evidently because no one else was familiar with the procedure.

21. H.O. 97/1.

22. Northumberland to Portland, July 30, 1798, H.O. 42/44. Portland wrote on the back of the letter: "There is no doing anything with this [illegible word] Duke but to find Persons to take the Lieuty. in Commission for there is no individual to take it. . . ." Northumberland to the King, Dec. 11, 1798, and Portland to the King, Dec. 13, 14, and 17, 1798, *Later Correspondence of George III,* III, pp. 166–68, No. 1891; 171–74, Nos. 1896–1899.

23. On November 1, 1792, Nepean informed Thomas Trigge, lieutenant governor of Portsmouth, that his letter of October 17 had followed Dundas to Scotland. H.O. 42/44.

24. IND 8913. Pollock's widow gave the index to the Home Secretary at that time, Lord Sidmouth.

25. Portland to the King, Oct. 3, 1800, *Later Correspondence of George III,* III, 421–22, No. 2254.

26. *The Times,* Nov. 4, 1797, according to *Later Correspondence of George III,* III, 474 n.

Throughout the years from 1782 to 1801 the Home Office remained a small and personal establishment. The amount of business that the Secretaries personally handled was remarkable.[27] Although before 1789 the volume of incoming correspondence was not great —sometimes less than twenty letters a day—even with the hectic pace in the 1790's the ministers seemed to be in touch with most daily developments, and the single permanent Undersecretary always was. The very smallness of the office itself—only four rooms—reflected the personal quality of the administration. It was an office administering to persons, not one administering programs and policies.[28]

27. D. M. Young, *The Colonial Office in the Early Nineteenth Century* (Imperial Studies, No. XXII, edited by Gerald S. Graham; [London, 1961]) , pp. 1–2, found this to be true well into the nineteenth century.

28. In writing this section on procedure I have found the following works of general use. Aylmer, *The King's Servants,* especially chap. vii; Edward H. Litchfield, "Notes on a General Theory of Administration," *Administrative Science Quarterly,* I (June, 1956) , 3–29; Edward and Gomer H. Redmond, "Comments on a General Theory of Administration," *ibid.,* II (No. 3, n.d.) , 235–43; Harold T. Parker, "French Administrators and French Scientists During the Old Regime and the Early Years of the Revolution," *Ideas in History: Essays Presented to Louis Gottschalk by His Former Students* (Durham, N.C., 1965) , pp. 83–109. I am also indebted to Professor Parker for many helpful suggestions.

Chapter Five

THE SECRET SERVICE

The leaders of all nations choose either regularly or occasionally to employ clandestine means to achieve certain goals. The eighteenth-century English term for these undercover operations was Secret Service.[1] The expression has seemed worth retaining for historical purposes, although espionage would now be a more common term —at least for operations against foreign governments.

For its Secret Service operations the British government relied upon the Secretaries of State. The Foreign Secretary had responsibility for the collection of intelligence within foreign countries. The Home Secretary saw to the management of the domestic Secret Service and also supervised the gathering of much intelligence on foreign (particularly French and Spanish) naval operations. In 1794 the War Department assumed the Home Office's responsibility for military intelligence.

From 1782 to 1801 the Treasury disbursed over £1,300,000 in Secret Service funds. Of this amount the Foreign Office spent £953,000, the War Department £220,000 (to 1800), and the Home Office £135,000.[2] There was no limit on the amount that Secretaries could draw from the Secret Service funds, provided that the money was for national defense or for the detection of treason. Payments

1. Secret Service to the eighteenth-century Englishman also entailed secret pensions granted by the king and expenditures by the court for elections. That aspect of the Secret Service did not concern the Home Office.

2. No accounts for Shelburne and North or for the Foreign Secretaries in 1782 and 1783 have come to light. Sydney spent £17,858.7.½. Copy of Nepean's statements of the 26th and 28th, 1791, before the Cursitor Baron of the Exchequer, Sydney Papers, Clements Library. Leeds spent about £24,000 a year or a total of £126,000. Cobban, *English Historical Review*, LXIX, 236. Grenville spent £831,267.10.7¼ from Feb. 24, 1790, to Feb. 20, 1801; £3,780 was spent while he was Home Secretary (A.O. 3/949). Dundas from May 11, 1792, to June 10, 1800, spent £255,093.1.4, of which at least £35,000 was spent while he was Home Secretary. A.O. 1/2122, roll 6; Home Office to the Treasury, Feb. 6, March 9, April 4, May 2, July 1, Sept. 9, Oct. 14, Nov. 12, 1793, and Feb. 1 and 19, March 6, April 18, June 6, 1794, H.O. 36/7–8. Portland spent £76,348.15.0 from Sept. 9, 1794, to the end of 1801. A.O. 1/2122, roll 7.

did not require the scrutiny of the Treasury. When the Secretaries began to run low on funds, they requested the Treasury to issue a warrant to reimburse them for a specified amount that they attested they had spent for Secret Service.[3] The financial arrangement had the advantage of limiting to a minimum the number of persons cognizant of clandestine operations.

The Secret Service monies spent by the Home Secretaries increased about sixfold in twenty years. Lord Sydney, from 1782 to 1789, spent an annual average of £2,600. Grenville expended about £1,900 during each of the two years he served as head of the Home department. The tenure of Dundas marked the great leap. He disbursed at least an annual average of £11,000 from mid-1791 to mid-1794. Portland averaged about £12,000 a year. The years of greatest demand were 1793 (£16,000), 1794 (£15,000), and 1798 (£14,517.12.6). The first two years marked the height of the campaign against the radical societies (and must have included some payments for acquiring military intelligence). The Irish uprising in 1798 accounted for the heavy expenditure in that year.[4]

The coming of the war vastly stepped up Dundas' expenditures, which can be followed for foreign Secret Service in Nepean's accounts in the Dundas Papers in the Duke University Library. Together with Nepean's more general accounts from 1782 to 1789 in the Sydney Papers in the Clements Library at the University of Michigan, they open up the story insofar as they are supplemented by letters in the Public Record Office. A report to the Treasury for the period from March 1792 to March 1795, in the former collection, gives figures of £13,100 for the year beginning May 15, 1792, and £24,210 for the remaining fourteen months of Dundas' tenure at the Home Office—for *foreign* Secret Service alone. Domestic expenditures of course likewise increased as the government began to struggle with radicalism. The Irish uprising of 1798 accounted for large amounts.

The reason for the involvement of the Home Office in domestic Secret Service affairs is obvious, but its concern with foreign clandestine activities requires explanation. Professor Alfred Cobban, who

3. H.O. 36 contains copies of the Home Office's requests to the Treasury for money. The original letters have been culled from the Treasury papers in the P.R.O. Itemized accounts were enclosed sometimes.

4. The Home Office letters to the Treasury are my source of information on yearly expenditures. H.O. 36.

has done indispensable spadework on the Secret Service, suggests that the responsibility was a carry-over from the Southern Department, which had conducted all relations with France and Spain. It was nearly always French and Spanish ports that attracted the attention of the Home Office.[5] To this plausible explanation one might add that as the Home Office had responsibility for military affairs until 1794, procuring naval intelligence may, with some logic, have fallen within its jurisdiction. The presence of Evan Nepean in the Office may also help to explain the attachment of some foreign Secret Service. Nepean's naval service, as purser aboard different vessels from 1776 to 1782, may have determined that he rather than William Fraser, Undersecretary in the Foreign Office, should direct the collection of intelligence about French and Spanish ports. Fraser had no maritime experience.[6] It was Nepean who gave many of the detailed orders about the collection of naval intelligence. All copies of letters about Secret Service activities are in his own hand, as is the account book. In ordinary matters the clerks performed all such functions.

Much of the Home Office's attention in the early years focused on tidying up Secret Service business from the American Revolution. Over £5,500 went to settle debts incurred during that war. Joseph Hynson received £1,000 in 1784 in lieu of a pension of £200 a year bestowed for his services in Paris during the war. He had intercepted letters sent by two of the American commissioners, Benjamin Franklin and Silas Deane, in 1777, to the Continental Congress.[7] Hynson was a close friend of Silas Deane's secretary. Another spy, John Thornton, had been in receipt of a pension of £200 a year since January 5, 1779.[8] Thornton served as private secretary to Arthur Lee, another American commissioner in Paris during the war, and rendered important services to Britain by sending false military information through Lee to the American Congress.[9] Thornton, or

5. *English Historical Review*, LXIX, 254–55. 6. For Fraser, see below.

7. Aug. 30, 1784, Nepean's Secret Service Account; Samuel Flagg Bemis, "British Secret Service and the French-American Alliance," *American Historical Review*, XXIX (April, 1924), 479–84, 491–92.

8. Thornton to Thomas Orde, Aug. 3, 1782, enclosed in Orde to Nepean, Aug. 7, 1782, loose letters in Nepean's Secret Service Account.

9. Bemis, *American Historical Review*, XXIX, 483; see also a letter about Thornton in Benjamin Franklin Stevens (compiler), *B. F. Stevens's Facsimiles of Manuscripts in European Archives Relating to America 1773–1783* (25 vols.; London, 1889–98), III, No. 29, and letters in Francis Wharton (ed.), *The Revolutionary Diplomatic Correspondence of the United States* (6 vols.; Washington, 1889), I, 659–61.

(as his real name seems to have been, to judge from later entries in the account) Dumaresq, became active again in 1787 and 1788, and remained so all through Dundas' tenure at the Office.[10] A Captain Taylor, who had supplied Lord George Germain, Lord Shelburne, and Nepean with intelligence, received a settlement of £1,262.9.6 for his services.[11] Another £446.0.8 went to reimburse Vice-Admiral Sir Edward Hughes for money expended by him for Secret Service in the East Indies, where he served as commander-in-chief from July 1778 to the end of the war.[12] Joseph Brant, the Mohawk chieftain, was granted £1,449.14.9 in 1786 in consideration of damages sustained by him and his sister from the depredations of American troops.[13] Granting the money from Secret Service funds evidently avoided claims by other Indians.[14]

The Home Office's Secret Service had a more vital aspect than paying old debts, for Nepean often actively engaged in the collection of intelligence. He had several means by which he accomplished that end. Richard Oakes, a London merchant, and Thomas Taylor, master of Lloyd's Coffee House, regularly provided information of intelligence value. Informers—persons who volunteered information for various reasons—provided a certain number of useful reports. Among the most profitable sources of information were small boats sent from England to observe the activities in different French and Spanish seaports. The Channel Islands, near the French coast, were another rich mine of intelligence. On occasion the Home Office actually sent spies—persons under orders to engage in active collection of intelligence in closed areas.

Oakes, a dealer in hardware, though somewhat amateurish, nevertheless proved to be a valuable source of intelligence. On May 24, 1782, for instance, he sent information on the number of ships in the enemy fleet intending to act in the English Channel and also related a brief history of his source of information. In 1781 an official high in the Marine Department of France had made overtures to a friend of Oakes in France. In return for £5,000 down and £25,000 at the

10. Dumaresq was undoubtedly a member of the prominent family of that name on the island of Jersey. A. C. Saunders, *Jersey in the 18th and 19th Centuries* (Jersey, 1930), *passim*. Dundas Papers, Duke University MSS.

11. Aug. 17, 1782; Feb. 15, 1783, Nepean's Secret Service Account.

12. Feb. 24, 1784, *ibid.*; *DNB*, X, 172–75.

13. March 31, 1786, Nepean's Secret Service Account.

14. Sydney to Lieutenant Governor Henry Hope, April 6, 1786, and Sydney to Brant, same date, Shortt and Doughty (eds.), *Documents Relating to the Constitutional History of Canada, 1759–1791*, II, 805–809.

end of the war, the official promised to furnish the British government with every move of the French Cabinet. Oakes had told the official, through his friend, that he could not make such a proposal with any hopes of success, as the war had proved very costly for England; but that if the Frenchman could furnish him with information he would see what he could do. By this contact, Oakes claimed, he had had the means of furnishing the British government with "almost Everything of Consequence during the last twelve months." Oakes complained, however, that the effort had cost him much both in time and money and requested £500.[15] The government evidently valued the information, for Oakes received £1,050 from Secret Service funds for the last half of 1782, and another £400 in the first half of 1783.[16]

In addition to serving as a channel for this important French official, whoever he was, Oakes performed other services. In 1782 he accompanied a Madame de Vitre and a Monsieur Reboul to Ostend on some mysterious intelligence mission.[17] Oakes brought Madame de Vitre back to London in 1784 on the advice of the British ambassador to France, the Duke of Manchester, to avoid having her case made a public concern between England and France.[18] Her "case" referred to a pension that she had requested to compensate for the loss of her husband aboard the *Lizard* in 1775 while he tried to hold Quebec for the British.[19] The government granted the pension, which she received through the British ambassador in Paris.[20] Sympathy alone, it appears, did not beget her recompense, for Oakes stressed her importance for keeping open his sources of information in France.[21] Madame de Vitre's son worked in the office of the Comte de Vergennes, minister of foreign affairs.[22]

At times Oakes must have been too expansive in his promises, for Nepean had to reprimand him at one point. In justifying himself, Oakes gave the little information that is known about him. He referred to his work in the councils of the city of London and to his great success as a merchant. During the war he fitted out five privateers at his own expense for a descent upon Zeeland, which failed

15. May 24, 1782, H.O. 42/1. The notice of Oakes's bankruptcy referred to him as a hardwareman. *The Times,* Feb. 8, 1792.

16. Nepean's Secret Service Account.

17. Sept. 10, 1792, *ibid.*

18. Oakes to Nepean, April 6, 1784, H.O. 42/4.

19. Mme Jeanne de Vitre to Sydney, Jan. 14, 1784, No. 3 East Street, Red Lion Square, H.O. 42/4.

20. Oakes to Nepean, April 6, 1784; Mme de Vitre to Nepean, Feb. 12 and May 30, 1784, H.O. 42/4.

21. Oakes to Nepean, April 6, 1784, H.O. 42/4.

22. Oakes to Nepean, Dec. 26, 1783, Holborn Bridge, H.O. 42/3.

only for lack of troops.[23] In all he had lost over £44,000 during the war and had given the government most of his time from 1781 to 1783.[24]

Oakes's losses failed to daunt him, for whenever trouble threatened, he was ready with information. Several times foreign powers attempted to entice away British seamen; Oakes reported the incidents.[25] When civil war in the Netherlands appeared imminent in 1787, Oakes made a secret mission to Flanders for which he received £400.[26] Sometimes his intelligence came rather circuitously. On October 19, 1788, Oakes informed Nepean that the preceding night he had seen the Russian agent, who had just received letters from Henry Hope, an important banker in Amsterdam, reporting that the Danish forces had surrounded the King of Sweden. The letters also contained further particulars on the war between Sweden and its opponents, Denmark and Russia.[27] Circuitous though it was, the information was substantially correct.[28]

During the crisis with Spain in 1790 over Nootka Sound in northwestern America, Oakes produced an account of the size of the Spanish fleet that he had got from a Spanish merchant in London.[29] Oakes relied upon a French merchant for news of developments at the court of Louis XVI during the crisis.[30] Throughout June 1790, Oakes furnished information on the activities of the French and Spaniards by means of a person named Royre. This man had access to the Spanish minister in London and also to the Duke of Orleans, cousin of Louis XVI, who had arrived in London October 21, 1789.[31] During the Nootka Sound crisis Oakes also acted as agent for employing small craft to spy on the Spanish ports.[32]

What part Oakes would have played in gathering intelligence

23. Oakes to Nepean, June 28, 1782, H.O. 42/1.
24. Same to same, Jan. 25, 1784, H.O. 42/4.
25. Oakes to Nepean, July 30, 1783, H.O. 42/3 and same to same, Jan. 25, 1784, both from Holborn Bridge, H.O. 42/4.
26. Aug. 5 and 24, Oct. 6, Nov. 6, Dec. 7, 1787, Nepean's Secret Service Account. Professor Cobban's *Ambassadors and Secret Agents: The Diplomacy of the First Earl of Malmesbury at the Hague* (London, 1954) considers the Dutch crisis in detail, but does not have any reference to Oakes's mission.
27. Cleveland Court, H.O. 42/13. See Cobban, *Ambassadors and Secret Agents,* pp. 113, 127, 196, for information on Hope (1736–1811) and also the *Gentleman's Magazine,* LXXXI (March, 1811), 292–93.
28. J. H. Rose, *William Pitt and National Revival,* p. 495.
29. Oakes to Nepean, May 12 and 15, 1790, Cleveland Court, H.O. 42/16.
30. Oakes to Nepean, May 18, 1790, Cleveland Court, St. James's Place, *ibid.*
31. Oakes to Nepean, June 11, 16, 17 (2), 26, and 30, 1790, *ibid.*; *Later Correspondence of George III,* I, 446, n. 1.
32. Nepean to John Cartwright Morris, May 12, 1790, copy, H.O. 42/16. Oakes sent additional letters on Spanish affairs to Nepean Oct. 22, 19, and 30, 1790, H.O. 42/17.

during the wars of the French Revolution will never be known. On March 21, 1791, he hastily informed Nepean that he had been arrested for expenses incurred in keeping open a "large number of houses" during the armament against Spain. He planned to flee to the East Indies. The Secretary to the Admiralty, Philip Stephens, would speak to Nepean about giving him £300.[33] Undaunted to the last, on that very same day, Oakes was sending intelligence about Russia to Nepean.[34] The last record of this interesting and quite useful man is a letter that he wrote from Calcutta on New Year's Day, 1793. The indomitable Oakes offered to send his impression of the state of business in India as soon as he got settled, and enclosed some books as gifts for Dundas and the King.[35]

Thomas Taylor, master of Lloyd's Coffee House, provided a regular means of communication on naval affairs. Lloyd's had developed a remarkable news service about shipping during the latter half of the eighteenth century. The Admiralty drew very heavily for information not only upon the master but also upon the managing committee at Lloyd's.[36] Nepean's connection, however, seems to have been solely with Taylor, master from 1774 until his death June 6, 1796.[37] Since it was Taylor's business to keep the books of arrivals, departures, and losses of ships, to copy the port letters, and to see to the prompt posting of all intelligence received, his position as a source of information on naval matters was unique and valuable.[38]

During the Nootka Sound crisis, for instance, Taylor sent Nepean copies of letters received by London merchants from their correspondents in Bristol that conveyed accounts of the sighting of Spanish vessels by the captain of a ship that had recently docked.[39] From Portsmouth came reports from a merchant captain who had sighted Spanish ships off Cape St. Mary.[40] In August, Taylor sent information obtained at Dover from a captain who had seen the

33. H.O. 42/18. 34. *Ibid.*

35. To Dundas, H.O. 42/24. His wife Elizabeth Oakes wrote to Nepean on June 18, 1792, to ask for a small sum. Her son Richard William had gone to India as midshipman in December 1790, but had now returned and needed another berth. June 18 and 28, 1792, H.O. 42/20.

36. D. E. W. Gibb, *Lloyd's of London: A Study in Individualism* (London, 1957), p. 71.

37. Taylor was born about 1746. *Gentleman's Magazine,* LXVI (June, 1796), 530.

38. Charles Wright and C. Ernest Fayle, *A History of Lloyd's from the Founding of Lloyd's Coffee House to the Present Day* (London, 1928), pp. 169, 203; for more on Taylor see pp. 169–70, 213, and the portrait opposite p. 170.

39. June 2, 1790, H.O. 42/16.

40. Taylor to Nepean, Lloyd's Coffee House, June 25, 1790, *ibid.*

Spanish fleet near Oporto.[41] On November 2, Taylor relayed information about the Russian fleet,[42] and a year later about trouble in Guadeloupe and St. Lucia.[43] Following the rupture with France, Taylor again sent reports.[44] Taylor's information generally dealt in specifics such as the number, description, location, and time of observation of enemy ships; consequently, the intelligence had great value, and as will appear later, was put to good use by Nepean.

Some information came unsolicited from informers. One of the most interesting of these, semiliterate Mary Tonkin of Swansea, Glamorganshire, South Wales, wrote to Grenville in March 1790 that she had just returned from Faro in Spain,[45] and enclosed considerable information about shipbuilding at the port.[46] In June she wrote again. The tone was noticeably different. Nepean, she said, had sent her for her information about Spain only five guineas, which had been "disagreeably received." The journey alone had cost her thirty guineas. She had now returned from France and expected that her services would be more adequately rewarded. If not, she would be obliged to enter some foreign service. The postscript of the letter assumed an abusive tone: "I ask you a civil question. Shall I sell the English Fleet, or save it from ruin? You force me to do it." Admiral Barrington and his twelve sail of the line, she warned, would have a hearty drubbing. She closed by asking that her compliments be given to Philip Stevens, secretary to the Admiralty, who was a blackguard and betrayer of the King's secrets.[47] How many cranks like Mary Tonkin the Office had to tolerate is unknown. Sometimes, however, unsolicited information proved to be quite valuable, and then as now authorities could ignore it only at their peril.

An important source of naval intelligence came from the use of small boats, such as luggers and cutters. In November 1784 Nepean

41. Same to same, Aug. 26, 1790, same place, *ibid.*
42. Same to same, same place, H.O. 42/17.
43. Taylor to Nepean, Nov. 14, 1790, Spencer Bernard MSS, O.E. 2/27; and Nov. 16, 1791, same to same, O.E. 2/40.
44. Same to same, Feb. 24, 1793, H.O. 42/24; and July 18, 1793, C.O. 166/1. Many letters may be in the Admiralty correspondence or elsewhere, as Taylor surely sent more than are in the H.O. or C.O. papers, but the pattern is clear from the examples given.
45. Faro is in Portugal, not Spain. She may have meant Ferrol, an important naval port in northern Spain.
46. Mary Tonkin to Rt. Hon. Grenvell [*sic*], Swansea, H.O. 42/16.
47. Same to Granville [*sic*], June 30, 1790, White Horse Cellar. Spelling and punctuation of the quotation is modernized and corrected.

advanced £150 to one Captain Phillips to enable him to undertake a journey to Toulon and other ports in France to observe the size and state of the naval forces and arsenals.[48] Phillips reported from Toulon in March 1785.[49] Later in 1785 Captain Robert Le Geyt, commander of a Post Office packetboat on the run from Dover to Calais and Ostend,[50] received over £150 for trips to Normandy and Brest.[51] The gathering of intelligence on enemy naval dispositions by packetboat commanders occurred fairly often in the eighteenth century.[52]

From 1785 to 1787, during the civil disorders in the Netherlands, a flurry of spying occurred. Le Geyt again went to Brest and St. Malo.[53] A Captain Blankett received £92 for watching the French squadron at Brest.[54] Joseph Stewart, a successful merchant in Sandwich, Kent, who had been instrumental in the capture of a French spy in 1781,[55] received £80 for the hire of his vessel to watch the French on the coast of Flanders.[56] Captain Dumaresq, probably the same man who had served as private secretary to Arthur Lee, also made trips to Brest between November 1787 and June 1788 to report upon French ships preparing for the East Indies.[57]

During the crisis over Nootka Sound in 1790 the use of small craft on spying missions became a regular and almost systematic practice. All the letters concern the dispatching of small craft to French and Spanish ports. Nepean approached Richard Oakes in May 1790 about employing two cutters. Oakes got in touch with a shipping concern in Dover—Mills, Ladd, and Jell—that evidently acted as agent for small, independently owned boats. Nepean spelled out the terms of the agreement to John Cartwright Morris, captain and owner of one of the cutters. For the *Alert* cutter, the government would pay £80 per month for a minimum period of three months. In case of capture by any foreign power, the government would be answerable for the cost of the vessel, tackle, and furniture. Upon

48. Nepean's Secret Service Account.
49. Cobban, *English Historical Review,* LXIX, 250.
50. *Tenth Report of the Commissioners Appointed to inquire into Fees . . . in Public Offices: The Post Office,* Appendix 12, p. 890, *PP 1806* (309), VII. Le Geyt, probably a member of the prominent Jersey family of that name, died on April 7, 1792, at Canterbury. *Gentleman's Magazine,* LXII (April, 1792), 390.
51. May 24, July 12, and Oct. 12, 1785, Nepean's Secret Service Account.
52. Kenneth Ellis, *The Post Office in the Eighteenth Century: A Study in Administrative History* (London, 1958), pp. 35–37, 61.
53. July 31, Sept. 22, 26, 1787, Nepean's Secret Service Account.
54. July 23, 1787, *ibid.*
55. He died on August 27, 1789. *Gentleman's Magazine,* LIX (Sept., 1789), 864.
56. Nov. 20, 1787, Nepean's Secret Service Account.
57. Sept. 20, 1788, *ibid.*

Morris' return Nepean would pay any bills drawn upon him by the owners for the amount of the freight that he carried for the sake of a legitimate appearance.[58]

To Mills, Ladd, and Jell, Nepean sent the necessary passes for two vessels, to be employed in addition to the craft of Morris, and cautioned them that only those entrusted with the mission should have knowledge of it. He hoped that the commanders of the two vessels were reliable. The *Diligent* cutter would receive £75 per month for three months, and the *Friendship* £50 per month for the same period. If their service proved satisfactory, the government might extend the bargain for a longer period of time.[59]

Nepean's copies of instructions to two of the three commanders survive and illuminate the purpose of the missions. Morris had orders to determine "the *actual state of the Maritime Force at Ferrol*," but left the mode of executing the assignment to the captain. The names and class of the ships, Nepean said, were necessary and an account of the military, if obtainable without great difficulty, was desirable. Morris was to report by express as soon as he reached England.[60] Although Morris and three other captains all failed to collect reliable information on their voyages in mid-1790,[61] Nepean persisted in sending out these small ships until the Nootka Sound crisis ended in the fall of 1790.[62]

When hostilities with France began to threaten in late 1792, Nepean once more relied upon cutters to gather intelligence. He employed a firm of merchants and bankers in Dover—Fector and Minet—to act as his agent for hiring these useful captains. In response to the firm's request for licenses for two cutters,[63] Nepean wrote that he was sending the licenses through the customs collector at Dover, but "I advise the Masters by all means to *keep their old Licenses,* and in case they should be examined in a foreign Port, the

58. May 12, 1790, H.O. 42/16. 59. To Richard Jell, May 27, 1790, secret, *ibid.*

60. May 12, 1790; Nepean to Robert Griggs, master of the *Friendship,* May 27, 1790, H.O. 42/16.

61. Morris to Nepean, June 1, 1790, Falmouth; Morris (Dover) to Oakes (Cleveland Court, London), June 10, 1790, enclosed in Oakes to Nepean, June 11, 1790; Griggs to Nepean, June 16, 1790, *Friendship,* Falmouth; John Matthews (*Isabella,* Ramsgate) to Wilsford (Swithen Street, Lombard) [n. d., but after July 1790]; John Simmons to Nepean, *Diligent,* Dover pier, Aug. 6, 1790, H.O. 42/16.

62. John Mills to Nepean, July 18, 1790, Falmouth; Griggs to Nepean, Aug. 22, 1790, Dover; Nepean to Mills, Aug. 30, 1790, H.O. 42/16; Mills to Nepean, Sept. 29, 1790, Falmouth, H.O. 42/17.

63. Fector and Minet to Nepean, Dec. 9, 1792, H.O. 42/23. William Minet, *Some Account of the Huguenot Family of Minet* (London, 1892).

more their proceedings appear irregular, the better. By producing *only* their old Licenses, they would hardly be suspected." [64]

The firm came to handle considerable secret business. They had authorization to purchase large numbers of small foreign craft, especially cutters at Ostend that might be used against England. Nepean's letter to Fector on February 2, 1793, reveals both that the banker bought ships for the government and that he was entrusted with the discretion of selecting the ports to which he was regularly to send ships:

> I shall be glad if you can send over one or two of your vessels to any of the ports nearly opposite to you to which shipping may resort, with a view of observing whether since the embargo any alteration is making the fitting of any of the shipping now detained? I mean with a view to enable them to accommodate troops, to receive stores &c.
>
> Whether any of the rigging, stores &c of the vessels detained are taken for the equipment of other vessels?
>
> Whether any assemblage is making of fishing vessels or any other small craft, which seems calculated for the transportation of troops across &c.
>
> It is very desirable that we should receive information upon these and all other points of a similar nature regularly, and I should think you might so manage that business by means of your own vessels, that when one might be on her return the other might be going over. You are the best judge as to the ports but I should think those which are the nearest to us the best because the intelligence would be more expeditiously obtained than from ports that may be more distant.[65]

Nepean continued to send vessels to the French coast during early 1793. Captains went to the Scheldt, Cherbourg, and Le Havre.[66] At least two American vessels, at the instigation of Home Office, sailed to Boulogne on intelligence missions.[67] The increasing flood of émigrés in 1793 brought heavy charges on the Secret Service for their relief, for sending some of them to Santo Domingo and Martinique (July 1793–January 1794), and for the formation of a Loyal Emigrant regiment under Claude-Louis, Comte (later Duc)

64. Nepean to Peter Fector, Dec. 25, 1792, secret, H.O. 42/23.

65. Secret, spelling modernized, H.O. 42/24. As an example of disbursements to this firm, they received £1029 on April 25, 1793; £716 on July 22 and October 7; and £700 on March 7, 1794. Dundas Papers, Duke University MSS.

66. Nepean to Stephen Hunt, Dec. 22, 1792; Nepean to David Puttee, captain of the *Peggy*, Dec. 22, 1792, H.O. 42/23; Nepean to Hunt, Jan. 19, 1793; Nepean to Putee, Dec. 25, 1792, and Feb. 3, 1793, H.O. 42/24.

67. Bundock to William Huskisson, June 25, 1793, No. 23 Billiter Lane, London, H.O. 42/25.

de La Chastre (1745–1824), which went with the ill-fated expedition to Flanders in 1794.[68]

The Channel Islands of Guernsey, Jersey, Alderney, and, to a small extent, Sark provided another source of information for Nepean's Secret Service. The lieutenant governors of the islands frequently transmitted information that they had gleaned from seamen who continually plied the waters between the islands and France.[69] In January 1788 Nepean paid the lieutenant governor of Jersey, Philip Fall (or Falle), £81.13.0 for the hire of a vessel and the pay of an officer from Jersey to go to Brest to inspect the naval forces there.[70] During the war with France the Channel Islands became the center of the entire royalist movement. Professor Cobban contends, quite rightly it appears, that the British government was confident that it would not become involved in hostilities with France.[71] Not until late 1792, as we have seen, did Nepean begin to send out spies. Fall made the first move by sending intelligence of French activities in late December 1792.[72] By mid-January 1793 Nepean became interested. He wrote to Fall:

> I understand that the French are equipping at L'Orient, Rochefort, etc. and if you can find a fit Person, I mean a person conversant with shipping, it will be extremely desirable that you should send him to those places as soon as possible. It is very material that he should bring intelligence of the *Names* of the ships which have sailed and of those remaining in these ports with their conditions—viz. whether they are manned and fit for sea, Building, Equipping, or lying up as Hulks, and as I am in possession of a list of the whole Navy of France, I can from a reference to it at once ascertain their force.[73]

Nepean also had the lieutenant governor of Guernsey send a man to examine the fleet at Brest. The Chevalier du Laurens was dispatched into Brittany, and Peter Le Mesurier, governor of Alderney, sent information obtained from French smugglers.[74]

68. Nepean's Secret Service Accounts in Dundas Papers, Duke University MSS. The sums for relief of émigrés are to be found especially in Nepean's personal settlement, August 1, 1797, with Charles Long at the Treasury, for sums expended April 1793–January 1795. For La Chastre, spelled in the accounts Chatre, see *Biographie Universelle . . . Supplément*, LXIX, 287–290.

69. Various reports may be found in H.O. 98/1–5 (Jersey), H.O. 98/23–24 (Guernsey), and H.O. 98/40 (Alderney).

70. Jan. 9, 1788, Nepean's Secret Service Account.

71. "The Beginning of the Channel Isles Correspondence, 1789–1794," *English Historical Review*, LXXVII (Jan., 1962), 38–39.

72. Dec. 20, 1792, H.O. 98/2.

73. *Ibid.*

74. Cobban, *English Historical Review*, LXXVII, 41. The Dundas Papers in Duke University MSS show outlays in Guernsey and Jersey in the summer and autumn of 1793.

The Home department actually sent some agents directly into foreign countries or took into its employ persons already resident in Europe. As we have seen, Madame de Vitre was in receipt of a pension while she resided in France. Oakes himself made occasional trips into Flanders and France on intelligence missions. John (or Thomas) Green had received payments in 1782 for his part in searching for smugglers in Sussex who were carrying intelligence to the French. After Green moved to Flanders, he received stipends, evidently for information that he provided.[75] In 1784 Monsieur de St. Marc reported on the engineers whom the French government had ordered to examine the state of defenses along the French coast.[76] On October 8, 1787, Nepean paid £50 to Alexander Catmure, who later served as a guard for the King, for a trip to Dunkirk to observe the troops and ships.[77] On the same day the Undersecretary paid one Tencate for a similar mission to Calais. Lieutenant George Paris Monke,[78] a naval officer, went as a spy to Dunkirk and Gravelines to examine the state of the French navy. In October he reported on the French ports at Toulon and Marseilles. He managed to gain entry to Toulon by following the mail packet disguised as a Frenchman. Monke continued to send reports from Toulon, Flanders, and other places through early 1789, sometimes via the British embassy in Paris. In all he received £1,290 from September 13, 1787, through April 1789.[79]

The Home Office participated in other aspects of foreign Secret

75. Nepean's Secret Service Account, *passim*. Green's reports were not in the Home Office papers. Green may well have been John Richards Green (1757–1818), who fled to Flanders in 1782 to escape imprisonment for debt. He later assumed the name of John Gifford, returned to England, and served the government as an active antiradical pamphleteer. *DNB,* VII, 1184.

76. Feb. 2, 1784, Nepean's Secret Service Account; Cobban, *English Historical Review,* LXIX, 239.

77. Oct. 2 and 8, 1787, March 18, 1788, Nepean's Secret Service Account; Oct. 29, 1790, Contingent Account, H.O. 82/3. Nepean thought well of Catmure. Nepean to Colonel Francis Edward Gwynne, equerry to the King, June 6, 1790, H.O. 42/16. As surveyor of windows in Westminster, Catmure received £90 a year. *Eighth Report of the Select Committee on Finance: Tax Office,* First Series, XII, Appendix A.1, p. 228.

78. Monke, only son of an officer of the Royal Horse Guards, entered the Navy in June 1775 as a midshipman. During the war he saw active duty under Lord Rodney. In 1790 he was appointed to command the *Speedwell* cutter and was employed "on various services, under the orders of Lord Howe." In 1792 he captured a smuggling cutter off the Yorkshire coast. Shortly before the war with France, Monke made a trip to Hamburg to bring over British sailors wrecked off the coast of Jutland. During the course of this assignment he seriously impaired his health and resigned his command in August 1793. He subsequently commanded other ships and was promoted to commander in March 1797 and to post captain on January 12, 1810. On December 18, 1810, he ran his ship aground and was not employed thereafter. *Annual Biography and Obituary,* XIV (1830), 428–29. He died on November 14, 1828, at Dunkirk.

79. Nepean's Secret Service Account; Cobban, *English Historical Review,* LXIX, 250.

Service on occasion. During the crisis in Holland it actually took part in supplying the supporters of the royal party with gunpowder. Sir James Harris, ambassador to the Netherlands, informed the Foreign Secretary, Lord Carmarthen, on August 28, 1787, that "we endeavoured to concert means to convey into the Brille [a royalist stronghold] the quantity of powder your Lordship mentions as being ready at Harwich [the port in Essex]. If we once get it safe to the Brille, it may easily be brought in small quantities here" by means of fishing boats.[80] Nepean sent Thomas Daw, one of the senior Home Office clerks, to Harwich to receive the dispatches from Harris. Although Daw apparently did not get the orders,[81] the Home Office paid £1,353.13.7 in October on account of the sloop *Polly* and its cargo of gunpowder.[82]

A mysterious and hurried transaction occurred in late December 1792. Nepean informed Fector that he must be ready on the morning of the 29th to carry a person across the bay. He sent a letter from the Admiralty to order cruisers to assist the cutter and one from the Treasury to prevent revenue vessels from interfering with her. The government would pay for the cutter if she were taken.[83] Captain John Hawes made the trip, which landed one Lauzun at an undisclosed destination.[84]

In February 1794 William Windham engaged in a correspondence with Dundas and Nepean for the purpose of returning Monsieur de La Robière, an aide-de-camp to a French royalist commander, to France. Windham, who was to become Secretary at War in June 1794, had interested himself in the royalist movement and actively supported it. Nepean handled the details relative to the passage, and the Home Office defrayed the cost. This expedition went very ill, for winds and bad weather delayed the embarkation, and then the French drove the ship carrying de La Robière back to Plymouth. Not till later did he succeed in returning to France.[85]

80. [Malmesbury, James (Harris), first Earl of] *Diaries and Correspondence of James Harris, First Earl of Malmesbury*, edited by James Howard, third Earl of Malmesbury (4 vols.; London, 1844), II, 362.

81. Daw to [?Nepean], Aug. 30, 1787, Harwich, P.R.O. 30/8/128 (Chatham Papers).

82. Oct. 17, 1787, Nepean's Secret Service Account. On August 17 Daw received £20 for his expenses to Harwich.

83. Dec. 28, 1792, secret, H.O. 42/23.

84. Peter Fector and Minet to Nepean, Dec. 31, 1792; John Hawes to Dundas, Dec. 19, 1792, *ibid.* Possibly this agent was David Lauzun, a king's messenger. He was serving in 1774 and retired on October 10, 1795. Ambrose Vincent Wheeler-Holohan, *The History of the King's Messengers* (London, 1935), p. 278.

85. *Diary of the Right Hon. William Windham, 1784 to 1810*, edited by Mrs. Henry Baring (London, 1866), pp. 302, 309–310; letters from Windham to Dundas, Feb. 8, 9, 11, 12, 17 (2), and 24, 1794; Joseph Banfield to Nepean, April 11, 1794, Falmouth;

Simply collecting the information about the activities of foreign government does not suffice to provide usable intelligence. Someone must collate and analyze the raw intelligence and prepare an intelligence estimate. Only one such document prepared by the Home Office has come to light, but it provides an excellent idea of how information gathered by the Secret Service was put to use. On September 26, 1787, Nepean prepared an intelligence estimate of the distribution of the French navy. His knowledge of the French West Indian fleet came from a letter sent by a respected planter on St. Kitts, letters received by the master of Lloyd's, a report sent by Commodore Gardiner to the Admiralty that mentioned French ships moving to the United States in order to avoid the hurricane season, and a Boston newspaper's account of the arrival of the French squadron. Nepean concluded that only one French squadron operated in the western waters, but that when the hurricane season passed in October, the French would be "equal to the execution of any attack which may be meditated against our islands in our present impotent state."

Nepean also had to know the location of the French ships that remained in Europe. Information from Horace Walpole, the British ambassador to Portugal, and from a merchant captain's account, sent by the lieutenant governor of Guernsey, led Nepean to suspect that about fifteen French vessels were bound for Brest. Captains Le Geyt and Blankett, whom Nepean ordered to Brest, reported a flurry of activity caused by the provisioning and readying of ships. Further reports from Admiral Lord Hood, a French merchant captain (sent by the lieutenant governor of Jersey), and Blankett confirmed the presence of between fifteen and twenty ships at Brest. Other intelligence from the Channel Islands and Captain Blankett described the preparations at Cherbourg and L'Orient.[86]

The importance of this intelligence estimate may be seen at once by the tone of a Cabinet minute of October 11, 1787, about two weeks after Nepean prepared the précis:

> It is humbly submitted to your Majesty that in consequence of farther information respecting the preparations supposed to be made in the ports of France, Rear Admiral Hotham be directed to communicate to the Admiralty any intelligence he shall receive from the cutters employed

---

Dougal McDougal to unknown recipient, April 18, 1794, aboard the *Earl of Chatham* at Penzance.

86. This long, interesting précis found its way into C.O. 318/4.

to obtain information of troops being under embarkation at the ports of Dunkirk, Calais or Boulogne, . . . and to keep the ships under his command in readiness to proceed as he may be farther directed.[87]

Two days later the Cabinet advised that "a detachment of five ships of the Line should be immediately prepared for foreign service, and proceed to the Leeward Islands. . . ." [88]

When in 1794 the creation of the office of Secretary for War no doubt relieved the Home department of the unusual responsibility of foreign Secret Service, Nepean became Undersecretary in the new office. The Channel Islands correspondence passed into the hands of Philip d'Auvergne, Duc (or Prince) de Bouillon, and continued to play a significant role in the counterrevolutionary movement in France.[89]

Within England itself a permanent Secret Service existed from at least 1782 through 1791, and no doubt longer. William Clark, who headed the service, employed and paid two other agents. Each man received five shillings a day when actively employed, and one shilling a day when unemployed. Expenses such as coach hire were also paid by the government. Clark may have been the Bow Street officer of the same name, but most of the other Secret Service operatives have sunk into historical oblivion. From the atrocious spelling of surviving letters it may be assumed that some were scarcely literate. The accounts do not clearly indicate the names of the two operatives besides Clark except in 1791, when Isaac and Simon Smith were on the payroll. Prior to that year three names appear more than once. James Johnstone was engaged in August 1784 in watching the French minister to England and other persons. In 1785 he made a trip to Brest for which he received £105. The last entry mentioning him is March 31, 1786. One Murphy appears in March 1784 and in August 1786. George Hart also appears twice, but both times in the fall of 1788.[90]

Though the account books are missing for 1790, the almost daily reports in the Home Office papers from August through November 1790 identify another agent—George Parker, who was sufficiently illustrious to find his way into the *Dictionary of National Biography*. Parker, born in 1732, enjoyed a varied career in the navy and

87. *Later Correspondence of George III*, I, 342. 88. *Ibid.*, I, 343.

89. Cobban, *English Historical Review*, LXXVII, 50; much material on Bouillon is in F.O. 95, H.O. 69, P.C. 1, and W.O. 1. 90. Nepean's Secret Service Account, *passim*.

the army and had actually seen service under General James Wolfe at Quebec. But he spent most of his years as a traveling actor and lecturer in England and Ireland. Parker's great corpulence had forced George Coleman, dramatist and part owner of the Covent Garden Theatre, to decline his services as an actor.[91] In 1784 Parker accompanied the celebrated Irish priest Arthur O'Leary to Dublin at the request of the Chief Secretary for Ireland, Thomas Orde.[92] He evidently had some part in reorganizing the police in Dublin.[93]

The Home Office employed Parker from August through November 1790 in following the Venezuelan revolutionary Colonel (later General) Francisco de Miranda.[94] This was to be his last employment under the government. In January 1791 he wrote Nepean to inform him

> of the dreadful situation that my wife and family are in—by all that [is] just and sacred we are starving. O! Sir, you did not use to want humanity.
>
> I am so lost and dejected, that I sink under my troubles, and have not courage enough to combat with them; and all this is owing to my not having the least employment from my patron Mr. Nepean. . . . I little thought that I should ever be left to want bread, and the common necessities of life—besides every moment in expectation of a rapacious and cruel landlord seizeing [*sic*] the very *Bed* we lie on, as every other article is in pawn, that only excepted.[95]

Parker confessed that he had dragged out the surveillance of Colonel Miranda for six weeks when two or three days would have sufficed, but resorted to that trick only because Nepean had told him that it would be the final employment.[96] Perhaps it is not without significance that the post from which Parker generally observed Miranda's lodgings was a tavern. From later letters with which Parker continued to bombard Nepean, it appears that he had written an impertinent letter or two and had boasted that he had been hired to follow Miranda. But he was starving and his wife was ill from the reception that Mrs. Nepean had accorded her when she called at his house, and he himself was too ill to walk across the room, and his child was ill, and could Nepean not help?[97] After 1793

91. *DNB*, XV, 235–36.

92. W. J. Fitzpatrick, *Secret Service Under Pitt* (2nd ed.; London, 1892), p. 230; but Fitzpatrick errs in identifying him as Richard Parker who was hanged for his part in the mutiny at the Nore in 1797 (pp. 277–279).

93. Parker to Nepean, Jan. 20, 1791, No. 3 Oakley Street near the Turnpike, Westminster Bridge, H.O. 42/17.

94. Reports in *ibid.* 95. Jan. 1791, *ibid.* 96. *Ibid.*

97. Parker to Nepean, May 13, June 2, and two without dates, H.O. 42/25.

Parker seems to have given up asking. The wife and child are not mentioned in the *DNB,* and were probably rhetorical creations. Although his wit and humor had brought him the friendship of men like Dr. Samuel Johnson and Sir Joshua Reynolds, in later years Parker was reduced to selling gingerbread nuts at fairs and races. He died in the Coventry poorhouse in April 1800, aged sixty-eight.[98]

Without an organized and trained secret service, the government doubtless not uncommonly employed many George Parkers. To have hired more reputable men would have been expensive and difficult to justify, at least in peacetime, to an inquiring Parliament. In fairness, however, it should be pointed out that William Clark served as head of the little Secret Service in a trusted capacity for at least ten years, apparently without complaint.

These agents performed a wide variety of functions. Many of their cases involved the investigation of persons suspected of being in the secret employ of foreign nations. In 1782 Clark made a trip to Brighthelmstone and Portsmouth in search of a Monsieur Pelivé suspected of conveying intelligence to France.[99] Captain Ottendorf received £135 in 1782 and 1783 for providing intelligence of certain persons employed by the French in London.[100] John (or Thomas) Green was active in late 1782 in search of two smugglers employed to carry intelligence to France.[101] Captain John Haddock, commander of a Customs cutter at Rye, assisted him.[102]

The agents spent considerable time in observing various foreign ministers and persons supposedly connected with them. The reasons are not always clear. Johnstone, from August 1784 to at least April 1785, watched certain persons engaged by the French minister, particularly a Madame d'Eon. She was followed till July 1786.[103] Between September 5 and 28, 1784, two men observed the motions of Prince Caramanicio, the ambassador from the Kingdom of the Two Sicilies.[104] The Spanish ambassador, the Marquis del Campo, was

98. *DNB,* XV, 235–36. 99. Sept. 25, 1782, Nepean's Secret Service Account.
100. Oct. 11, 1782, Feb. 1, 1783, *ibid.*
101. Aug. 20, Oct. 1, 31, 1782, March 10, 1783, *ibid.*
102. March 18, 1783, *ibid.; Fourth Report of the Select Committee on Finance, 1797: Customs,* First Series, XII, Appendix F., pp. 84; or possibly Henry Haddock, master of the *Scourge,* a customs vessel, who was killed by smugglers off Dungeness Point, Kent. Sept. 1, 1783, *London Chronicle.*
103. Nepean's Secret Service Account. Mme d'Eon could not have been the notorious transvestite, the Chevalier Eon de Beaumont, as he did not return to London till after November 17, 1785. Cynthia Cox, *The Enigma of the Age: The Strange Case of the Chevalier d'Eon* (London, 1966), pp. 113–14, 124.
104. Nepean's Secret Service Account incorrectly calls him the Venetian ambassador.

observed from September 29 through October 12, and again from October 29 through December 30, 1784.[105] In October and November 1786 a Monsieur Le Toure, suspected of being employed by the French, was under surveillance.[106] From December 31, 1787, to January 24 of the next year Count Browne had a watch upon him for the same reason.[107]

Agents immediately began to observe the new ambassador from France, the Marquis de la Luzerne, and his friend the Chevalier de Ternant, a lieutenant general of cavalry in the Dutch service.[108] From the date of their arrival, January 25, 1788,[109] to June 30, Clark and his men followed them. In August 1788 Colonel Trapp, an Irishman in the service of France, had a watch placed upon him.[110] Thereafter the records are scanty, for the principal account book ends. In June 1791 two men observed one O'Callaghan, employed by the French and Spanish ambassadors to obtain intelligence regarding the navy.[111]

By no means should all these clandestine activities be considered foolish. During the civil war in the Netherlands (1785–1787) the French supported the republican faction, whereas England supported the stadholder. In September 1787 François Barthélemy, French chargé d'affaires in London, received orders from the Count de Montmorin, French foreign minister, to send spies to the English ports to observe the preparations. In the course of that autumn Barthélemy sent five different spies on several trips to the ports.[112] Nepean's payment of four guineas to a Captain Collett, employed by the French minister in obtaining accounts of the state of equipment at Portsmouth and Chatham, to induce him to disclose other persons similarly employed [113] indicates that the Secret Service had its proper uses.

Another source of frequent concern to the Secret Service involved the loss of seamen and artificers to foreign nations. In August 1782

105. *Ibid.* 106. He was observed Oct. 11–Nov. 17, *ibid.*

107. *Ibid.* Philip George Browne (1727–1803), Count von Browne in the Holy Roman Empire, and fourth Earl of Browne in the Jacobite Peerage of Ireland. He was an officer in the Austrian service. *Complete Peerage,* II, 347.

108. For La Luzerne and Ternant see Cobban, *Ambassadors and Secret Agents,* pp. 185, 194.

109. Carmarthen to the King, Jan. 24, 1788, *Later Correspondence of George III,* I, 360–61.

110. Dec. 31, 1788, Nepean's Secret Service Account. He was followed July 26–Aug. 20, 1788. 111. Oct. 31, 1791, *ibid.*

112. Cobban, *Ambassadors and Secret Agents,* p. 190; for Barthélemy see below.

113. Feb. 11, 1788, Nepean's Secret Service Account.

John Swindell, an engineer at Stockport, Cheshire, offered to provide information on a club formed by a large number of artificers who planned to emigrate to the United States. The aid of an American ship of war that would rendezvous with their ship at sea had supposedly been promised by Benjamin Franklin.[114] Nepean immediately sent Clark to gather any further intelligence. "He is a person," Nepean told Swindell, "in whom you may place the utmost confidence, and who will communicate to you the mode we have adopted for apprehending the persons you mention. . . ."[115] Clark sent a full report with the names of several of the intended emigrants, the name of the Londonderry firm supplying the ship, and the information that the organizer of the movement had his passport concealed in the heel of his boot.[116] The move against the emigration evidently was successful, as poor Swindell had to flee Stockport after his enemies threatened and finally shot at him.[117]

In October 1783 Clark went to a tavern in East London in quest of foreigners supposedly enticing seamen; two of his men followed Robinson, captain of an American privateer, who was suspected of the same designs.[118] Sydney informed the lord justice clerk in Edinburgh that Dr. John Witherspoon, president of the College of New Jersey and (former) member of the American congress, was encouraging emigration and should be watched.[119] While Witherspoon and Samuel Seabury, first episcopalian bishop in North America, were in London, Murphy observed them.[120] In 1788 George Hart followed the Russian ambassador, Count Woronzow, while he was engaging seamen for the Russian service.[121] The next year a man tailed Colonel Trapp, this time employed by the Empress of Russia to hire seamen.[122]

Several purely domestic matters occupied the attention of the

114. Swindell to Thomas Townshend, Aug. 3, 1782, Stockport, H.O. 42/1.
115. Aug. 6, 1782, *ibid.*
116. Clark to ?, Aug. 8, 1782, Leake [Nottinghamshire], H.O. 42/1.
117. "Case of John Swindell," June 23, 1784, H.O. 42/4. Swindell received at least £52.10. from Secret Service funds as a reward. April 19, 1783, Nepean's Secret Service Account.
118. Dec. 10, 1783, *ibid.*
119. Aug. 16, 1784, H.O. 103/1. For Witherspoon (1723–94), see Allen Johnson and Dumas Malone (eds.), *Dictionary of American Biography* (20 vols. and supplements; New York, since 1926), XX, 434–38; hereafter *DAB.*
120. Aug. 26, 1786, Nepean's Secret Service Account. For Seabury (1729–96), see *DAB*, XVI, 528–30.
121. Nov. 15, 1788, Nepean's Secret Service Account. He was followed from August 24 to October 10, 1788.
122. June 6, 1789, *ibid.* He was followed from May 4 to June 6, 1789, and possibly longer.

Secret Service. In late 1784 while the East India Company was considering a successor to Warren Hastings, Clark paid some person in the office of the Company to bring him daily accounts of the proceedings.[123] There is also a payment of one guinea to the porter of East India House.[124] George Leonard Staunton, created an Irish baronet in October 1785, private secretary to Lord Macartney, governor of Madras, had returned from India in January 1785. Pitt and Dundas supported Macartney for the governor generalship of Bengal, but on January 21 Staunton called upon Dundas' opponent, Edmund Burke. Major John Scott, Warren Hastings' spokesman, informed Hastings that "Staunton . . . has been talking to Burke, for which Mr. Dundas, as he told me to Day, will mark him." [125] Dundas was a man of his word, for from January 26 to February 18, the day following the election of Macartney by the court of directors, one and sometimes two men followed Staunton.[126]

Various other persons also came under surveillance. A Mr. W_____ was followed from the 7th to the 23rd of January, 1783—probably William Weddell, M.P.[127] During the Regency crisis agents watched the houses of Richard Brinsley Sheridan and the Duke of Portland in order to observe persons who frequented them.[128]

An understandable object of inquiry by the Secret Service was Lord George Gordon. The government had not forgotten the terrible London riots of 1780 that bear his name. Men trailed him for much of the time from 1784 to the end of 1786. On November 19 Gordon donned a Dutch naval uniform with his Highland broadsword slung over his shoulder to express his sympathy for the Dutch Protestants who were being oppressed by the papist Austrian Emperor. He became involved with a large number of unemployed sailors whom he tried to rally to the Protestant cause. Gordon remained a disturbing influence in the eyes of the authorities.[129] For at least the last half of 1786 men watched Gordon continuously [130]—

123. Oct. 19, 1784, *ibid.* The reports began on September 13.

124. Dec. 31, 1784, *ibid.*

125. *Correspondence of Edmund Burke,* V, 206–207.

126. Nepean's Secret Service Account; for Staunton (1737–1801), see *DNB,* XVIII, 1000–01.

127. *Ibid.* The person followed often called upon Lady Rockingham. Weddell was her brother-in-law.

128. Dec. 31, 1788, *ibid.* A report on Sheridan, Dec. 6, 1788, is in the Clements Library.

129. Percy Colson, *The Strange History of Lord George Gordon* (London, 1937), pp. 138–41.

130. Dec. 31, 1786, Nepean's Secret Service Account.

not without cause. In November he began to distribute handbills, the products of a disordered mind, that gave the authorities reason to fear riots.[131] Fortunately nothing came of the threat. Although Gordon's case falls more under the jurisdiction of the police of London than the Secret Service, government officials probably thought that because of the horrible damage done during the Gordon riots in 1780, Lord George warranted the strictest attention. The period of observation lasted a long time, longer perhaps than the London magistrates at Bow Street could undertake. Gordon ceased to be a problem in 1786 when he was committed to prison for publishing a libel against the Queen of France, and except for a short time in 1787, he spent the rest of his days in Newgate, where he died in 1793.[132]

The Home Office had some connection with the Secret Service in Ireland, though such matters were usually handled by the Irish Chief Secretary. The Home Office might give certain directions, but expenses were usually met by the Irish Secret Service fund.[133] The sole entries in Nepean's Secret Service account book relating strictly to Ireland are in 1784. The spy Murphy followed Arthur O'Leary, a priest who had taken an active part in the agitation in 1782 and 1783 in behalf of Irish nationalism, to determine whether he was communicating with the French ambassador regarding the disturbances in Ireland.[134] A spy followed O'Leary in London from May 20 through September 6 of 1784.[135] Nepean was evidently satisfied as to O'Leary's dependability, for from September the priest began to receive a pension from the Irish Secret Service fund in return for information on the designs of the Irish Catholics, with whom he had ingratiated himself. It was also at this time that George Parker went to Ireland for the same purpose.[136]

Unfortunately there is no intelligence estimate for the domestic Secret Service comparable to the one Nepean prepared on the French navy. Most of the intelligence acquired by the domestic Secret Service did not require elaborate analysis. Once the agents had uncovered illegal proceedings, the local authorities probably arrested the persons involved.

131. Sydney to the King, Nov. 5, 1786; and the reply, same date, *Later Correspondence of George III*, I, 257–58. 132. Colson, pp. 188–90.

133. Fitzpatrick, *Secret Service Under Pitt*, *passim*; and Aspinall, *Politics and the Press*, pp. 411–13. 134. March 7, 1784, Nepean's Secret Service Account.

135. Dec. 31, 1784, *ibid.*

136. *DNB*, XIV, 1017–20; Fitzpatrick, *Secret Service Under Pitt*, pp. 230 ff.

The Secret Service, as conducted by Evan Nepean, had its first interest in the activities of France and Spain. Nepean used men like Oakes and Taylor, informers, vessels, and spies as sources of information. Although it would require an examination of the French and Spanish archives to be certain of the accuracy of the reports, the conclusions that he drew from them violated none of the principles of modern military intelligence. Nepean's planning—the first phase of the intelligence cycle—is obscure from lack of evidence. The results of the remaining three phases indicate that the first was sound. Planning entails determining requirements and priorities, the proper allocation of available collection means, the selection of collection agents, and the supervision of the execution of orders. His collection of information—the second phase—may appear crude, but he had no modern technical devices to assist him. He did, for example, establish a fairly regular service of small craft to patrol the French coast in late 1792; and his information from Oakes and Taylor was usually regular and accurate. The government no doubt combined reports from these sources with information received by the Foreign Office from internal sources in France to form a more complete intelligence estimate. The précis of 1787 indicated that Nepean had processed and collated his intelligence (the third phase) in a suitable manner, and recorded, evaluated, and interpreted it for his superiors in a clear style. The use and dissemination (phase four) of the estimate depended upon higher echelons. One ought to remember, of course, that the Home Office had only one part in acquiring intelligence about foreign nations, and that in this sense a single Secret Service did not exist.

The Home Office made irregular use of its Secret Service staff of three men for domestic purposes. The quality of the agents may not always have been high, but absence of any definite evidence about most of them precludes an evaluation. The laws against emigration of seamen and artisans were taken seriously, and the agents closely watched suspected persons. Watching foreign ambassadors was a regular occurrence and was not without justification. The Secretaries might have the agents attend the motions of persons for personal or political reasons, but this happened on remarkably few occasions. All in all, the Secret Service of the Home Office performed a useful purpose in both foreign and domestic affairs.

Chapter Six

THE PRESERVATION OF PUBLIC ORDER

The Home Office in the eighteenth century had executive responsibility for the administration of certain police affairs. This jurisdiction, however, entailed much less than it does today. Local officials such as sheriffs, mayors, and justices of the peace had the authority to manage nearly all affairs affecting the preservation of public order. Local officials generally investigated a crime, arrested the culprit, bound him for trial at the local quarter sessions, and committed him, if convicted, to the local jail. The Home Office seldom had any part in this process. The same held true for London, but to a lesser extent, as the Office did have certain supervisory powers over the London magistrates. The present Home Office supervises the operation and upkeep of nearly all prisons,[1] but the eighteenth-century Office had virtually no responsibility for them. "It was no part of the duty of the Secretary of State . . . to know what the local authorities were doing [regarding the prisons]. He received from them no annual or other reports. He regarded it as beyond his function even to remonstrate with any local authority. . . ."[2]

The Home Office did, however, enter the area of public order at several important stages. The Secretary served as a channel to the king for petitions asking mercy for criminals, as supervisor of the transportation of criminals to areas beyond Europe, and as magis-

1. Newsam, *The Home Office,* chap. xiv.

2. Sidney and Beatrice Webb, *English Local Government,* VI: *English Prisons under Local Government* (London, 1922), p. 29; also chaps. i-ii. The Webbs's *English Local Government* (9 vols.; London, 1906–29) remains the standard authority on the subject and is rich in detail on the process of local administration of criminal laws. On July 7, 1791, Dundas did direct Drs. Carmichael Smyth and David Pitcairne to investigate the medical facilities of the King's Bench and Fleet Street prisons. H.O. 42/21. Each received £52.10 (Dec. 3, 1792, H.O. 82/3). See also Dundas to Lords Kenyon and Loughborough, Jan. 24, 1792, and same to Charles Grey, Feb. 6, 1792 (H.O. 43/3). For Pitcairne (1749–1809) and Smyth (1714–1821) see William Munk, *The Roll of the Royal College of Physicians of London* (2nd ed.; 4 vols.; 1878–1955), II, 353–57, 383–85.

trate in special cases involving crimes against the state. The Home Office's relationship to law enforcement in the counties, London, and in respect to aliens are sufficiently important to merit discussion in separate chapters.

All petitions to the king that sought pardons or reductions in sentences for convicts passed through the office. The petitions came either from the judges who had initially sentenced the prisoners, the prisoners themselves, or from private persons in behalf of a convict. The Home Secretary submitted directly to the king all recommendations for mercy by the judges of all the circuits except that for London and Middlesex. The recorder of London, before whom cases at Old Bailey were tried, submitted his report to the Secretary at the end of each session.[3] The Secretary sent the recorder's letter to the king,[4] who directed the Secretary to notify the recorder of the date that he would hear the report. The Secretary also notified the "nominal" cabinet of the date selected for the report.[5] The "nominal" cabinet, sometimes referred to as the "hanging cabinet," to be distinguished from the "efficient cabinet," always heard the recorder's report and advised the king on the extension of the royal mercy.[6]

When a petition came directly from a convict, or far more often, from some one or more persons on behalf of a convict, the Home

3. James Adair (?1743–1798), recorder of London 1779–89, to Lord North, April 28, 1783, H.O. 42/2.

4. North to the King, April 29, 1783, *Correspondence of George III,* VI, 368.

5. The King to North, April 30, 1783, *ibid.,* p. 369.

6. There are copies of four lists sent to members of the nominal cabinet dated April 15, April 26, April 30, and June 1, 1782. It is interesting to compare them with the list in Arthur Aspinall and E. Anthony Smith (eds.), *English Historical Documents, 1782–1832* (English Historical Documents, XI; London, 1959), pp. 86–87. Four offices in 1810 did not exist in 1782; otherwise the lists are identical except in the following particulars. The Master of the Horse was not summoned in 1782. Viscount Weymouth attended in April, through he did not become Groom of the Stole till May. The Commander-in-Chief and the Master General of the Ordnance both attended (or were anyway invited). In addition, the lists were sent to the Duke of Northumberland (1714–86) who had no Cabinet office or other important post, though he was Lord Lieutenant of Middlesex. Lord Gower held no office at this time, but presumably was invited because of his importance. For some reason the Duke of Leeds (1713–89) was invited, though his most important post had been Cofferer of the Household from 1756 to 1761. Lord Ashburnham (1724–1812), Groom of the Stole from 1775 to 1782, also continued to be summoned. Although he held no office again, he still received the summons in 1810. The letters are in H.O. 42/1. The one for April 30 omits (probably accidently) Rockingham and Fox, but adds Thomas Townshend, Secretary at War.

Leon Radzinowitz, *A History of English Criminal Law and Its Administration from 1750* (3 vols. to date; New York, 1948–1957), I, 107–37, has an excellent treatment of the use of the royal prerogative of mercy. For the Cabinet see Arthur Aspinall, "The Cabinet Council, 1783–1835," *Proceedings of the British Academy,* XXXVII (1952), 145–252, and Sir Lewis Namier, "The End of the Nominal Cabinet," *Crossroads of Power* (New York, 1962), pp. 118–23.

hired by the Treasury transported the convicts; consequently, the Home Office had limited concern with the actual details of the transportation. The affairs of New South Wales, of course, like those of other colonies, did fall under Home Office jurisdiction.

The Office entered the picture primarily before the convicts embarked on the ships. It had considerable supervisory authority over the activities of the contractors who kept the hulks moored in the Thames, at Plymouth, and at Portsmouth. The hulks served as receptacles for the convicts till they could be transported. Often, especially before 1787, prisoners passed their entire sentences aboard the hulks. The Secretary of State issued the orders to the superintendents of the hulks to release prisoners to the transports, and to free convicts who had received pardons. The Secretary also examined the accounts of the superintendents before they were submitted to the Treasury. When complaints arose about the superintendents, the Secretary ordered proper persons to investigate.[25]

The Home Office directly entered the law enforcement scene in one particular instance. Whenever government planned to seize persons suspected of treason, the Secretary of State issued the warrants for their arrest to the king's messengers. The warrants did not always specify the names of the persons to be arrested; sometimes only the occupants of a certain building were indicated.[26] If necessary the Secretary ordered the Post Office to intercept letters of suspects. He issued any orders respecting the privileges that state prisoners might receive,[27] and also examined and approved all bills submitted by attorneys for prosecuting persons charged with treason. The Treasury then paid them.[28]

It has proved impossible to draw nice distinctions between the role of the Home Secretary either in suppressing treason or in preserving public order and the general movement against English

25. Much information on the system is in H.O. 11/1 and H.O. 13/1–13; *Twenty-eighth Report from the Select Committee on Finance: Police, including Convict Establishments, 26 June 1798*, First Series, XIII, 344–426; and in the obituary of Aaron Graham, inspector of convicts, *Annual Biography and Obituary*, IV (1820), 402–22. Eris O'Brien, *The Foundation of Australia (1786–1800): A Study in English Criminal Practice and Penal Colonization in the Eighteenth Century* (2nd ed.; Sydney and London, 1950) deals in depth with the subject. See also A. G. L. Shaw, *Convicts and the Colonies* (London, 1966), pp. 1–78.

26. For example, Portland to Charles Sylvester and assistants, April 19, 1798, H.O. 13/11.

27. Portland to the lieutenant of the Tower of London, March 9, 1798; William Wickham to Sir Francis Burdett, April 11, 1798, *ibid.*

28. King to Charles Long, June 23, 1796, H.O. 36/9.

Secretary sent the petition to the judge before whom the convict had been tried and sentenced. The recommendation of the judge usually determined the Secretary's course of action.[7] If the recommendation was favorable, he sent the petition and report to the king; if the judge's report was unfavorable, he appears not to have sent either document to the sovereign. Once the judges submitted their reports and the king considered them, the Home Office would not take any action on additional petitions on behalf of a particular convict unless new evidence as to his guilt arose.[8]

If the king granted a pardon, the Home Office prepared a warrant under the royal sign manual, signed by the king and countersigned by the Secretary. The Secretary of State then sent the warrant to the judge, who commuted the death sentence.[9] Virtually all pardons involved prisoners under sentence of death; exceptions were extremely rare.

Pardons might be either free or conditional. Only a few were free, usually in cases where the innocence of the person convicted had been established. Grenville, as a matter of principle, never applied to the king for a free pardon for a capital convict.[10] The most frequent condition specified in pardons was transportation beyond the seas, usually for seven or fourteen years or for life; less than seven years was rare. Service in the navy, where escape was difficult, or, infrequently, in the army might be the condition, although before 1790 this was seldom granted.[11] It became common after the outbreak of hostilities with France to pardon convicts on condition that they enter one of the services.[12] Some convicts also received pardons upon condition that they give security for their good behavior, or consent to do hard labor for a period of time, usually one year. Occasionally a person might be allowed to transport himself beyond the seas.[13]

Remissions of parts of a sentence might also be granted by the

7. The reports are in H.O. 47/1–28.
8. Nepean to the Mayor of New Sarum, Dec. 27, 1784, H.O. 13/2.
9. James Adair to North, Nov. 3, 1783, H.O. 43/3; Radzinowitz, I, 199–210.
10. Nepean to Edmund Wigley, Aug. 21, 1790, H.O. 13/8.
11. The Duke of Leeds, acting for Grenville, to the Marquis of Salisbury, Oct. 15, 1790, H.O. 13/8.
12. King to John Harrison, Feb. 16, 1797, H.O. 13/11; Portland to the sheriff of London, Sept. 5, 1800, H.O. 13/13. The East India Company rejected all requests to take convicts before 1792. Dundas to John Noble, mayor of Bristol, Sept. 12, 1792, H.O. 13/9. But it took them by 1794. Dundas to the justices of the assize, Norfolk Circuit, April 1794, *ibid.*
13. Examples of all types of conditional pardons may be found throughout the classification H.O. 13.

king. A remission could reduce one or more years of a sentence without any condition attached, or could require that in return for the remission the convict serve in the navy or find security for his good behavior during the rest of his sentence. The notorious adventurer and swindler Major James George Semple, for example, had to find £1,000 in security (put up by himself) and £200 in surety (put up by others) before the remainder of his sentence would be remitted.[14] Employers sometimes would provide security for convicts whom they wished to hire.

The Home Secretary also served as the channel through which the king received applications for respites or reprieves, although the Secretary could order a respite without the king's authority when the case did not allow time to consult the sovereign.[15] The king usually granted them in cases where some new evidence had appeared, or when the report of a judge on a petition for mercy could not be obtained before the execution was to take place.[16] The Home Office directed all respites, which were usually for a specified period, or occasionally indefinite, to the sheriffs of the various counties concerned.

The Home Secretary often went to considerable lengths to obtain information about pardons and respites. When the commissioners of excise requested a respite for a counterfeiter, the Office consulted the solicitor of that board to determine how far a respite for the offense was consistent with the security of the revenue of the realm.[17] John King inquired what means the Admiralty had of devising ways to prevent the desertion of convicts who might be pardoned upon entering the navy.[18] Scrope Bernard asked Alderman John Boydell, a well-known engraver and print publisher,[19] who had signed a petition attesting to the good character of a man sentenced to seven years' transportation, whether he would answer for the man's entering the East India Company's service if he were to be pardoned.[20]

14. Portland to the Recorder of London and the keeper of Bridewell, May 3, 1800, H.O. 13/24. For Semple see *DNB*, XXII, 1179, and Joseph W. Reed, Jr., "Boswell and the Major," *Kenyon Review*, XXVII (March, 1966), 161–84, which adds some information not in the *DNB*.

15. Sydney to the King, July 22, 1788, *Later Correspondence of George III*, I, 383–84; Grenville to same, Aug. 3, 1789, *ibid.*, pp. 436–37; Dundas to same, Sept. 7, 1791, *ibid.*, p. 559.

16. For a printed example see Sydney to the King, April 11, 1786, and the reply, same date, *Later Correspondence of George III*, I, 217–18.

17. Draft to John Vivian, Aug. 22, 1795, H.O. 13/10.

18. To John Harrison, Feb. 16, 1797, H.O. 13/11.

19. *DNB*, II, 1012–14.

20. Sept. 8, 1790, H.O. 13/8.

Although the Secretaries denied many requests for respites
pardons simply because the judge had submitted an unfavo
report, they occasionally refused on other grounds. Usually
intended that such rejections would ensure that the culprits s
as examples for their crimes. Grenville, in refusing to order a r
for two forgers, wrote that "the situation of this country in resp
its Commercial dealings, renders it necessary that the Cri
Forgery should be punished with rigour, and it has been a g
rule not to pardon it. . . . It is thought that those delays whe
Fate of the Convicts is certain are cruel toward them, and
tendency very much to weaken the effect of the Example."
Dundas refused to present a petition for pardon on behalf of
convicted of stealing packages en route from manufacturing
to the coast, as the chairman of the quarter session that tri
reported that such pilfering had seriously injured commerce
extension of clemency in this case would be productive of
mischiefs in the Country."[22]

The business relating to pardons greatly increased duri
period—perhaps a reflection of the growth of a more huma
view of crime. Dundas had to employ a clerk specifically as k
criminal registers; the post remained upon the establishm
many decades. The keeper maintained an account of all con
in order to distinguish between old and new offenders and
cate any increase or decrease in the various types of felon
register evidently assisted the Secretaries in deciding wheth
to advise the king to grant a particular pardon. The keeper
a register of all references to judges and of all pardon
officer greatly facilitated the administration of criminal affai

The Home Office also exercised supervisory control i
relating to the transportation of criminals beyond the
separation of the American colonies from the Empire en
being used as a depository for undesirables. After some
attempts to settle convicts in Africa,[24] the government d
send them to New South Wales and adjacent areas. C

21. To Mr. Williams, Sept. 2, 1789, H.O. 13/7.
22. To Lord Walsingham, July 12, 1792, H.O. 13/8.
23. *Sixteenth Report, 1797*. Appendix M, p. 235. The register of felo
is in H.O. 26/1–8, 56 (more full than the registers 1–8). The register
1797–1812 is IND 13979, 13980.
24. Sydney to the Africa Committee, Dec. 14, 1784, H.O. 43/1; Mi
Committee of the House of Commons on Transportation, 1785, H.O. 7/1.

radicalism that began after the outbreak of the French Revolution. In the first place, the actions of the government in London represented a small part of the antiradical movement, for local justices of the peace and other officials and various loyalists associations conducted sporadic but effective prosecutions and intimidation campaigns without the government's participation. In the second place, the activities of the Home Office were but a part of the government's response to radicalism, for the ministers used spies, propagandists who wrote pamphlets and newspaper articles, publications such as the *Anti-Jacobin Review,* outright prosecutions, and Acts of Parliament to cope with the menace to the governing class. Although the Home Secretary issued the warrants for the arrest of persons suspected of treason and (sometimes with an Undersecretary) interrogated the suspects in the office or before the Privy Council, Pitt himself must have had the deciding voice in preparing such moves. The absence of the Secret Service accounts presents the gravest obstacle—for without them it is impossible to know which government office paid, let alone directed, the numerous spies whose letters and reports on suspected persons and societies fill the Home Office's, Privy Council's, and Treasury solicitor's papers.

A detailed study of the government's move against radicals (and there is none) must be approached from the point of government as a unit, not from the viewpoint of a single office. Contemporary officials probably did not have a distinct picture of a given office's responsibilities, as the antiradical movement was largely a pragmatic one. An "army of government spies and informers" is a faulty analogy to describe such a loose affair. The great variation in the value of the reports of the spies reflects the absence of any concerted system.

Because of these inherent difficulties, it has been necessary to treat the role of the Home Office in the antiradical movement in the broadest and most general sense. A few examples, where one might like a profusion of details, must serve to illustrate general problems and the Home Office's attempts to meet them.

Chapter Seven

PUBLIC ORDER IN THE COUNTIES

In ordinary times little correspondence passed between the Home Office and the officials in the counties and provincial cities (several of which were counties in and of themselves). The Secretaries did have to approve the appointments of justices of the peace and deputy lieutenants, and the king pricked all sheriffs. The lord lieutenants of the counties, the sheriffs, the justices of the peace, the mayors, and the town clerks were generally the persons to write to the Secretary of State when writing became necessary. As indicated in the preceding chapter, local officials handled almost all business relating to the enforcement of laws and the apprehension of criminals without disturbing the executive government in London. Only in extraordinary circumstances did they have to inform or ask for assistance from the Secretary of State for the Home department. Before 1789 little difficulty arose in the counties that could not be dealt with on the spot. In 1782 a justice of the peace in Kent did have to report an outbreak of contagious distemper among the cattle in the area around Deal,[1] in order that the Secretary could refer the matter to the Privy Council, which then issued a quarantine to prevent the infection from spreading.[2]

The main correspondence between the Home department and local officials arose from riots and disorders that could not be controlled at the local level, and invariably required the use of troops. Since the Secretary of State had to issue the orders for the movement of troops within Great Britain, applications always came to him. In March 1783, for instance, Lord Sydney received notice that riots were occurring near Newcastle-under-Lyme, Staffordshire. Although he would ordinarily have asked the King's commands, time pressed

1. John Carter (1723–1810) to Thomas Townshend, Nov. 19, 1782, Deal, H.O. 42/1.
2. Townshend to the Lord President, Nov. 20, 1782, H.O. 43/1.

him to make a decision.[3] He wrote to the Lord Lieutenant of Stafford to defer demobilizing the militia of the county till further orders.[4] He then ordered the Secretary at War and the Commander-in-Chief to issue the necessary orders for the movement of troops to Newcastle-under-Lyme.[5]

Not till 1789, however, did any appreciable activity occur. From that time the Home Office began to interest itself more and more in the preservation of public order. Discontent among the lower classes, the growth of radicalism encouraged by the revolution in France, and open sedition caused the disorders in the counties to become painfully frequent. The government seems to have become suspicious of the motives of rioters almost immediately after the fall of the Bastille. On July 29 the magistrates at Wrexham, Denbigh (North Wales), reported that the colliers had rioted over the high price of corn, but they suspected other motives. The magistrates requested troops.[6] Grenville replied that if their suspicions that the real object of the riots was not the price of corn proved correct, he would be glad to receive "the most early information thereof from you."[7] The entire Thirty-fourth Regiment marched to Wrexham,[8] but the continuation of the riots forced Grenville to dispatch more troops.[9] In August 1789 troops had to disperse between two and three hundred rioters at Leeds who objected to the introduction of some new spinning machines.[10] In October 1790 Grenville sent troops to overawe mobs at Whitby and Malton.[11]

Advising magistrates as to the proper course of action to follow to check civil disorders constituted one of the most important duties of the Secretary of State. The Secretaries always expected to be informed of any tendencies to riot.[12] The normal procedure, upon receiving a request from a magistrate for troops, was to notify the Secretary at War to dispatch the troops from the nearest military garrison to the scene of the disorders. The Home Office usually inserted in the *Gazette* an offer to pardon any person not immedi-

3. Sydney to the King, March 13, 1783, *Correspondence of George III,* VI, 275–76.
4. To Earl Gower, March 13, 1783, H.O. 42/2.
5. Sydney to the King, March 13, 1783, *Correspondence of George III,* VI, 275–76.
6. July 29, 1789, to the Secretary at War, H.O. 42/15.
7. Aug. 4, 1789, H.O. 43/3.
8. G. W. Yonge to Nepean, Escot, Aug. 2, 1789, H.O. 50/381.
9. Grenville to the magistrates, Aug. 15, 1789, H.O. 43/3.
10. Mayor, recorder, and alderman of Leeds to Grenville, H.O. 50/381.
11. H.O. 50/382.
12. For example, Dundas to the mayor of Bristol, Oct. 1793, H.O. 42/26.

ately involved in the riots who expressed a willingness to give information on his fellow rioters. If the property damaged belonged to the government, the *Gazette* notice might also contain the offer of reward for information. Although the government would advertise in the *Gazette* the king's pardon for damage done to private property, the person injured had to provide the money for a reward.[13]

The Secretaries did not always limit themselves to such relatively passive behavior. The riots in Birmingham in July 1791, known as the "Priestley riots" because of the damage done to the home and laboratory of the radical Dr. Joseph Priestley, brought sharp, quick action.[14] Joseph Carles[15] and Benjamin Spencer,[16] two Birmingham magistrates, apprised Dundas on July 15 of the disorders that had begun on the preceding day—the anniversary of the fall of the Bastille.[17] Dundas received the letter on the morning of the 16th and immediately dispatched a messenger to Nottingham with directions to the commanding officer of the Fifteenth Light Dragoons to send three troops to Birmingham.[18] The next day, as the riots continued unabated, Dundas ordered the sheriff of Warwick to summon the magistrates and gentlemen of the county to suppress the riots,[19] and asked the Lord Lieutenant, the Earl of Aylesford, to assist the troops. Aylesford was confidentially to convey his opinion of the cause of the riots and a description of the persons against whom the rioters had directed their violence.[20] Dundas at the same time requested that the undersheriff of Warwick, John Brooke, provide information to a messenger about the number and force of the rioters.[21] Dundas also ordered more troops from near London, Nottingham, and Manchester to proceed to Birmingham.[22] On the 18th Dundas took the precaution of warning the sheriffs of Worcester, Stafford, Oxford, Shropshire, and Northampton to be ready to act in case the riots spread, and if necessary, to call upon the military. They were also to enforce the laws against vagrants, since a number

13. Portland to Thomas Bernard, Nov. 27, 1800, H.O. 43/12.

14. R. B. Rose, "The Priestley Riots of 1791," *Past and Present,* No. 18 (Nov., 1960), 68–88.

15. Carles (1740–96), a local landowner of Brown's Green, Handsworth, was a J. P. in both Staffordshire and Warwickshire, *ibid.,* p. 80.

16. Spencer (c. 1744 to Sept. 2, 1823) was vicar of Aston in Warwickshire and rector of Hatton in Lincolnshire from 1780 till his death. Foster, *Alumni Oxonienses,* IV, 1333.

17. H.O. 42/19.

18. Dundas to Carles and Spencer, H.O. 43/3.

19. *Ibid.*

20. To Heneage (Finch), fourth Earl of Aylesford (1751–1812), July 17, 1791, *ibid.*

21. *Ibid.*

22. A list of all units dispatched to Birmingham is in H.O. 42/19.

of disorderly persons were coming from London to Birmingham.[23] Dundas dispatched John Townsend[24] and Thomas Carpmeal,[25] two of the Bow Street runners, to identify any Londoners who might have come to Birmingham for no good reason.[26]

On July 21, after the riots subsided, Dundas directed William Chamberlayne, solicitor to the Treasury, to leave for Birmingham to take depositions on the riots to enable the government to decide whether or not to order a special commission for the more speedy trial and punishment of "any such of the offenders as may appear to be objects for possible example." To add solemnity to the proceedings, an attorney named Lister and Nicholas Bond, a Bow Street magistrate, assisted Chamberlayne.[27] There is no need to pursue the course of the Priestley riots further, but they do provide an example of the extensive action that the Home Office could take in times of crisis. Ordinarily, however, the Secretary had only to signify his approval of steps that the magistrates had already taken to restore order.

The greatest exertions came in response to the proceedings of the various corresponding societies and other groups whose aims entailed some alteration in the constitution, legal or otherwise. In 1792 Dundas wrote to the mayor of Bristol that he had heard of a number of associations in that city whose purpose allegedly was to obtain information on constitutional questions:

> I believe I may venture to express an opinion that many if not most of these associations, have been established for the most mischievous purposes. It is therefore extremely desirable that their Proceedings should be carefully attended to; . . . every good Citizen and Wellwisher of our Excellent Constitution should unite in pursuing every legal and prudent means of suppressing them.[28]

Dundas may perhaps be excused for his apprehensions, for in October 1792 reports poured in of radical societies in Brimingham, Cambridge, Chester, Derby, Ipswich, Leicester, Liverpool, Manchester,

23. H.O. 43/3.
24. Townshend, later chief of the Bow Street police, died on July 10, 1832, aged seventy-three. The *Gentleman's Magazine,* CII (July, 1832), 91, has a long eulogy.
25. Thomas Carpmeal died on December 31, 1807, aged sixty. *Ibid.,* LXXVII (Supplement, 1807), 1240.
26. Dundas to Carles and Spencer, July 20, H.O. 43/3.
27. *Ibid.* Bond died on June 2, 1807, aged sixty-four. The *Annual Register,* XLIX (1807), pp. 579–80, has a long obituary that praises his good qualities as a magistrate. Chamberlayne later resigned as solicitor to become a commissioner for auditing the public accounts. He died on November 11, 1799, at Cooley, near Reading. *Gentleman's Magazine,* LXIX (Nov., 1799), 1004.
28. To John Noble (father of Richard H. Noble, a clerk in the office), Sept. 12, 1792, H.O. 13/9.

Sheffield, Stockport, and Yarmouth in England and from Dumfermline, Edinburgh, Glasgow, and Perth in Scotland as well as from other cities.[29]

On May 21, 1792, the king issued a proclamation against seditious meetings and publications. In late 1792 Dundas began his second-hand direction of the campaign against radicalism in Scotland with the assistance of the Lord Advocate, Robert Dundas. Spies attended the "National Convention" that met in Edinburgh in December 1792. The following August the Scottish court sentenced Thomas Muir, the most gifted radical leader, to fourteen years of transportation. The next month T. F. Palmer was sentenced to seven years. In January 1794, W. Skirving, secretary of the Scottish convention, and Maurice Margot, delegated by the London Corresponding Society to attend the Scottish convention, followed Muir and Palmer to New South Wales. The trials broke the back of radicalism in Scotland.[30]

In May of 1794 in London the king's messengers arrested Thomas Hardy, secretary of the London Corresponding Society, John Thelwall, John Horne Tooke, and other members of both the London Corresponding Society and the Society for Constitutional Information. The juries failed to convict the arrested parties, but the prosecutions nearly choked the reform movements.[31]

Such direct steps on the part of the government were unusual, but throughout the period the Secretaries generally encouraged the sternest measures against the elements that displayed open aversion to the constitution. Following a second series of riots in Birmingham in 1795, Portland informed the magistrates of that city:

> I very much approve your exertions in dispersing the Rioters, and I trust that the speedy Trial and punishment of such of those who have been secured, as shall be found the most guilty, will operate as a salutary example to all Persons who are unfortunately misled by the instigations of Individuals who evidently aim at the destruction of all Order and Government.[32]

29. H.O. 42/22.

30. Philip Anthony Brown, *The French Revolution in English History* (London, 1918), pp. 95–99. Additional information on Scotland may be found in Henry W. Meikle, *Scotland and the French Revolution* (Glasgow, 1912); George W. T. Omond, *The Arniston Memoirs: Three Centuries of a Scottish House, 1571–1838* (Edinburgh, 1887), pp. 226–45; Edward Hughes, "The Scottish Reform Movement and Charles Grey, 1792–94: Some Fresh Correspondence," *Scottish Historical Review*, XXV (April, 1956), 26–41.

31. Brown, pp. 118–50. E. P. Thompson, *The Making of the English Working Class* (New York, 1963), though polemical in tone, contains much information on the radical movement, and the footnotes contain the most extensive bibliographical information on radicalism in the late eighteenth century.

32. June 25, 1795, H.O. 43/6.

In many cases the Home Office did not rely solely upon the random information that the magistrates happened to submit. The Secretary often requested especially detailed intelligence that could be obtained only by planting spies in the meetings of the groups suspected of seditious behavior. It appears, however, that the local magistrates found the necessary spies or provided the necessary details themselves. John Brooke, undersheriff of Warwick during the Priestley riots, became a principal source of information for the Birmingham area. On October 12, 1792, Nepean asked him to send a report about arms supposedly manufactured in Birmingham and Sheffield for distribution in Ireland.[33] On November 6 Nepean again wrote to Brooke, this time to ask him to find some trustworthy person to attend a suspected debating society. "I would readily pay him for his trouble, and I should think that he might, the day after each debate, give me information of the *Question discussed,* and the general tendency of the arguments held by different people upon it."

Nepean also wanted more reports about arms to Ireland.[34] Brooke furnished the desired information, or as much as he could uncover. On November 8 he reported the number of weapons that were being manufactured for shipment to Liverpool, but could not determine their final destination.[35] The collector of customs at Liverpool also made an extensive search of the records of shipments in canal boats, in wagons, and in the warehouses of the African merchants. He directed all packages large enough to contain arms to be opened on the pretense of looking for manufacturing machinery forbidden to be exported.[36] The search for arms evidently failed, but Brooke continued to relay reports on the debating society,[37] which evidently was never a subject of court action. Another agent who was a beneficiary of the Office in the amount of £200 a year was Charles Stuart (1792–?), who was a scribbler, and occasionally reported such horrifying intelligence as "Perhaps you do not know that the

33. H.O. 42/22. Brooke, an attorney, engaged in land speculation in Birmingham; he laid out the suburb of Ashted. His bankruptcy in 1793 did not seem to deter him from reporting to Nepean. He served as chairman of the Loyal True Blues—an antiradical society in Birmingham. The government must have valued his services, for he was appointed barrack master for the area. Brooke was also secretary to the governors of King Edward's School in Birmingham and later became a coroner for the county of Warwick. He died on June 26, 1802. The best sketch of him is by Philip D. Chatwin (ed.), in Vol. V of *The Records of King Edward's School, Birmingham* (Publications of the Dugdale Society, XXV), pp. xi–xiv. See also *Gentleman's Magazine,* LXXII (July, 1802), 689, and R. B. Rose, *passim.* 34. Private, H.O. 42/22. 35. *Ibid.*

36. Ar. Onslow to Nepean, Nov. 15, 1792, Customs House, Liverpool, *ibid.*

37. Several reports bound together with Nov. 21, 1792, on the cover, *ibid.;* Nepean to Brooke, May 6, 1793, H.O. 42/25; Brooke to Nepean, May 6 and 27, 1794, H.O. 42/30; Nepean to Brooke, June 23, 1794, H.O. 43/5.

Paynites now meet in *chapels!*" (Stuart [February 9, 1793] to Nepean, accounts, and a few other letters, in Dundas Papers, Duke University MSS). King inherited Stuart when Portland took office.

At various times the Office also directed persons to undertake investigations. Dundas requested that the Bishop of Hereford make an inquiry concerning a minister in a parish in his diocese who had preached an improper sermon.[38] Colonel Duncan Campbell of the Ninety-eighth Regiment was told to investigate a sergeant in his unit who had written an improper letter.[39] Robert Parker, an attorney at Halifax, Yorkshire, received orders to conduct an inquiry into possible sedition, for which the office would reimburse him.[40] In 1798 W. Watson, Farnsfield, Nottinghamshire, investigated sedition at Nottingham and at nearby Mansfield.[41] The Home Office generally tendered the legal services of the solicitors of the Treasury to any magistrate who suggested a prosecution for sedition that had a chance of success.[42]

The office seems to have sent out other investigators directly from London. James Walsh made many trips to Ireland and to several places in England from December 1792.[43] It was Walsh who spied upon William Wordsworth at Nether Stowey, Somersetshire, in 1797.[44] Nepean sent William Metcalfe to Shropshire in 1793 and later to Worcestershire, where he remained three months. He then went to Liverpool to inquire into some riots. (Later he sent reports on the London Corresponding Society.)[45] Edward Gosling went in search of suspicious persons in 1794.[46] In 1800 Portland relied upon Aaron Graham, a Bow Street magistrate, to assist and advise county

38. To John Butler (died 1802), bishop since 1788, March 21, 1794, H.O. 43/5.

39. Sept. 27, 1794, *ibid.*

40. Portland to Parker, Nov. 20, 1795, H.O. 43/7.

41. W. Watson to Portland, May 21, 1798, H.O. 42/43.

42. For example, Dundas to John Lloyd, Haverfordwest, Pembroke, Jan. 24, 1793, H.O. 43/4; Portland to magistrates of Birmingham, March 14, 1796, H.O. 65/1; Grenville to the magistrates at Ipswich, Nov. 17, 1792, H.O. 43/4.

43. "Mr. James Walsh attending the Home Department." His salary from December 1, 1792, to February 28, 1796, was £622.2.6. H.O. 42/38. The Contingent Account (H.O. 82/3) records payments of £396.18.0 from February 1, 1791, to July 2, 1792. Part of the payments before mid-1792 were for Walsh's investigating the plundering of a Dutch ship that had run aground in Cornwall.

44. The letters are in H.O. 42/41, but are printed in A. J. Eagleston, "Wordsworth, Coleridge and the Spy," *Coleridge: Studies by Several Hands on the Hundreth Anniversary of His Death,* edited by Edmund C. Blunden and Earl Leslie Griggs (London, 1934). See also F. M. Todd, *Politics and the Poet: A Study of Wordsworth* (London, 1957), chaps. ii–v, Appendix B, pp. 229–31, and George W. Meyer, "Wordsworth and the Spy Hunt," *American Scholar,* XX (Winter, 1950/51), 50–56.

45. William Metcalfe to Portland, Jan. 5, 1795, H.O. 42/34.

46. Dundas to the mayor of Plymouth, June 27, 1794, H.O. 43/5; Gosling to Wickham, June 30, 1794, H.O. 42/31. Gosling had been a spy on the meetings of the London Corresponding Society and testified at the trial of Thomas Hardy. Brown, pp. 142–43.

magistrates in the suppression of riots. Through Graham, Portland also found out the state of mind of the inhabitants and the capability of the magistrates. Sometimes the alarms were false. In Birmingham the magistrates had sent for troops without good cause. Graham reported "that the Inhabitants and troops had been equally astonished on the arrival of the latter who to shew how much they were so on finding that the place was not in a state of confusion struck up the favorite air—'Oh dear what can the matter be?' "[47]

The county magistrates certainly formed the first line of defense against disorder, but lacking a national police or even organized local police forces outside of London, the Home Office had to rely upon the military whenever force became necessary. In June 1792 Colonel Oliver de Lancey, deputy adjutant general, made a useful tour to determine the loyalty of the various regiments stationed in the counties. At the same time he reported to Dundas on the disposition of the people in many of the large manufacuring towns; and recommended the construction of barracks near several of these cities in order that troops might always be available for immediate action.[48] The King concurred, and erection of the barracks began at once.[49] Later, German soldiers occupied these quarters. Several times the Secretary of State had to order the Secretary at War to remove troops from various towns because of suspicions as to the loyalty of the troops or because of clashes that had taken place between the troops and local residents.[50] The barracks, of course, prevented the soldiers from causing unnecessary friction with the townspeople as well as serving to keep a ready force at hand.

Confusion frequently arose from doubt concerning the extent of

47. Graham to King, Dec. 26, 1800, Birmingham, H.O. 42/55. See also same to same Dec. 29 and 31, Wolverhampton, *ibid.*, and same to same April 13, 1801, Sheerness, H.O. 42/61; and Portland to the Treasury, April 22, 1801, H.O. 36/11. Graham, born at Gosport, Hampshire, in 1753, went to sea at the age of fourteen. He served as secretary to Admiral Edwards, governor of Newfoundland 1779–82, and acted as chief justice of that colony. Graham served as inspector of convicts till shortly before his death on December 24, 1818. *Annual Biography and Obituary,* IV (1820), 402–22.

48. June 13, 1792, private, H.O. 42/20; extract printed in Arthur Aspinall (ed.), *The Early English Trade Unions* (London, 1949), pp. 4–6.

49. George III to Dundas, Aug. 29, 1792, 4:30 P.M., Weymouth, H.O. 42/20; not printed in the *Later Correspondence of George III.* Other material on the barracks may be found in the same bundle. De Lancey served as barrack master general 1794–1804. See also J. R. Western, "The Volunteer Movement as an Anti-Revolutionary Force, 1793–1801," *English Historical Review,* LXXI (Oct., 1956), 603–614.

50. De Lancey to Nepean, Nov. 30, 1792, Manchester, H.O. 42/25; magistrates at Sheffield to Dundas, May 10 and 11, 1792, H.O. 42/20; reply, May 14, 1792, H.O. 43/4; Portland to Lt. Col. Gerald Noel Edwards, colonel of the Rutland Regiment of Fencibles, July 23, 1794, H.O. 43/5; A. H. Lloyd, mayor of Winchester, to Portland, Oct. 12, 1794, H.O. 42/33.

the authority of the magistrates over the military. The subject dragged on until Portland ended the controversy by consulting the law officers. After 1796 the magistrates could call out the military even if open rioting had not broken out, but they had to be present personally to do so. Once the troops were called out, the magistrates had authority over their general movements.[51]

A certain amount of compassion for the poor often marked the orders of the Secretaries of State. Dundas wrote to the magistrates of Whitehaven, Cumberland, that he was sending troops,

> but even then it will be worthy of your Consideration, provided Lord Lonsdale should stop the working of his [coal] Mines, which I understand is the occasion of the present Tumult, to form some plan either by Subscription or otherwise, for the subsistence of People who will thereby be deprived of Employment, for without the establishing of some System of that Sort, it appears to me that Riots must inevitably take place, and when once begun it is difficult to determine what may be the Consequences.[52]

Often Dundas and Portland wrote to overzealous magistrates to tell them that the men whom they had arrested for making seditious remarks ought to be released with a reprimand, as they had been quite drunk at the time of the speech.[53]

The Secretaries generally attempted to distinguish between disorders fomented by propagandists demanding political reforms or more drastic measures and those arising from the two other most common causes—strikes or combinations of laborers for higher wages and better conditions, and agricultural distress resulting in a shortage of food and grain. The unrest, seldom leading to riots, among laborers seems to have been limited very largely to the years 1792 and 1799. Dundas reacted more sharply to them than did Portland. It is perhaps fortunate that the more tranquil-minded Duke of Portland headed the Home Office in the critical years 1794–1801. When Henry Blundell, mayor of Liverpool, warned Dundas in 1792 that the carpenters at Liverpool planned to strike,[54] Dundas directed Boundell to pursue "every legal and constitutional

51. Portland to Lord De Dunstanville (Tehidy Park, near Redruth, Cornwall), Aug. 27, 1796, H.O. 43/8. Sir Francis Basset (1757–1835) had been created Baron De Dunstanville on June 17, 1796. *DNB,* I, 1297–98.

52. Sept. 16, 1791, H.O. 43/3.

53. Some examples are Dundas to Robinson Shuttleworth (Preston, Lancashire), April 8, 1794; to magistrates in Warwick, June 21, 1794, to dismiss a deranged man; to Anthony Pechell, July 10, 1794, to release a prisoner who had apologized for his behavior; to Charles Westbourne (Evesham, Worcester), July 10, 1794, H.O. 43/5; Portland to James Cook (Grantham, Lincoln), Oct. 14, 1794, H.O. 43/6.

54. May 27, 1792, H.O. 42/20; extract printed in Aspinall, *Early English Trade Unions,* pp. 2–3.

means of suppressing such combinations and of bringing the Ringleaders to punishment."[55]

In 1799 Parliament actually passed several acts against combinations. The fear of treason remained strong, and the propertied class were uneasy about any gatherings. Even after the acts were passed, John King, at Portland's direction, wrote to a magistrate regarding a combination among the Lancashire weavers. They ought to manifest "to the weavers the readiness of the magistracy to take into consideration the difficulties under which they at present labour . . . and . . . to guard them against being led away by ill-disposed and seditious persons who . . . endeavour to inveigle them into illegal proceedings and breaches of the public peace."[56] But, of course, the Home Office had the responsibility to act when it received reports of illegal combinations. The only manner in which the workers' meetings could be checked to determine whether their plans were illegal entailed the planting of spies. Although the Hammonds have railed against the use of such spies,[57] it is difficult to conceive of any other approach that the authorities could have taken. The procedure followed in such cases was to send the reports of the spies to the law officers, who determined whether or not prosecution should be undertaken. The Home Office followed the same policy in regard both to meetings of radical societies and allegedly seditious statements by individuals. Many such reports, as we have seen, the Secretaries did not bother to send to the law officers, but advised the magistrates to drop any proceedings.[58]

The shortages of grain reached acute stages in 1795 and again in 1800 and presented the Home Office with another task—that of corresponding with the magistrates on the relief the government planned to afford. Generally the office referred letters relating to shortages of grain to the Privy Council, whose responsibility it was to find effective means of relieving distresses caused by lack of food. But often the office corresponded directly with the magistrates. In 1795 Portland wrote to a magistrate near Mold, Flintshire, that "you

55. May 30, 1792, H.O. 43/4; printed in full in Aspinall, *Early English Trade Unions,* p. 3.

56. To Thomas Butterworth Bayley, Nov. 11, 1799, H.O. 43/11; a long extract is printed in Aspinall, *Early English Trade Unions,* pp. 28–30.

57. J. L. Hammond and Barbara Hammond, *The Skilled Labourer, 1760–1832* (London, 1919), p. 67. For the combination laws see M. D. George, "The Combination Laws," *Economic History Review,* VI (April, 1936), 172–78; and the same author's "The Combination Laws Reconsidered," *Economic History,* I (May, 1927), 214–28.

58. Many examples of this may be found in H.O. 43/11, especially for 1799; see also Aspinall, *Early English Trade Unions,* pp. 20–36.

must be sensible that His Majesty's confidential Servants use every means in their power to remedy the present difficulties; . . . and that you will endeavour as much as possible to lessen the evils complained of."[59]

Portland perhaps appeared at his best in 1800 when the shortage of grain, or rather, the mistaken belief that the scarcity was an artificial one calculated to reap profits for farmers and dealers, caused tumults in many counties. He set forth his ideas, firm but not harsh, on how to deal with the disorders in a letter in September of 1800 to the town clerk of Nottingham, and more fully in a letter, remarkable for its clarity and common sense, to the Duke of Marlborough, Lord Lieutenant of Oxford. The Cabinet read his letter to Marlborough and insisted that it be published for the salutary effects that it might have in restoring order.[60] The letters both to Marlborough and to the town clerk of Nottingham appeared in many newspapers. The essence of the policy to be followed appears in the letter to the town clerk:

> Whereever any reduction in the price of a commodity has been effected by intimidation, it has never been of any duration; and, besides, by throwing things out of their natural and orderly course, it almost necessarily happens that the evil, instead of being remedied, returns with increased violence. According to the best information I have been able to procure, and as far as my experience extends, I am satisfied, that whenever a scarcity of provisions exists, or is seriously to be apprehended, the only means which can tend effectually to obviate it, and to prevent the grain from rising to an excessive price, consists in holding out full security and indemnification to all farmers and other lawful dealers, who shall bring their corn, or other commodities, regularly to market, and in giving early notice of a determined resolution to suppress at once, and by force, if it shall unhappily become necessary, every attempt to impede, by open acts of violence, or by intimidation, the regular business of the markets.[61]

The letter to Marlborough[62] explained in more detail the causes of the scarcity and the pointlessness of using violence. Portland realized the danger of compromising with lawlessness, however understanda-

59. To Rhual, Oct. 29, 1795, H.O. 43/7.

60. Portland explained the publication in another letter to Marlborough, Oct. 23, 1800, private, H.O. 42/52.

61. Sept. 10, 1800, printed in the *Annual Register,* XLII (1800), Appendix to Chronicle, pp. 141–44. Portland wrote similar letters on September 11 to the mayor of Chesterfield and to the magistrates of Birmingham, H.O. 43/12.

62. Printed in the *Annual Register,* XLII (1800), Appendix to Chronicle, pp. 141–43. Lord Holland, certainly no admirer of Portland, thought well of the soundness of the doctrine set forth in the letter. Holland, *Memoirs of the Whig Party,* I, 166–68.

ble the causes might be. He sharply rebuked the mayor of Bunbury, Cheshire, for failing to use the military to disperse a riot. "Every such concession on the part of the Civil Power must inevitably tend to encourage further attempts to riot and insurrection, and be the means of increasing the present price of Grain to the most alarming extent."[63]

In late 1800 the Home Office served as the collecting agency for information about the harvest of that fall which was gathered from the parish clergy and local officials in all parts of England. By acquiring this information the government had some means of determining which areas would require assistance, but the scope of government activity remained limited. This appears nowhere more clearly than in letters from Portland to Heneage Legge and from John King to Sir Christopher Willoughby in 1795. In response to Willoughby's complaints about the scarcity of wheat in his neighborhood, King explained that the government could not adopt a plan for the general direction of charities, and all relief had to vary according to local conditions.[64] Portland advised Legge (of Aston Hall, near Birmingham) that "it is to the exertions and liberality of gentlemen in general, that Government must look in the present moment of distress, for the effectual relief that can be afforded to the country at large."[65]

Eighteenth-century statesmen envisioned the central government as interfering in local affairs in the natural order of things only when emergencies so demanded. That the government at Whitehall should make laws and regulations for the management of society never occurred to men like Dundas and Portland. Despite the pervasive and continuing unrest in the countryside, no system of national police materialized. Whether for civil unrest or for the relief of threatened famine, the government relied upon the local officials and landed aristocracy for assistance. If absolutely necessary, the military could provide support. The Home Secretary provided only a haphazard coordinating center for the preservation of public order in the counties.

63. Sept. 13, 1800, H.O. 43/12.

64. King to Sir Christopher Willoughby [1748–1808], Bt., of Baldon House, Oxford, July 3, 1795, H.O. 43/6.

65. Portland to Legge [1747–1827], July 13, 1795, printed in John Alfred Langford, *A Century of Birmingham Life* (2 vols.; Birmingham, 1868), II, 55. Similar letters in 1795 are in H.O. 43/6. For the general situation during times of crop failure see Donald Grove Barnes, *History of the English Corn Laws from 1660 to 1846* (London, 1930), pp. 69–86; and C. R. Fay, *The Corn Laws and Social England* (Cambridge, 1932), chaps. iii–iv.

Chapter Eight

PUBLIC ORDER IN LONDON

The Home Office enjoyed a peculiar relationship to the maintenance of public order in the city of London. The police and magistracy of London and Westminster before 1792 consisted of thirteen magistrates sitting at various places in the city, although the Lord Mayor, the sheriff of London, and other officials had some limited duties regarding public order. The magistrates heard cases on misdemeanors and weighed the evidence in cases of persons accused of a felony to determine whether they should be bound over to a higher court. At least ten of the justices were "trading" justices, that is, they earned a large part of their livelihood by collecting the fees and fines due them as magistrates. Most of these ten exemplified the worst possible traits for a justice of the peace. Although several managed to stay one step ahead of the law, at least three had found lodging in the King's Bench or Fleet Street prisons at one point in their lives. Fortunately, the three magistrates who sat at Bow Street, together with six officers known as runners and a patrol of about sixty men, maintained a respectable level of efficiency and competence. It was this office that did most of the "thief-taking" for the metropolis.[1]

In 1792 Parliament passed the Middlesex Justices Act, which brought a long overdue reform to the magistracy. Nearly all the trading justices were removed. In their places the Act provided for the establishment of seven public offices in addition to the one at Bow Street. (In 1798 the Thames Police Office was added.) The offices had locations at strategic positions in the area in order to afford adequate protection to the entire metropolis. Each office had three magistrates, appointed by the Home Secretary, and from six to

1. Radzinowitz, III, 1–62, has by far the best account of the early police of London. Gilbert Armitage, *The History of the Bow Street Runners 1729–1829* (London, 1932) is largely anecdotal.

ten constables.[2] Dundas went to considerable lengths to insure that the offices had only competent and respectable men.[3] The Act gave the Secretary of State extensive powers over the London magistrates. The receiver of the public offices, who collected all fees and fines and paid all salaries and expenses, submitted the accounts to the Secretary of State for his approval; the Secretary then sent them to the Treasury.[4] The receiver, John Reeves, or the magistrates also consulted the Home Secretary about extraordinary purchases and about the appointment and removal of clerks and officers.[5] In July 1793 Dundas ordered Reeves to perform the same duties for the office at Bow Street as he did for the seven public offices;[6] thereafter the Home Office also exercised supervisory jurisdiction over Bow Street. In August 1793 Dundas actually removed one of the Bow Street magistrates for making an unauthorized trip to Paris.[7] And in 1795 King ordered the Bow Street magistrates to make a full report about their having allegedly forced an apprentice to enter the navy or army,[8] and later rebuked them for failing to cooperate with the other offices.[9]

The Secretary and Undersecretaries handled metropolitan police problems as they arose. No Home Office official had direct responsibility for London, but Richard Ford, a magistrate at Shadwell from 1792 and later at Bow Street, managed a great deal of the correspondence and business relating to the London police on behalf of the department. In 1794 and 1795 he served successively both Dundas and Portland by taking testimony at the Privy Council during the examination of persons accused of treason.[10] He had to take leave

2. Radzinowitz, III, 108–37.

3. For example, Dundas to Lord Onslow, June 22, 1792, H.O. 43/4. Nepean to Onslow, and reply, July 7, 1792, H.O. 42/21; Dundas to Lord Sommers, April 17, 1794, H.O. 43/5. Among those appointed were Patrick Colquhoun (1745–1820), a distinguished authority on police (*DNB,* IV, 859–61); Aaron Graham; Nathaniel Conant, who was knighted when he became chief of the Bow Street office (died 1822); Philip Neve, a barrister (*Annual Biography and Obituary,* IX [1825], 444–45); John Floud, "whose talents advanced him to . . . [the office of magistrate], where he displayed them to great advantage" (*Gentleman's Magazine,* LXX [May, 1800], 486); and Benjamin Robertson, an amateur botanist of distinction who died worth £100,000. *Ibid.,* (Supplement, 1800), p. 1294.

4. John Reeves to Dundas, Aug. 1, 1792, H.O. 42/44; Richard Ford to Reeves, July 11, 1795, H.O. 65/1; King to Charles Long, April 21, 1795, H.O. 36/9.

5. King to Bow Street magistrates, Aug. 2, 1796, H.O. 65/1; Richard Ford to Reeves, July 11, 1795.

6. Dundas to Reeves, July 13, 1793, H.O. 43/4; same to same, July 10, 1794, H.O. 43/5.

7. Major Mitchell to Dundas, Aug. 13, 1793, St. George's Row, Hyde Park, H.O. 42/26.

8. Jan. 25, 1795, H.O. 43/6.

9. Feb. 3, 1795, H.O. 65/1.

10. Portland to the Treasury, May 13, 1795, H.O. 36/9.

from his office of magistrate at Bow Street early in 1794 in order to devote his time to duties in the Home Office.[11] In January 1795 a new entry book separated police business from general correspondence.[12] Although John King continued to sign most of the letters, Ford evidently composed them.[13] Portland had a high opinion of Ford's abilities and exchanged much correspondence with him from October 1794 through August 1795 regarding riots in London and the activities of the London Corresponding Society.[14] During a disorder in London in 1797 it was Ford who remained at the Home Office to receive reports from all the police officers two or three times in the course of the evening.[15] Ford received £500 per annum for his services.[16] From August 7, 1800,[17] till January 1801 he also acted as superintendent of the Alien Office. In January he succeeded Sir William Addington as chief magistrate at Bow Street,[18] resigned his post as superintendent, and probably gave up his other duties at the Home Office. He was knighted on December 16, 1801,[19] and continued to head the office at Bow Street till his death on May 3, 1806, aged forty-eight.[20]

Prior to 1792 the Home Office interfered only sporadically in the operations of the justices within the metropolis. When a wave of robberies swept the city in 1782, Townshend wrote to the magistrates, the Lord Mayor, and other officials to demand that they hold

> frequent Sittings for this purpose, by calling before you the proper officers under your direction, and giving them the strictest orders and Warrants from time to time, as there shall be occasion, to search for and apprehend Rogues, Vagabonds, idle and disorderly Persons, in order to their being dealt with according to Law; and . . . proceed with rigour . . . against all persons harbouring such offenders . . . [and] against [those] who keep the said night houses or cellars, Tippling or common Gaming House. . . .[21]

11. Ford to Nepean, n.d., received May 5, 1794, H.O. 44/42.
12. H.O. 65/1.
13. Ford to Edward Finch Hatton, March 19, 1801, Bow Street, H.O. 42/61.
14. Portland MSS, PwF 3,928–3,943.
15. March 4, 1797, *Later Correspondence of George III*, II, 549–50.
16. Portland to the Treasury, May 13, 1795, H.O. 36/9.
17. Warrant, H.O. 38/8.
18. *Annual Register*, XLIII (1801), Appendix to Chronicle, pp. 1–2.
19. *Ibid.*, p. 62.
20. *Annual Register*, XLVIII (1806), pp. 530–531. Richard Ford was the son of James Ford (1717–95), a physician. From his father Sir Richard inherited an interest in the Drury Lane Theatre. Some correspondence between him and Sheridan may be found in *The Letters of Richard Brinsley Sheridan*, edited by Cecil Price (3 vols.; Oxford, 1966). Ford had four illegitimate children by his mistress, Mrs. Jordan the actress, but before 1790 she transferred herself to the Duke of Clarence, later King William IV. *DNB*, X, 1082.
21. To the Lord Mayor, Oct. 20, 1782, and to the high steward of Westminster, the chairman of the sessions of the peace of Middlesex, and justices of the peace for Middlesex, Westminster, Surrey, and the Tower Hamlets, Oct. 22, 1782, H.O. 43/1.

The magistrates had some success in seizing a variety of "loose, idle, and disorderly persons," of whom at least seventeen "elected" to serve in the navy. The magistrates continued to make reports on their proceedings for some time thereafter.[22] In 1783 when some seamen threatened to riot, Lord North directed the Lord Mayor to assemble the city magistrates. The Commander-in-Chief at the same time readied a detachment of troops at the Tower of London to assist the civil authorities.[23] A riot over the introduction of the shop tax in 1785 obliged Lord Sydney

> to send to the Lord Mayor of the city of London and the Magistrates of Westminster that they might take the necessary measures for preserving the peace. He likewise sent to the Marquis of Lothian [commander of the Life Guards], and the Adjutant General, that the military might be in readiness to support the civil power in the prevention of disorder.[24]

In 1787 Nepean wrote directly to the commanding officer at the Tower to prepare to assist the civil magistrates in case anything came of threats received by the Lord Mayor to burn some flour mills near the city.[25]

After 1791, although the Home Office did not interfere in the daily business of the magistrates, it regularly intervened in cases of riots or threatened riots. In some instances, the Office might do no more than send warnings that it had received of threatened disorders. At other times the magistrates were ordered to take some particular action. In November 1792 an anonymous informer warned Nepean that a mob would descend upon Kennington Common to burn an effigy of the Duke of Brunswick.[26] Nepean ordered the magistrates at Southwark to stop it.[27] Evidently the alarm was false, for the newspapers do not mention the incident. Later that same month Nepean warned the magistrates at Great Marlborough Street of an impending riot scheduled to take place on Sunday. Only one magistrate should attend, in order to avoid suspicion, but the others ought to be prepared to act if necessary.[28] The magistrates remained, as did the constables, till 2 A.M.; but nothing happened.[29]

22. See especially James Keen, high constable of Kensington, to Sydney, March 17, 1783; and William Mainwaring, chairman of the Middlesex Sessions, to Sydney, March 8, 1783, H.O. 42/2. 23. North to the Lord Mayor, April 18, 1783, H.O. 42/2.

24. Sydney to the King, June 15, 1785, *Later Correspondence of George III*, I, 165.

25. Aug. 6, 1787, secret, H.O. 43/3. Other instances of correspondence with the Bow Street magistrates occurred before 1792, but not a great many.

26. From "A Friend to Good Order," Nov. 5, 1792, H.O. 42/22.

27. Nov. 5, 1792, noon, *ibid.* 28. Nov. 28, 1792, secret, H.O. 43/4.

29. Nathaniel Conant (?1746–1822) to Nepean, Nov. 25, 1792, 2 P.M.; magistrates at Worship Street to Nepean, Nov. 26, 1792, H.O. 42/22.

Patrick Colquhoun, a magistrate at Worship Street and a distinguished reformer of the police, explained the incident: "I am aware that under the present circumstances there will be many false alarms which renders it of very great importance to adopt such measures as shall precisely ascertain the truth without exhibiting to the public Eye the Idea of any interference on the Part of Magistrates."[30] On both occasions in November the military had been in readiness.[31]

By no means were all alarms false. A typical action by the Home Office occurred in 1794 during severe rioting in London. Portland sent a circular letter to the magistrates ordering them to call upon the chairmen in their respective districts of the Association for the Preservation of Liberty and Property against Republicans and Levellers to inform them that they might have to assist the magistrates.[32] The next day, as rioting continued, Portland also ordered the magistrates to have the church wardens swear in extra constables.[33] Colquhoun reported that the use of special constables and the readiness of the military had restored tranquillity.[34]

In certain cases the orders from the Home Office to the magistrates were far more explicit about how a riot should be ended. When word reached the Office on June 26, 1795, that the London Corresponding Society had called a general meeting for August 29 in St. George's Field, it immediately notified all the magistrates.[35] On the 27th Portland warned the Lord Lieutenant of Surrey[36] and the next day, the Lord Mayor and the commanding officer of the Horse Guards to be in readiness.[37] The Home Office coordinated the activity of the civil authorities with that of the military on the day of the riot. King ordered the magistrates to read the Riot Act and indicated the precise locations of the military units on which they could draw for support.[38]

30. To Nepean, Nov. 26, 1792, No. 51 Charles Square, Hexton, H.O. 42/22.

31. Sir George Yonge, Secretary at War, to the King, Nov. 25, 1792, *Later Correspondence of George III,* I, 630–31.

32. Aug. 20, 1794, H.O. 43/5. The Association, founded on November 20, 1792, by John Reeves, often proved useful by providing extra constables in times of need. The best, though disparaging, account of the Association is Eugene Charlton Black, *The Association: British Extraparliamentary Political Organization 1769–1793* (Harvard Historical Monographs, LIV; Cambridge, Mass., 1963), pp. 233–74; see also Austin Mitchell, "The Association Movement of 1792–1793," *Historical Journal,* IV (1961), 56–77; and Donald E. Ginter, "The Loyalist Association Movement of 1792–93 and British Public Opinion," *ibid.,* IX (1966), 179–90.

33. Aug. 21, 1794, *ibid.*

34. Colquhoun and William Browne to Portland, Aug. 23, 1794, Worship Street, Shoreditch, H.O. 42/33.

35. H.O. 65/1.

36. To Lord Onslow, *ibid.*

37. *Ibid.*

38. King to the magistrates at Union Hall and Queen's Street, 3 P.M., *ibid.*

Occasionally the office directed the magistrates to undertake certain other tasks. In December 1792 Nepean ordered the Bow Street magistrates to have their constables arrest persons writing seditious words on walls.[39] In 1795 the owner of the New Circus Theatre displayed advertising bills and posters that offended the government. King directed the Bow Street magistrates to send for the owner "and represent to him, not in a public manner, that if he persists in making similar allusions in his Bills, it may be the means of the Magistrates refusing a renewal of his license."[40] Later that year Portland sent Richard Ford information on which of the public houses had been frequented by foreigners and other undesirables. The information was to be put to use when magistrates met to license houses.[41] Obviously, the government had various more or less unobtrusive means by which they could exercise control in London.

The Home Office made use of means other than the magistrates to preserve order in London. The use of spies to report on various societies was a favorite way of acquiring intelligence. Local officials probably planted most spies with the Office's approval. In November 1792 Patrick Colquhoun informed Nepean that he had spoken to an intelligent foreman of one of the principal manufacturers in Spitalsfield, who would insinuate himself into the different societies and bring Colquhoun information.[42] He had some credit with the weavers from the time that he had served as magistrate for the area and would make use of it. Another example of local initiative in the London area occurred in 1799 when Henry Thornton, M.P. for Southwark, informed Wickham that a distiller in the area named Benwell had reported that one of his employees had offered a coworker a shilling a meeting to attend a society at Wandsworth. Any person accepting had to spend sixpence at the meeting and take a secret oath.[43] Wickham's reply typifies a common practice:

The Duke of Portland would therefore particularly wish that the Person who gave the information to Mr. Benwell could be induced to become a Member of the Society—the more so, as the circumstances of money being given to any Members of a Society (excepting when under prosecution) is quite new.

You will perhaps be so obliging as to speak to Mr. Benwell on this

39. Dec. 10, 1792, H.O. 43/4. 40. April 18, 1795, secret, H.O. 43/6.
41. Portland to Ford, Aug. 29, 1795, copy, Portland MSS, PwF 3,944.
42 Colquhoun to Nepean, No. 51 Charles Square, Hexton, Nov. 26, 1792, H.O. 42/22.
43. King's Arms Yard, Coleman Street, April 2, 1799, H.O. 42/47.

subject, and engage him to take such steps as he shall think most likely to give him a knowledge of the members, views, and constitution of this Society; and I am sure the Duke of Portland will at all times feel himself particularly obliged by any information with which you can furnish him, on a subject so important to the peace of Society.[44]

The government itself probably planted other spies, although the absence of the Secret Service accounts prevents a clear understanding of which government office was responsible. At least two government undercover agents insinuated themselves into membership in the secret committee of the London Corresponding Society. One of these, William Metcalfe, wrote:

Mr. Nepean requested that I would attend to the disaffected Societies, and endeavour to find out their intentions and designs. . . . I engaged in that unpleasant business, and very shortly afterwards procured myself to be admitted a Member of the London Corresponding Society where I carried myself so void of Suspicion that I was appointed a Tything Man by which I had an opportunity of attending the Committee of Delegates from the several Divisions of the Society, and at length was chosen of the Secret Committee in which situation I was at the time of the commencement of the late prosecutions and might still have been, but that my name having been included in the list of witnesses to be called for the Crown together with my having been . . . present at and contributing to the apprehension of La Maitre and the other persons charged with the horrid design of assassinating the King, I was immediately denounced in the Society, and it consequently became impossible for me any longer to furnish Government with the information of their proceedings.[45]

The Home Office kept close watch on the radical societies after 1791. Richard Ford sent frequent reports about the L.C.S. to Portland, while the Secretary was out of town.[46] Ford was still receiving information on the L.C.S. in 1798.[47] Luke Ideson, vestry clerk of St. James, Westminster,[48] took transcripts of the proceedings of the Westminister Forum in Brewer Street.[49] A complaint laid before the magistrates about the Forum had been submitted to the vestry and eventually to Portland. Ideson, whom Portland ordered to investi-

44. April 3, 1799, private [copy], *ibid.*

45. To Portland, Jan. 5, 1795, Tallow Chandler's Hall, H.O. 42/34. The other spy was "Citizen" Groves (Thompson, *English Working Class,* pp. 133–35, 153, 156, 489, 494). Paul Lemaitre was a London watchmaker, accused in 1795 of plotting to kill the King with a poison needle fired from a blow gun. *Ibid.,* pp. 140 n., 464–65.

46. Reports from Oct. 1794 to Dec. 1795, PwF 3928–3943, Portland MSS.

47. Packet dated March 12, 1798, H.O. 42/42.

48. Ideson died on July 12, 1799, aged sixty. *Gentleman's Magazine,* LXIX (July, 1799), 630.

49. Ideson to King, Dec. 6, 1797, Poland St., H.O. 42/21.

gate, had to hire constables to protect the shorthand writers from abuse at the meetings.[50] A letter from Portland to the King in 1796 conveys an impression the extent of the reporting on radical societies:

> The Duke of Portland humbly begs leave to lay before your Majesty a report of Thelwal's [a leading radical] second lecture & to request your Majesty's commands respecting his continuing to transmit to your Majesty the accounts which he conceives it to be his duty to have given him regularly of everything that passes at this & the other Academies & seminaries of sedition.[51]

The Home Office had a vague relationship with the London press, but unlike the Treasury, it does not seem to have made systematic uses of the press to stamp out radicalism. The Secret Service account of Nepean records no payment to a newspaper. The Home Office may have favored certain newspapers, such as *The Times,* with news items, but there was certainly no concerted subsidy. Perhaps it subsidized some pamphleteers and writers for the newspapers.[52] Dundas had considerable success in ordering the subsidization of the loyal press in Edinburgh, but attempts in the English counties must have been most irregular.[53]

One special police duty of the Home Department related to guarding the King. The office hired and paid out of the contingent account five officers whose job it was to serve as guards at Windsor, Kew, St. James's, or Weymouth. They received £100 per annum till 1801, when the salary doubled.[54] No regular guards were stationed at the royal residence until 1789, when two were appointed. The number rose to five by 1792. The guards (often Bow Street constables) prevented undesirable persons (often lunatics) from approaching the King. In February 1789 a deranged young man had actually wandered through Kew Palace during the King's illness before the porter stopped him. Lord Sydney sent a messenger to Kew to carry

50. Ideson to Wickham, Aug. 27, 1798, Poland St., H.O. 42/44.

51. Feb. 14, 1796, *Later Correspondence of George III,* II, 458–59. Page 843 in the index of Thompson, *English Working Class,* is excellent for following the course of events in London during this period. H.O. 42/21 has copies of minutes of the Society for Constitutional Information from October 1792 through January 1793.

52. Lucyle Werkmeister, *The London Daily Press 1772–1792* (Lincoln, Nebraska, 1963), p. 359. Mrs. Werkmeister was unable to determine which agents worked for the Treasury and which worked for the Home Office. I doubt that Nepean and Dundas actually supervised the writers in a consistent fashion. The Treasury usually managed the press and no doubt continued to do so.

53. Aspinall, *Politics and the Press,* pp. 351, 413.

54. H.O. 82/3.

the man to the Home Office.[55] After Thomas Augustus Smith Murray, an imposter claiming to be a half-brother of George III, made a considerable nuisance of himself in late 1789, guards always remained near the King.[56] The growth of disorders in the 1790's insured that they would remain.

The mounting fear of radicals, the control over the public offices in the metropolis, the use of spying, which was more regular than that in the counties, and even the introduction of a permanent system of guards for the King had drawn the Secretary of State into a more direct part in the process of preserving order in London than had ever before been the case.

55. [Robert Fulke Greville] *The Diaries of Colonel the Hon. Robert Fulke Greville, Equerry to His Majesty King George III,* edited by F. McKno. Bladon (London, 1930), pp. 222–23.

56. Nepean to Bernard, Nov. 10, 1789, 12 P.M., Spencer Bernard MSS, O.E. 7/4; printed in Higgins, *The Bernards of Abingdon,* III, 132–33. Nepean spent much time in investigating Murray's claim and made several trips before he discovered that Murray's alleged mother, said to have been a member of the Atholl family, never existed. Many papers relating to Murray are in H.O. 42/17.

Chapter Nine

THE ALIEN OFFICE

The disorders that began in France in 1789 brought to England large numbers of foreigners, many of whom had seditious intentions. Ironically, the spur to the government's first action came from Dundas' expectation that the Duke of Brunswick's army would take Paris, and consequently drive many of the radicals to seek refuge in England.[1] Although that expectation proved to be totally without foundation, the sentiment expressed by John Walter, editor of *The Times,* that the presence of French émigrés was causing disaffection,[2] obliged government to take some steps to control the influx.

Although initial measures were fairly sporadic, the Home Office regularly received information about aliens. The main sources of information were officials at the southern ports. At various times in the fall of 1792 the lieutenant governor of Portsmouth,[3] a justice of the peace at Gosport,[4] a post office official at Dover,[5] the collector of customs at Dover,[6] and at Harwich,[7] and others reported that hundreds of Frenchmen had arrived and often gave information about them, such as their identity and supposed political views.

The collector of customs at Dover also sent copies of French newspapers to the Home Office. The Secretary sometimes relayed especially significant news from such papers to the King.[8] Persons in either the Home or Foreign Office apparently culled them for intelligence of developments in France. The Office evidently confiscated

1. Dundas to Lords Kenyon and Loughborough and to the Lord Chief Baron, Sept. 12, 1792, H.O. 43/4. 2. Walter to Dundas, Oct. 29, 1792, H.O. 42/22.

3. Lt. Gov. (Sir) Thomas Trigge to [Dundas], Sept. 13, 1792, H.O. 42/21.

4. Thomas Curry to Dundas, Sept. 12, 1792, *ibid.;* reply, Sept. 13, H.O. 43/4. Curry died on January 3, 1803. *Gentleman's Magazine,* LXXIII (Jan., 1803), 89.

5. R. Gibbon to Nepean, Dover, Sept. 25 and 28, 1792, H.O. 42/21.

6. Peter Newport to Nepean, Nov. 5, 1792, Dover; same to Charles Long, Nov. 12, H.O. 42/22.

7. Wm. Crowder to [Charles Long], Nov. 12, 1792, Harwich, *ibid.*; also a list of foreigners arrived since April 1, 1794, H.O. 42/29.

8. Portland to the King, June 14, 1795; same to same, Nov. 10, 1795, *Later Correspondence of George III,* II, 354, 418.

French papers with some regularity, as John Heriot, editor of the government papers, the *Sun* and the *True Briton,* complained of the seizure of his French papers.[9]

One interesting letter illustrates an action taken by the Office during the early years. In September 1792 a Mr. Ross, a perfumer at Walworth in London, received a peremptory order to report to the office of the Secretary of State to provide information about French emigrants whom he was harboring. "If you fail [to come], you will most assuredly answer for the consequences at your peril."[10] How many persons received similar notices is unknown.

The first concerted step to check aliens came on December 1, 1792. Intelligence of open sedition and worse on the part of some aliens who had recently landed at ports in Kent and Essex prompted Nepean to write to the Reverend Philip Salter, an Essex justice of the peace.[11] The government determined that agents had to be stationed on the roads from such ports as Harwich and Dover to examine all foreigners proceeding to London. Any armed persons were to be taken before a magistrate, who had orders to detain them if they failed to give a satisfactory account of themselves. The government would then decide what to do with them. Nepean sent Patrick McManus, one of the police officers guarding the King, to Chelmsford to examine the foreigners. "It is possible," Nepean wrote

> that in the performance of this service some steps may be necessary to be taken not exactly justifiable by Law, but in times like the present, when dangerous incendiaries are daily resorting to this Country, avowedly with mischievous intentions, it is not necessary to be very nice. If therefore in giving your assistance in this business any prosecution should be commenced against you for any thing of that sort, I am authorized to assure you of the fullest support from Government on any occasion.[12]

The British government obviously feared the French and their potentially dangerous presence and saw no reason to extend the full benefit of English law to aliens seeking to subvert it. But a few days

9. To Portland, Aug. 3, 1795, H.O. 42/35. See also Aspinall, *Politics and the Press,* pp. 399–403. Only newspapers favorable to the government may have received French papers.

10. Unsigned, Sept. 26, 1792, but evidently the original letter, since the broken seal and postmark appear on the letter. Ross evidently brought the letter to the office when he came. H.O. 42/21.

11. Salter (1746–1829) had been ordained in 1771 and served as rector of Shenfield, Essex, 1772–1829. Venn and Venn, *Alumni Cantabrigenses,* Pt. II, V, 406.

12. Secret, H.O. 42/23.

after writing to Salter, Nepean cautioned a magistrate at Dartford, near London, not to commit any foreigners to jail for any cause that he would not also commit an English citizen for. Persons examining foreigners should be careful to treat them with every civility.[13]

Parliament quickly responded to the situation by passing a law that provided the executive with great discretionary powers in regard to aliens. Lord Grenville introduced the Alien Bill into the House of Lords on December 19, 1792. Only three members spoke against its passage.[14] Dundas, in the Commons, stressed the necessity for the government to have a check upon potentially dangerous aliens. Many members of the Opposition lent their support to the bill.[15]

The Alien Act, which received the royal assent on January 8, 1793,[16] directed that the masters of ships provide lists of all foreigners to the customs office at the port of arrival. All aliens arriving after January 10, 1793, had to register with the customs offices as soon as they disembarked, surrender any arms that they carried, and remain at the place of arrival until a magistrate or the Secretary of State granted a passport for them to come inland. Magistrates sent copies of any such documents they issued to the Home Office. An alien who arrived after January 1, 1792, had to obtain a passport before changing his place of abode. The Act also gave the king the authority to issue a proclamation ordering nonresidents to leave the realm, and to restrict arrival to specified ports of entry. The Secretary of State might issue warrants to deport any undesirable aliens. The magistrates could require foreigners to reside in a specific area and require householders to present accounts of such persons residing in their houses.[17] The very threat of the passage of such a bill, *The Times* reported, had had a good effect. Many Frenchmen decamped, including Rotondo, who had beheaded the Princess de Lamballe. "The metropolis is already cleared of hundreds of the French vermin, who come hither to breed rebellion and assassination. . . ."[18]

To the Home department fell the responsibility for the central

13. To John Scott, Dec. 7, 1792, H.O. 43/4.
14. Debates on Dec. 21, 22, 26, 1792, Debrett, *Parl. Reg.,* XXXVI, 24, 37–64. Only Lords Guilford, Lansdowne, and Lauderdale opposed it.
15. Dec. 25 and 31, Jan. 2 and 4, 1793, *ibid.,* XXXIV, 208–37, 240–302. Lord Titchfield, Lord Beauchamp (whose speech is particularly sensible), Sir Gilbert Elliott, and Thomas Grenville were among the opposition members who voted for the bill.
16. House of Commons, *Journals,* XLVIII, 91.
17. *Statutes at Large,* 33 George III, c. 4.
18. Jan. 2, 1793. Jan. 19 also refers to the good effect of the bill.

administration of the Alien Act. The story of the Home Office's action is largely one of implementing and tightening the basic law. In order to regularize procedures, the Secretary appointed a superintendent and (eventually) two clerks who formed the Alien Office.[19] The two Undersecretaries of State also received appointments as superintendents. William Huskisson became the first superintendent on January 10, 1793.[20] Temporary clerks served at first,[21] but by October 15, 1795, Charles M. Lullin became chief of passports and licenses.[22] By at least June 1798 Henry William Brooke held the post of chief clerk.[23]

William Wickham succeeded Huskisson July 11, 1794, but remained in office only till the 9th of December of that year, when he became chargé d'affaires in the Swiss cantons. Thomas Carter, Portland's private secretary, served from December 9, 1794, to February 1798. Charles William Flint, who had accompanied Wickham to Europe in 1796 as his confidential secretary, became superintendent, on July 5, 1798.[24] Wickham, however, requested Flint's assistance in Europe,[25] and Richard Ford replaced him on August 7, 1800.[26] Flint again became superintendent on February 19, 1801.[27]

Almost the first action of the Secretary of State after the passage of the Act was to have the King issue a proclamation restricting the residence of aliens to the area around London unless they had passports exempting them.[28] The Alien Office printed special forms

19. The Alien Office, originally on Whitehall, moved to Crown Street, Westminster, in July 1798. *The Times,* July 6, 1798.

20. Dundas to the Treasury, Feb. 4, 1794, H.O. 36/8. For Huskisson's appointment, see *The Huskisson Papers,* edited by Lewis Melville (London, 1931), pp. 18–19; and C. R. Fay, *Huskisson and His Age* (London, 1951), pp. 66–67.

21. William Bowra was clerk by November 2, 1794, till October 10, 1795. Contingent Accounts, H.O. 82/3.

22. Lullin, born about 1774, was pensioned at £637 per annum in 1816 when the Alien Office establishment was reduced. He was still living in 1839. *PP 1839* (142–III), XXXI, 656.

23. Brooke, born about 1772, retired in 1813 because of ill health on a pension of £600. *Ibid.* He died on April 15, 1842, at Walmer, Kent. *Gentleman's Magazine,* n.s., XVII (May, 1842), 564.

24. Warrant, H.O. 38/8.

25. Wickham to Grenville, July 15, 1800, H.M.C., *Dropmore Papers,* VI, 269–70. Wickham sent Flint back in January 1801. Same to same, Jan. 13, 1801, Vienna, *ibid.,* p. 419.

26. Warrant, H.O. 38/8.

27. *Ibid.* Flint, born in Scotland between 1775 and 1778, received his education at Edinburgh before entering the Foreign Office in 1793 (Fitzpatrick, *Secret Service Under Pitt,* pp. 349–50). He served in the Irish Office of the Home department in the early nineteenth century and was appointed Undersecretary in 1827. He was knighted on May 29, 1812, upon acting as proxy for Sir Henry Wellesley at his installation as Knight of the Bath. He retired in March 1832 and died on January 19, 1834. *Gentleman's Magazine,* n.s. I (Feb., 1834), 228.

28. Feb. 4, 1793, *London Gazette.*

to distribute to customs officials and others for use in submitting information about all foreigners.[29] It also issued all passports and licenses both to nonresidents and to British citizens who requested to go abroad. When a foreigner wished to become a naturalized citizen, the Alien Office made inquiries about his character.[30] When necessary, the Secretary issued a warrant to a king's messenger to deport an undesirable alien.[31] He also directed magistrates to expel seditious aliens residing in restricted areas.[32]

In early 1796 Portland complained to the Privy Council that foreigners were evading the Act by landing anywhere they chose.[33] By Order in Council of March 23, 1796, persons who were not British citizens might disembark only at Gravesend, Dover, Yarmouth, and (later) Falmouth.[34] The next step was the appointment of permanent inspectors at each of the four ports, who were to assist the customs officials in executing the Act of 1793. When any alien came under suspicion the inspector was to accompany him to London, or else delegate the duty to some responsible person. Upon arrival in London the inspectors surrendered the foreigners and their baggage to the magistrates at Great Marlborough Street. After the magistrates examined them and their baggage, they sent any particulars to the Duke of Portland's office. The aliens who aroused no suspicion could proceed to London, after making the necessary declaration to the customs officials, but the inspector submitted a regular list to the Undersecretary of all arrivals and departures.[35]

Six men served as inspectors during the period. Several were actually customs officers. John Mazzinghi, however, held the position of recorder of aliens for the city of London under the direction of the Lord Mayor.[36] Mazzinghi served at Gravesend till his dismissal before December 11, 1798.[37] Peter Newport held the post of inspector at Dover till his death on September 30, 1799.[38] He had long been collector of customs at that port. James Walsh, Jr., who com-

29. Copies of some of these printed forms are in H.O. 1/2–3.
30. For example, John Benson (died 1827) clerk to the House of Commons to [?Dundas], March 6, 1794; R. Chamberlain, mayor of Exeter to [Dundas], March 13, 1794, H.O. 42/28.
31. For example, Dundas to Frederic Courvoisier, Nov. 30, 1793, H.O. 42/27.
32. For example, Dundas to the mayor of Bristol, Jan. 2, 1794, H.O. 43/4.
33. To the Lord President, March 16, 1796, H.O. 43/7.
34. Privy Council Register, P.C. 2/145.
35. King to John Mazzinghi, Feb. 18, 1796, H.O. 5/1.
36. Mazzinghi to Huskisson, Dec. 2, 1793, H.O. 1/1.
37. Wickham to James Reeves, Dec. 11, 1798, H.O. 5/4.
38. *Gentleman's Magazine,* LXIX (Oct., 1799), 903.

manded a Customs cutter, served as inspector at Yarmouth from 1796 to 1798 and then replaced Mazzinghi at Gravesend.[39] Samuel Humphrey Pellew, collector of customs at Falmouth, acted as inspector by January 5, 1800.[40] Benjamin Fuller Stowe succeeded Newport both as collector and as inspector.[41] George J. Hake succeeded Walsh at Yarmouth.

The inspectors, who received annual salaries of £100, furnished the Alien Office with much information, and certainly tightened the control over nonresidents. Often an inspector had two or three cutters to assist him. So serious was his duty considered that he had sole command of the vessels, despite the wishes of the commissioners of customs.[42]

Other restrictions upon aliens soon followed. In the summer of 1796, all London householders had to furnish the Alien Office with an account of any foreign residents.[43] Another act in 1798 extended the provisions of the original to some classes of aliens formerly exempted, and also provided that foreigners had to take out licenses in order to reside in England, not just secure a passport to come to London. The Secretary of State or the superintendents had to issue a passport to aliens wishing to leave the kingdom.[44] A royal proclamation of July 15, 1798, again demanded a general registration of all aliens with the Lord Mayor or the magistrates.[45]

During an invasion scare in July 1801 Portland forbade the landing of any persons coming from French or Dutch ports at either Dover or Gravesend.[46] He sent Brooke, chief clerk of the Alien Office, to superintend the coast from Dover north to Whitstable in

39. He died on December 1, 1824, aged fifty-seven. *Ibid.*, XCIV (Dec., 1824), 571.

40. Flint to Pellew, Jan. 29, 1801, H.O. 5/6. Pellew was the eldest brother of Admiral Lord Viscount Exmouth and of Admiral Sir Israel Pellew. *Burke's Peerage*, 99th ed., p. 732. He died on February 18, 1843, aged ninety, having been collector of customs for nearly fifty years. *Gentleman's Magazine*, n.s., XIX (May, 1843), 536. C. Northcote Parkinson, *Edward Pellew Viscount Exmouth, Admiral of the Red* (London, 1934), p. 102, mentions a biography of Samuel Pellew that I was unable to locate.

41. He was appointed inspector on October 5, 1799. Flint to Stowe, H.O. 5/5. The last *Royal Kalender* to list him is for the year 1825.

42. A captain received £20 per annum, a first mate £10, a second mate £5, and a seaman £1.1.0. They worked for and were paid by the Board of Customs. Flint to Walsh, May 31, 1799, H.O. 5/5. See also Charles Greville to James Hume [died 1819], secretary to the commissioners of customs, Sept. 14, 1796, H.O. 5/2; and same to same, May 10, 1800, H.O. 5/5.

43. *The Times*, Aug. 3, 1796. "This enquiry seems to be extremely proper at the present moment."

44. *Statutes at Large*, 38 George III, c. 50. 45. *London Gazette*.

46. Flint to Stowe, July 21, 1801; same to same, July 23, 1801, H.O. 5/6.

order to prevent unauthorized communications. Stowe performed the same function from Dover to Lydd.[47]

The memoirs of François Barthélemy provide an insight into the functions of the Alien Office. Barthélemy had been French chargé d'affaires in England in the 1780's and thereafter French ambassador to Switzerland. In 1799 he came to England as a refugee. When his ship docked at Portsmouth, Brooke was there to meet it. On July 12, 1799, Brooke escorted Barthélemy and his companions to Barnes, six miles from London (near Richmond), where they were lodged in a comfortable house guarded by Edwards, a police officer. The house in fact served as a prison. After Charles Flint came to visit them on the 12th, Barthélemy recorded that he knew at once that he was under suspicion for his supposed sympathies with the French Revolution while he was ambassador to Switzerland. Flint had been chief secretary to William Wickham, the British envoy (and spy) in Switzerland. Grenville refused to see Barthélemy, and Portland gave orders that he was to be detained. Brooke, Flint, and Richard Ford came frequently to see the Frenchman and asked questions about France. Barthélemy gave general replies, but was careful to testify to his aversion to the Revolution. On August 13 Portland granted Barthélemy permission to leave. The Frenchman dined that day with Flint and Brooke, after which Brooke conducted him and his companions to London and then to Sheerness, whence they embarked on the 18th.

Flint and Brooke must both have known French quite well and in general been smooth and diplomatic. Less well-known aliens under suspicion may not have received such gentle treatment.[48]

The basic work of the Alien Office, in short, was to keep a regular check upon all foreigners entering and leaving the kingdom by

47. Flint to Stowe and Brooke, July 24, 1801; Portland to the Treasury, July 28, 1801, H.O. 5/6.

48. The account is taken from *Mémoires de Barthélemy 1768–1819*, edited by Jacques de Dampierre (Paris, 1914), pp. 399–404. The memoirs unfortunately do not contain any relevant material regarding the Secret Service while Barthélemy was a member of the French embassy in England in the 1780's. The account for those years is most sketchy. His papers, *Papiers de Barthélemy 1792–97*, edited by Jean Kaulek (6 vols.; Paris, 1886–1910) have no relevant information. For Barthélemy (1747–1830), see J. Balteau and others (eds.), *Dictionnaire de Biographie Française* (28 vols. to date; Paris, since 1933), V, 665–66. He was created a marquis in 1818.

Edwards was probably Henry Edwards, one of the King's guards at Windsor, although he did not receive an official appointment till March 3, 1800. He was the only police officer to receive free house rent. (Contingent Accounts, H.O. 82/3.) Or the man could have been John Edwards, a king's messenger.

means of passports and registrations—much as is done today. Wickham expressed this purpose in 1794:

> The Duke of Portland surprized me very much yesterday by desiring me to take upon myself the management of all matters that in any way related to the Aliens, and in particular to procure as soon as possible accurate returns of them all, to open some channels of Information by which better intelligence might be obtained of their several views and proceedings, with the intent . . . that the whole might be reduced to something like a regular system.[49]

But the Alien Office had an additional purpose that lies buried in obscurity. Wickham wrote to Portland in 1801 in order to impress upon the Duke the importance of the office:

> Indeed I always considered it as the Chief and Singular merit of the Institution, that from its very nature, no other Office could ever know any thing of what was passing there, unless instructed from the Fountain Head.
>
> I am persuaded that it would be sufficient for Your Grace to take Mr. Pitt for one half hour only into the Office and shew him the different Official Books, Secret as well as Public and the manner in which the Registers of each kind are kept.
>
> A mind like his could not fail to see at once that without bustle, noise or anything that can attract Public Attention, Government possesses here the most powerful means of Observation & Information, *as far as their Objects go,* that ever was placed in the Hands of a Free Government,—that in observing Foreigners resident here, much curious information respecting the ill intentioned of our Own Countrymen and Concerning Foreigners resident abroad, has been, and must continue to be indirectly obtained.[50]

The disappearance of the registers and other material veils from the historian this fascinating aspect of the Alien Office's function.

49. To Thomas Brodrick, Sept. 5, 1794, H.O. 1/2.

50. Jan. 3, 1801, copy, Vienna, private and confidential, Pelham Papers, Add. MS 33, 107, ff. 1–4.

Chapter Ten

IMPERIAL, DIPLOMATIC, AND MILITARY DUTIES

The reorganization in 1782 left to the Home Office the responsibility for the administration of the Empire—the North American and West Indian colonies, an African outpost near the mouth of the river Gambia, and Gibraltar. Also within imperial administration were Ireland, the Channel Islands, and the Isle of Man. There was also a formal correspondence with Scottish officials. The temporary British possession of Toulon from August to September 1793 and of Corsica from February 1794 to October 1796, and the acquisition of several French and Dutch possessions in the Caribbean, added these areas to the responsibility of the Home Office. Diplomatic duties consisted of conducting foreign relations with Algiers, Morocco, Tripoli, and Tunis. The Home Secretary also issued the official instructions to Lord Macartney before he began his famous mission to China. Military responsibilities included the executive direction of the war from 1782 to 1783 and again from 1793 to July 1794 and the handling of correspondence regarding the militia and certain volunteer and associated corps that were raised after 1793.[1]

The abolition of the Colonial Office[2] and the Board of Trade[3] in 1782 left nearly all responsibility for colonial affairs to the Home department.[4] The Privy Council, however, and a temporary commit-

1. The subjects mentioned in this paragraph, with the possible exception of the Barbary states and the Channel Islands, would require at least one volume each if I had attempted to trace the course of the Home Office's involvement with them. A description, and a brief one, of the Home department's administrative procedures for these areas of jurisdiction must suffice.

2. Margaret Marion Spector, *The American Department of the British Government, 1768–1782* (New York, 1940).

3. Arthur Herbert Bayse, *The Lords Commissioners of Trade and Plantations, Commonly Known as the Board of Trade, 1748–1782* (Yale Historical Miscellany, XIV; New Haven, 1925).

4. Manning, *British Colonial Government*, and Harlow, *Founding of the Second British Empire*, are indispensable. Mrs. Manning has a wealth of information about the general administration of the colonies. J. H. Rose and others (eds.), *The Cambridge*

tee of the Council quickly took upon themselves many of the duties of the old Board of Trade. The appointment of a standing committee on March 5, 1784, and the reconstitution of the Board of Trade and Plantations on August 23, 1786, under the presidency of Lord Hawkesbury removed most of the duties regarding colonial trade from the Home Office's concern. The Treasury also handled much colonial business.[5]

From March 1782 the actual management of the details of colonial affairs insofar as the Home Office was concerned was vested in the person of Grey Elliott, who had been solicitor and clerk of reports to the old Board of Trade since December 26, 1777,[6] and acting secretary to the board since April 1780.[7]

In early 1782 Lord Shelburne directed Elliott to form a plan for transacting colonial business, to include the creation of a permanent establishment, which Elliott would head. He did indeed take over

---

History of the British Empire (7 vols.; Cambridge, 1929–40), has the most extensive bibliography. Among more recent works useful for this period are David Fieldhouse, "British Imperialism in the Late Eighteenth Century: Defence or Opulence?" *Essays in Imperial Government Presented to Margery Perham,* edited by Kenneth Robinson and Frederick Madden (Oxford, 1963), pp. 23–45; and A. F. McC. Madden, "The Imperial Machinery of the Younger Pitt," *Essays in British History Presented to Sir Keith Feiling* (London, 1964), pp. 173–93.

5. Charles M. Andrews, *Guide to the Materials for American History to 1783 in the Public Record Office of Great Britain* (2 vols.; Washington, D.C., 1912–14), I, 100–103; Anna Lane Linglebach, "The Inception of the British Board of Trade," *American Historical Review,* XXX (July, 1925), 701–727.

6. Great Britain, Public Record Office, *Journal of the Commissioners for Trade and Plantations from January 1776 to May 1782* (London, 1938), p. 125.

7. *Ibid.,* p. 343; historians have given only the most cursory attention to Elliott. Yet he was one of the few persons in the British government to have had any significant experience in the colonies. By January 1756 Elliott had become a planter in Georgia. Allen D. Candler (ed.), *The Colonial Records of the State of Georgia* (25 vols.; Atlanta, Ga., 1904–16), VII, 309. He gradually increased his holdings in both land and slaves; in 1764 he owned at least forty-one slaves (*ibid.,* IX, 129). The extensiveness of his holdings is indicated by the sum of £12,149.3.9¾ granted him by the government of Georgia after the end of the war as compensation for the confiscation of his estates. Caroline Price Wilson (ed.), *Annals of Georgia,* Vol. I: *Liberty County Records and a State Revolutionary Pay Roll* (New York, 1928), p. 182. Elliott became surveyor and auditor-general of Georgia in 1758 (Candler, VII, 811), and served as speaker of the House of Assembly of Georgia at its third and fourth assemblies in 1760 and 1761 (*ibid.,* XIII, 417–18, 473). On October 6, 1761, he took his oath as a member of the Council for that colony (*ibid.,* VIII, 581), and regularly attended its sessions till April 1770, when he embarked for England (*ibid.,* XI, 3). He acted as agent for Georgia 1773 through 1775 and perhaps till 1779. Ella Lonn, *The Colonial Agents of the Southern Colonies* (Chapel Hill, N.C., 1945), p. 396.

Unfortunately there is little information about Elliott's personal life. He evidently came from Scotland, where he must have been made a master Freemason before 1756. As a Presbyterian he became one of the founders of the first church of that denomination in Savannah. He served as grand master of the Freemasons of Georgia 1757–1773. William Bordley Clarke, *Early and Historic Freemasonry of Georgia, 1733/4–1800* (Savannah, Ga., c. 1924), pp. 55–59, 69–70. Elliott died on May 31 or June 1, 1787. *Gentleman's Magazine,* LVII (June, 1787), 548. References to Elliott are in Grace Amelia Cockroft, *The Public Life of George Chalmers* (New York, 1939).

the business, but no establishment was made nor any clerk appointed. The inattention of the Secretaries of State to the situation caused Elliott to fall far behind in his work. He begged Lord North to allow him to appoint three clerks and to secure some suitable apartments.[8] North strongly recommended that Elliott should be granted his request, for his only assistance came from occasional work done by the clerks in the Home Office.[9] The Treasury concurred, and in December 1783 the Plantation Department came into being—a subordinate unit of the Home Office. At North's suggestion, the fees formerly collected by the Board of Trade went to defray part of the cost of the new establishment; the Secretary, however, paid any additional sum.[10] Elliott received a salary of £500 clear of deductions, in addition to £250 that he received as compensation for the loss of his offices at the Board of Trade. He also attended most of the meetings of the committee of the Privy Council for trade and plantations, for which he was paid £400 in 1785.[11] In September 1784 he was elevated to the rank of Undersecretary.[12] The three clerks received £120, £100, and £80 a year, respectively. They had virtually no perquisites except stationery for their own use.[13] Elliott's office occupied some rooms on the ground floor of the Treasury Building. Furnishings included a stove, four desks, twelve leather chairs, two small Scotch carpets, and a firescreen for the fireplace.[14]

Elliott's duties as Undersecretary in the Plantation Department entailed

> preparing Commissions and Instructions for Governors in the Colonies; the examination of all Minutes of Councils and Assemblies; the Consideration of Laws passed by the Legislatures; and the transmission of those Laws for the opinion of His Majesty's Counsel in point of Law; and in some Cases the framing [of] Bills to be Laid before the Colonial Legislatures—a general attention to the Civil Administration of the Colonies, and regulations necessary to be made therein, and whether His Majesty's Instructions are duly Complied with; the preparation of Estimates of the Civil Establishments of the Colonies provided for by Grant of Parliament; and the correspondance [*sic*] upon those different heads.[15]

8. Memorial of Elliott to North, Sept. 10, 1783, H.O. 42/3.
9. Oct. 30, 1783, H.O. 36/4.
10. Richard Burke to Nepean, Dec. 11, 1783, H.O. 36/4.
11. *First Report, 1786,* Appendix 15, pp. 25–26.
12. Sydney to the Postmaster General, Sept. 18, 1784, H.O. 43/1.
13. *First Report, 1786,* Appendices 16, 17, 18, p. 26.
14. Nepean to John Calvert, Jr., Jan. 17, 1784, H.O. 43/1.
15. Elliott to North, Sept. 18, 1785, H.O. 42/3; see also *First Report, 1786,* Appendix 15, p. 25.

Elliott had to correspond with the Treasury, for example, when he submitted the estimates for the civil establishments of the colonies, when difficulties arose over the allowance of certain charges on the accounts submitted by the governors, and in cases involving grants of land, particular in St. John's (Prince Edward) Island.[16] Although the loss of the thirteen American colonies and of East and West Florida greatly reduced the amount of colonial business, the nature of the official correspondence with the remaining imperial possessions did not appreciably change. The description that Elliott gave of his duties remains essentially valid for the twenty years that colonial affairs rested with the Home department.

Precisely what part Elliott had in advising the Secretary of State on major decisions about the colonies is unknown. The several references to him by William Smith, later Chief Justice of Quebec, do not indicate that his influence carried far.[17] But it is difficult to imagine that the ministers would not have consulted Elliott on important measures. He certainly advised Lord Hawkesbury quite often regarding colonial trade.[18] Elliott's death in late May or early June of 1787 removed the only person capable of directing the management of colonial correspondence on a semi-independent basis. Lord Sydney's appointment of all three clerks in the Plantation Department to positions in the Home Office proper by January 9, 1789,[19] spelled the end of the Plantation Department.[20]

Scrope Bernard seems to have managed the details of colonial business for Lord Grenville, and after 1792 John King did the same for Dundas and Portland. The Secretaries, with Pitt's advice, probably made most important decisions. Grenville certainly had the principal role in the preparation of a new constitution for Canada in 1791. No clerks seem to have been designated specifically for the execution of colonial business, and no permanent establishment came into being. Colonial affairs failed to receive the strict attention they deserved. In 1794 Dundas, as Secretary for War, assumed responsibility for colonial military arrangements, but the Home Office

16. Elliott's letters to the Treasury cover the last 43 pages of H.O. 36/4. The first letter is dated November 7, 1783, and the last April 19, 1787.

17. *Diary of William Smith, passim.*

18. Liverpool Papers, Add. MSS 38,218–38,221; T. 1/635, No. 2200.

19. Sydney to the Postmaster General, Jan. 9, 1789, H.O. 43/2.

20. King must have erred when he wrote that the Plantation Office continued till October 1793 when the clerks entered the Home Office. He was also wrong as to the date of Elliott's death, which occurred in 1787, not 1788. King to Rose, Oct. 22, 1796, H.O. 36/10.

continued to handle all other matters till August 12, 1801, when the Secretary for War assumed full control over all colonial affairs.[21]

Related vitally to colonial and imperial affairs were the voyages of explorers to various parts of the world.[22] The Home Office nearly always issued the orders. Captain William Bligh of H.M.S. *Bounty* sailed under Lord Sydney's direction to transplant breadfruit from the Pacific Islands to the West Indies.[23] Captain George Vancouver, who explored the northern Pacific and the northwest coast of North America in the early 1790's, made his reports directly to the Home Secretary.[24] The Home department encouraged various explorations by the African Association. In 1787 Simon Lucas made an unsuccessful venture into the interior via Tripoli, and in the 1790's Daniel Houghton and Mungo Park entered the interior via the river Gambia.[25] Nor should the famous mission of Lord Macartney to China be forgot, since Dundas, probably because he was in charge of India, issued the orders and laid down the policy to be followed.[26]

Another duty entailed conducting official business with Scotland. Much correspondence passed between the Secretary of State and the magistrates in Scotland regarding riots and disorders, exactly as similar matters passed between the Secretary and English magistrates. Much formal correspondence required only the approval of the king. The Secretary and magistrates corresponded in regard to respites and pardons for criminals. When required, the Lord Justice Clerk and the Lord Advocate (instead of the circuit judges as in England) submitted reports on the advisability of pardoning criminals. If the king signified his approval, a warrant was made out by the Home Office granting the pardon or remission. The warrant, however, passed under the seal appointed at the union between Scotland and England rather than under the English seals.[27] The

21. Young, *The Colonial Office in the Early Nineteenth Century*, p. 11.
22. See Harlow's two volumes.
23. George Mackaness, *The Life of Vice-Admiral William Bligh* (2 vols. in 1; New York, 1931). On most of the expeditions, the Secretary consulted with Sir Joseph Banks, the unofficial scientific adviser to the government.
24. C.O. 5/187. Bern Anderson, *Vancouver: A Life, 1757–1798* (New York, 1931).
25. Robin Hallett, *The Penetration of Africa: European Enterprise and Exploration Principally in Northern and Western Africa up to 1830* (London, 1965) is indispensable.
26. Earle Pritchard, *The Crucial Years of Early Anglo-Chinese Relations, 1750–1800* (Pullman, Washington, 1936). For the exploration phase, Harlow, *Founding of the Second British Empire,* should be consulted. Dundas carried the direction of Anglo-Chinese relations to the War Department (the King to Dundas, June 19, 1795, *Later Correspondence of George III*, II, 355.
27. Out-letters, H.O. 104/1–3; in-letters, H.O. 102/1/18.

Home Office prepared the warrants and carried on the correspondence relating to the appointment of many Scottish officials in the government, universities, and church.[28] There was some formal communication with the moderator of the General Assembly and with the Lord High Commissioner of the Church of Scotland.[29] Through the Secretary of State the Crown granted many ecclesiastical presentations in its gift.[30] Portland informed an applicant that these presentations were disposed of on the recommendation of the county M.P.'s in whose areas the presentations lay "from their being supposed to be best acquainted with and most interested in consulting the wishes of the Heritors [landholders in fee in the parishes]. . . ."[31] In fact, Henry Dundas probably made the decisions, for he managed Scottish politics for the Crown.[32] On military affairs, especially the movement of troops within Scotland for the suppression of riots, the Secretary corresponded with the Commander-in-Chief in Scotland. Militia business was generally sent to the lord lieutenants of the counties, first appointed in 1794.[33]

Irish affairs also lay within the jurisdiction of the Home Office. The Lord Lieutenant of Ireland sent all dispatches not relating to finance directly to the Home Secretary to be laid before the king. Financial business went to the Treasury, but the king signified his pleasure on all matters to the Lord Lieutenant solely through the Home Secretary. The Treasury advised the Secretary of its decision, which he conveyed to the king's representative in Ireland. The Home Office extracted from the official letters received all material relating to other departments of government and transmitted them to the office concerned. Portland, for example, sent copies of all passages relating to the army to Dundas, Secretary for War. Dundas determined the course of action, consulting the Cabinet if necessary, and informed Portland of the decision. If the king approved, as he generally did, Portland sent the dispatch to the Lord Lieutenant.[34] Many of the dispatches between the Home Office and Ireland in-

28. Warrants, S.P. 44/413 (1780–83); H.O. 106/3. 29. S.P. 56/4–6.
30. *Ibid.* 31. To Charles Francis Greville, M.P., Nov. 1, 1800, H.O. 42/53.
32. Furber, *Henry Dundas, passim.*
33. H.O. 103/1–3. The best bibliography is in Stanley Pargellis and D. J. Medley (eds.), *Bibliography of British History: The Eighteenth Century, 1714–1789* (Oxford, 1951), pp. 403–416; but P. D. Hancock, *A Bibliography of Works Relating to Scotland, 1916–1950* (2 vols.; Edinburgh, 1959–60); and George S. Pryde, *Scotland 1603 to the Present Day* (London, 1962) should be added. For the militia see J. R. Western, "The Formation of the Scottish Militia in 1797," *Scottish Historical Review*, XXXIV (April, 1955), 1–17.
34. Explained fully in Portland to Dundas, Feb. 9, 1795, and reply, Feb. 13, 1795, H.O. 30/1.

volved little more than transmitting decisions made by other government departments. Military affairs in particular, such as the commissioning of officers, required a great deal of paper work.[35]

A large amount of formal correspondence also passed between the English and Irish governments. The King's Letters, so called, to the Lord Lieutenant, of which the Signet Office always took copies, conveyed the initial, formal instructions and the commission of the Lord Lieutenant. The King's Letters conveyed the royal approval of grants of titles of nobility, appointments of archbishops and bishops, military commissions, patents of invention, and many other official matters.[36]

The Secretary of State nearly always directed his dispatches to the Lord Lieutenant and vice versa; the Undersecretaries corresponded with the chief secretary to the Lord Lieutenant. Communication with any other Irish officials was extremely rare. No separate office or particular clerks dealt with Irish affairs. Even the most important dispatches were not entered in letter books, but copies were made on loose folio sheets; they are now in the bundles with the in-letters.[37]

It is seldom possible to be sure who directed the formulation of Irish policy. The Secretaries of State in this period probably consulted Pitt on any important decision. In 1795 Portland sought Pitt's opinion on a matter in a manner that indicates that the occurrence was normal:

> I send you enclosed a Letter I received Yesterday from the Lord Lieut. relative to the Irish Brigade upon which I should wish to have your sentiments before I answered it. After the various conversations which have passed upon this subject I take it for granted that You were satisfied that no Act of Parl. was necessary to enable the officers to serve. . . .[38]

When Thomas Pelham, later Earl of Chichester, prepared to go to Ireland as chief secretary, Portland wrote Pitt in order to arrange a dinner for Pelham to discuss matters with Camden, the Lord President; Spencer, First Lord of the Admirality; Pitt; and himself.[39] Within the Cabinet, of course, the Home Secretary may have had considerable influence on policy, but that probably arose from the

35. H.O. 123/1–4 contain many military warrants.
36. H.O. 101/1–2.
37. H.O. 100/1–103. H.O. 122/1–6 are letter books, but concern formal matters such as military promotions that did not require the writing of a King's Letter.
38. June 22, 1795, P.R.O. 30/8/168 (Chatham Papers).
39. March 9, 1795, *ibid.* The total failure of Earl Fitzwilliam as Lord Lietuenant involved much correspondence between Portland and Pitt.

man's standing with Pitt as an adviser rather than from his possession of the seals of the Home department.[40]

The Channel Islands of Alderney, Guernsey, Jersey, and Sark (part of the bailiwick of Guernsey) and the Isle of Man constituted a distinct administrative duty for the Home Office. The king in council governed the islands, although the local legislatures had considerable power. The Secretary directed correspondence to the governor of Alderney and to the lieutenant governors of Guernsey, Jersey, and the Isle of Man. The governorships were largely honorary posts. Communications usually involved military and militia affairs and domestic disputes. The Secretary of State, for example, finally had to order the appointment of a commission to settle judicial disputes in Jersey,[41] and another commission had to settle the hereditary claims of the Duke of Atholl in the Isle of Man.[42]

The sole remnant of diplomatic responsibility that carried over from the Southern Department to the Home Office pertained to relations between Great Britain and the four Barbary Coast states —Algiers, Morocco, Tripoli, and Tunis. Although no precise statement explaining why the Home Office retained Barbary affairs seems to be extant, the reason almost certainly is the proximity of the Barbary states to Gibraltar (under Home Office jurisdiction as a colony) and their importance to that outpost as a source of food. The comments of the governor of Gibraltar, General George Augustus Eliott, in 1785 indicate that Gibraltar was independent of the Barbary states for provisions, but that the ministers had not realized that fact in 1782 when the reorganization occurred.[43] Eliott's successor, General Charles O'Hara, informed Nepean: "I think . . . I may

40. Edith M. Johnston, *Great Britain and Ireland, 1760–1800: A Study in Political Administration* (St. Andrews University Publications, LV; Edinburgh, 1963), has much useful information; pages 77–78 deal specifically with the role of the Secretary of State. T. H. D. Mahoney, *Edmund Burke and Ireland* (Cambridge, 1960) contains more material than the title implies. See also G. C. Bolton, *The Passing of the Irish Act of Union: A Study in Parliamentary Politics* (Oxford, 1966); J. C. Beckett, "Anglo-Irish Constitutional Relations in the Later Eighteenth Century," *Irish Historical Studies*, XIV (March, 1964), 20–38; Richard Robert Madden, *The United Irishmen, Their Lives and Times* (7 vols.; Dublin, 1842–46).

41. H.O. 99/1; H.O. 98/1–6. The papers of Sir John Nicholl, a commissioner to Jersey, are in P.R.O. 30/42/1.

42. H.O. 99/16; H.O. 98/63–66; Dundas to Atholl, July 16, 1791, H.O. 43/3. For the Isle of Man see William Cubbon (ed.), *A Bibliographical Account of Works Relating to the Isle of Man* (2 vols.; London, 1933–39). A brief bibliography of the Channel Islands is in Sir F. Maurice Powicke and E. B. Fryde, *Handbook of British Chronology* (Royal Historical Society Guides and Handbooks, No. 2; 2nd ed.; London, 1961), pp. 199–201. Nearly all the histories of the islands are outmoded.

43. Eliott to Sydney, June 30, 1785, Gibraltar C.O. 91/32.

venture to give you joy of having got quit of this damned Barbary nonsense, And as to us Gibraltarians, We can eat and drink and laugh and play without the assistance of the Emperor of Morocco."[44]

The Secretaries and Undersecretaries corresponded with the one consul who served in each of the Barbary states. The consuls usually sent dispatches at least once a month, but the Home Office's replies were irregular. The consul to Tripoli received no official letter for over a year.[45] There was nothing to write. Although fascinating, Barbary affairs did not loom large in British councils of state. In referring to the consul at Morocco Nepean wrote: "When Payne went over as consul, his principal object was to get a few Animals for the Tower [zoo]. . . ."[46] Appropriately, Payne was also Keeper of Lions in the Tower.[47] When necessary, the Secretary of State probably consulted the Cabinet about the course of action to be taken, but often the dispatches contained routine business. To follow the tortuous windings of British policy in the Barbary exceeds the scope of an administrative study.[48]

The military duties of the Home Office may be divided into two general categories—executive direction of the war from 1782 to 1783 and from 1793 to July 1794 and correspondence regarding the militia and volunteer and associated corps. Connected with both these general duties was the power vested in the Home Secretary to signify the king's pleasure on the movement of troops within England. In 1782 the abolition of the Colonial Secretariat deposited the conduct of the war on the step of the Home Office. Such, no doubt, was Shelburne's wish. For the short period that that unhappy contest persisted, the Secretary of State drafted and sent the general orders to the principal army commander, Sir Guy Carleton,[49] and to the chief naval officers, Admiral Robert Digby and Admiral Hugh Pi-

44. June 23, 1788, Gibraltar, C.O. 91/35. Portugal amply supplied all their needs. Stetson Conn, *Gibraltar in British Diplomacy in the Eighteenth Century* (New Haven, 1942) considers the problem of Gibraltar and the Barbary states at various times during the century. 45. Simon Lucas to Dundas, Feb. 6, 1795, F.O. 76/5.

46. To Bernard, Bath, Nov. 8, 1789, Spencer Bernard MSS, O.E. 7/3.

47. For George Payne (c. 1729–1800) of Brooklands, Surrey, see Foster, *Alumni Oxonienses,* III, 1081; Owen Manning and William Bray, *History and Antiquities of the County of Surrey* (3 vols.; London, 1804–14), II, 789; *Annual Register,* XVIII (1775), 205; and *Gentleman's Magazine,* LXX (Dec., 1800), 1221.

48. In general for Anglo-Barbary relations, see Sir Godfrey Fisher, *Barbary Legend: War, Trade and Piracy in North Africa 1415–1830* (Oxford, 1957); M. S. Anderson, "Great Britain and the Barbary States in the Eighteenth Century," *Bulletin of the Institute of Historical Research,* XXIX (May, 1956), 87–107; and Hilda I. Lee, "The Supervising of the Barbary Consuls During the Years 1756–1836," *ibid.,* XXIII (Nov., 1951), 191–99. 49. C.O. 5/105–111.

gott.[50] The Home Office corresponded with other departments to coordinate the movement of troops and supplies to the areas of conflict, position the fleets, and insure home defense. The Home Secretary also conducted the peace negotiations that ended the war, although Fox, the Foreign Secretary, had his own representatives in Paris. Shelburne certainly dominated the official negotiations both as Secretary of State and as head of the Treasury, but Townshend signed and sent the various commissions and instructions, and Henry Strachey, Undersecretary in the Home Office, actually went to Paris as a chief negotiator. Townshend expressed the greatest reluctance to act without the concurrence of the Cabinet, probably for fear of being blamed for decisions that Shelburne had made.[51] Shelburne insisted that he not call a Cabinet, which would only entail further delay.[52] After the conclusion of the peace, American affairs passed to the Foreign Office.[53]

Whenever war threatened, the Secretary of State for the Home department issued the necessary orders to the remainder of the king's servants. In 1787 when war with France over the Dutch crisis threatened,[54] in 1790 when England and Spain nearly came to blows over Nootka Sound,[55] and in 1791 when war with Russia was contemplated, the Home Secretary issued the king's commands to prepare for war. From the beginning of the war with France till July 11, 1794, Dundas, as Home Secretary, provided executive direction of the war both on the Continent and in the colonies. The Home Office staff expanded by a few clerks during the war, but the paperwork must not have become unmanageable, for clerks had time to make copies of not only the outgoing letters but also the incoming dispatches to Sir James Murray, adjutant-general to the British commander,[56] the Duke of York. The executive function of the Secretary did not demand the keeping of the wealth of detailed records that other military departments maintained. The burden of the decisions of war rested principally upon Dundas (though always advised), but not the execution of the details implicit in the general

50. C.O. 5/186.

51. Townshend to Shelburne, July 27, 1782, copy in Nepean's hand, Sydney Papers, Clements Library.

52. Shelburne to Townshend, July 29, 1782, High Wycombe, *ibid.*

53. The most recent treatment of the peace is Richard Morris, *The Peacemakers* (New York, 1965). The relevant chapters in Harlow, *Founding of the Second British Empire,* should not be overlooked.

54. Cobban, *Ambassadors and Secret Agents.*

55. John M. Norris, "The Policy of the British Cabinets in the Nootka Crisis," *English Historical Review,* LXX (Oct., 1955), 562–80.

56. W.O. 6/7–8.

orders that he issued. The creation of a Secretary for War ended the Home Office's participation in this aspect of administration.[57]

The Secretary of State provided the means by which the king exercised control over the militia. Only with the Secretary's approval could troops be moved within England; if the troops formed part of the milita of some county, the Secretary issued the orders to the lord lieutenant of that county. The Home Office also corresponded with the lord lieutenants regarding the approval of deputy lieutenants whom they had nominated, the removal and promotion of militia officers, the appointment of regimental adjutants, and other matters. Sometimes the lord lieutenants submitted disputes over militia matters for the Secretary's decision.[58]

The Secretary communicated with the commanders of the Volunteer and Associated Corps—two distinct organizations that supplemented the militia in internal defense. Letters about the Associated Corps concerned the appointment of officers, which nearly always received approval, promotions, pay, equipment, etc.[59] Letters to the commanders of the Volunteer Corps concerned similar affairs, but after 1798 all such letters went directly to Dundas, not to Portland.[60] The small part that the Home Office had in the actual important decisions about the Corps may be seen from Portland's letter to William Windham:

> All applications for raising new Corps are referred by the Secretary of State to the person who is at the head of the Army & the Secy. of State has from that time no more concern in the business untill he acquaints the person who makes the proposal with the King's determination upon it, which is signified to the Secy. of S. by the Commander in Chief.[61]

Any military matter requiring an important decision undoubtedly (and reasonably) went to one of the military departments. The Home Office acted as a clerical agency for militia and related correspondence.[62]

57. The best bibliography of the British in the war is Aspinall and Smith, *English Historical Documents,* XI, 856–58. Vol. IV of Sir John Fortescue, *A History of the British Army* (13 vols. in 14; London, 1906–30) remains the best account of the army in the war. For the administrative aspect Richard Glover, *Peninsular Preparation: The Reform of the British Army, 1795–1809* (Cambridge, 1963) is excellent.

58. Out-letters, H.O. 51/7–12; in-letters, H.O. 50/17–39, 313/21.

59. H.O. 51/105; H.O. 43/10–13. 60. H.O. 50/40.

61. Aug. 20, 1796, Windham Papers, Add. MS 37, 845, ff. 73–74.

62. J. R. Western, *The English Militia in the Eighteenth Century: The Story of a Political Issue, 1660–1802* (London, 1965) provides an excellent account of the subject, though he does not specifically spell out the role of the Home Office. For an understanding of the Home Secretary's role in militia affairs during an invasion, see E. H. Stuart Jones, *The Last Invasion of Britain* (Cardiff, 1950).

Chapter Eleven

RELATED OFFICES

The Secretaries of State had particularly close and to some extent supervisory relations with several other government offices—the State Paper Office, the secretary of Latin language, the translator of the German language, the *London Gazette,* the king's messengers, the Signet Office, and the decipherers.

I

The State Paper Office originated in 1578 by a commission under the great seal and bore the official name Office of Her Majesty's Papers and Records for Business of State and Council. The usefulness and size of the office waxed and waned with the conscientiousness of the man at the head of the establishment—the Keeper of State Papers.[1] By the middle of the eighteenth century the State Paper Office consisted solely of two officers—the Keeper himself and the Collector and Transmitter of State Papers, an office added in 1726.[2]

Both offices were sinecures. Sir Stanier Porten, Undersecretary of State in the Southern Department, received the appointment to the office of Keeper of State Papers in 1773.[3] Porten, who found the office a sinecure when he was appointed, annually netted £108 from a gross of £160.[4] Thomas Ramsden, Undersecretary in the Southern Department from 1748 to 1750, had been appointed Collector and

1. F. S. Thomas, *A History of the State Paper Office* (London, 1849) is sketchy and in any case is but an extract from his more complete *Notes of Materials for the History of Public Departments* (London, 1846), pp. 41–43, 111–44, 170–71. *The Thirtieth Annual Report of the Deputy Keeper of Public Records, 25 February 1869* (London, 1869), and printed in H. of C. 4165, pp. 212–93; *PP 1868–69,* XXVI contains a valuable history and a calendar of documents. John Bruce's manuscript "History of the State Paper Office to 1800" is in S.P. 45/74; there is a printed copy in the P.R.O.

2. *Thirtieth Report of the Deputy Keeper of Records, PP 1868–69* (4165), XXVI, 215. All subsequent references are to the *Report* printed in *PP.*

3. Date of warrant Dec. 23, 1773, Great Britain, Public Record Office, *Calendar of Home Office Papers of the Reign of George III, 1760–1775* (4 vols.; London, 1878–99), IV, 150, No. 421.

4. *First Report, 1786,* Appendix 33, p. 33.

Transmitter of State Papers about 1744.[5] It was his duty to transmit to the Keeper of State Papers all documents that he might receive from the Secretaries of State, but he received not one paper during the forty-seven years he held the office. His net yearly salary was £500.[6]

Although the office of Keeper of State Papers could be traced directly to the one created in 1578, the real duties involving the records of the Secretaries of State had been in the hands of three Commissioners appointed by George Grenville in 1764. The original Commissioners—Sir Joseph Ayloffe (1709–1781),[7] Dr. Andrew Coltee Ducarell (1713–1785),[8] and Thomas Astle (1735–1803)[9]—were distinguished antiquarians. By 1786 only Astle, particularly noted as a paleographer and as owner of the finest private collection of manuscripts in England, was alive, though in 1781 another antiquarian, John Topham (1746–1803), had succeeded the deceased Ayloffe.[10] Ducarell died in 1785, but it was not till 1789 that a new warrant added Thomas Astle, Jr., to the Commission.[11]

The duties of the Commissioners consisted of receiving papers sent by the Secretaries of State, repairing and binding any that were decayed, preparing calendars and indices, and obeying whatever orders the Secretaries of State gave regarding the communication or transmission of any papers.[12] Each Commissioner received £100 a year, and £100 was provided for clerks and a like sum for binding and other expenses.[13] Throughout the period from 1764 into the nineteenth century the records themselves were housed in a crowded gallery in the Treasury, which, as it afforded no fireplace, limited the calendaring and sorting of papers to the summer months. A second group of documents found lodging in a horrid old house in Middle Scotland Yard, the cellar of which the Thames regularly filled at high tide.[14]

5. Ramsden, baptized on July 22, 1709, was the fifth son of Sir William Ramsden, Bt. He was admitted to Clare College, Cambridge, on June 16, 1727. He married Anne, daughter of Sir Philip Medowes, but had no issue. He died in April 1791. Venn and Venn, *Alumni Cantabrigienses,* Pt. 1, III, 417. He was also Latin Secretary. See below.

6. *First Report, 1786,* Appendix 35, p. 34.

7. *DNB,* I, 756–57.

8. *Ibid.,* VI, 84–86.

9. *Ibid.,* I, 675–77.

10. *Ibid.,* XIX, 983.

11. Bruce, "History of the State Paper Office," p. 21, S.P. 45/74. Astle, Jr., born January 20, 1767, lived at Gosfield Hall, Essex, owned by the Marquis of Buckingham. He had two children. *Burke's Landed Gentry* (5th ed.; 2 vols.; London, 1871), I, 629, under "Hills of Colne Park." He died in November 1820. *Gentleman's Magazine,* XC (Nov., 1820), 475.

12. *First Report, 1786,* Appendix 37, p. 35.

13. *Ibid.*

14. *First Report from the Select Committee appointed to inquire into the state of the public records of the kingdom, &c., July 1800,* First Series, XV, Appendix C.1, 68–69. It should be pointed out that the Commissioners had responsibility only for

The parliamentary commission in 1786 recommended that the sinecure offices of Keeper and of Collector and Transmitter of State Papers be abolished upon the death of the incumbents, and that the care of state papers should remain in the hands of the Commissioners, whose work the commission particularly praised.[15] Such, however, was not to be the case. The Secretaries objected to abolishing the offices on the grounds that the Keeper had once again (by 1792) become an efficient officer, and that the position of Collector and Transmitter provided them with one of the few means by which they could reward the long and diligent service of persons employed by the Secretaries.[16] Grenville had had his private secretary in the Foreign Office, Charles Goddard, appointed Collector and Transmitter on January 6, 1795.[17] The following October an Order in Council ended the general attachment of that office to both Secretaries of State by placing it on the permanent establishment of the Foreign Office.[18]

The office of Keeper of State Papers, vacant since Porten's death in 1789, once again regained its vitality in the person of John Bruce, former tutor to Henry Dundas' son Robert and a professor of logic and metaphysics at the University of Edinburgh.[19] In August 1792 Dundas wrote to Grenville that

> Mr. Bruce . . . has been employed by me writing an authentic history of India for these two years. I mean to continue him employed under me in various ways of compilation, and perhaps ultimately in arranging or aiding to arrange the records laying [*sic*] unknown at the India House. He is one of the Professors of philosophy in the University of Edinburgh, which it is necessary for me to cause him to resign. It has been always in my contemplation to provide for him through the means of the offices which the Commissioners have foolishly reported to be abolished.[20]

Dundas, of course, had his way in appointing Bruce.

It was the duty of this able man to search the records for precedents whenever the Secretaries ordered, to examine the circum-

---

those papers relating to the Secretaries of State. Other government departments had voluminous records.

15. *First Report, 1786,* p. 12. 16. *Sixteenth Report, 1797,* Appendix A.1, p. 310.

17. Patent Rolls 19–43 George III, p. 291, C.66.

18. *Sixteenth Report, 1797,* Appendix A.3, p. 313.

19. Patent Rolls 19–43 George III, p. 237, C.66. For John Bruce (1745–1826) see *DNB,* III, 107–108; Andrew Dalzel, *History of the University of Edinburgh from its Foundation* (2 vols.; Edinburgh, 1862), II, 444–47; Sir Alexander Grant, *The Story of the University of Edinburgh During its First Three Hundred Years* (2 vols.; London, 1884), II, 330–31.

20. H.M.C., *Dropmore Papers,* II, 306. The actual warrant for appointing Bruce keeper is dated July 5, 1792, H.O. 38/5.

stances leading to the establishment of the precedents, and to draw up reports on them. He performed a similar function in doing research on the ratifications of various treaties and making reports on them.[21] The Secretaries made much use of precedent to assist them in formulating plans in such different areas as the issuing of proclamations for the detection of treason, defense against invasion, and the Union with Scotland in 1707 insofar as it might serve as a guide for the Union with Ireland in 1800.[22] Bruce's salary remained at £160 (£132 after fees and taxes); he also received £196 net as Latin secretary.[23]

The renewed vitality of the Keeper and some friction between Bruce and the Commissioners,[24] apparently persuaded the Secretaries to abolish the office of the Commissioners, who had concentrated on cataloguing and arranging the old state papers rather than on making reports. A warrant revoked the establishment effective January 5, 1800. The senior Astle served without salary, but his son and John Topham both received pensions of £200 per annum each. Bruce received all papers on May 29, 1800, and from that time became effective keeper of all papers of Secretaries of State. His salary was raised to £500 per annum, and he was given an establishment of three clerks, a housekeeper, and a messenger. The regulations for the revitalized office, written in 1799,[25] remained in force till 1854 when the State Paper Office was transferred to the Keeper of the Rolls (the Public Record Office).[26] The history of the State Paper Office illustrates the general tendency in the Pitt Administration to make offices more efficient. The responsibility for the papers came to be centralized in a single officer with a regular staff and precise regulations.[27]

II

The sinecure office of secretary of the Latin language was attached to the Secretaries of State. Thomas Ramsden, also Collector and

21. *Sixteenth Report, 1797,* Appendix H.1, p. 324.

22. Bruce, "Historical Sketch of the State Paper Office," especially p. 22; the *DNB,* III, 107–108, lists his works.

23. *Sixteenth Report, 1797,* Appendix H.2, 4, p. 324. Bruce's net return as Keeper seems to have been higher than Porten's, which was £108. Porten apparently erred in his report.

24. Bruce, "Historical Sketch of the State Paper Office," p. 26.

25. *Ibid.,* pp. 19–23.

26. *Thirtieth Report of the Deputy Keeper of Records,* p. 223.

27. "Index to Offices," II, E.407. Charles F. Mullett, "The 'Better Reception, Preservation and More Convenient Use' of Public Records in Eighteenth-Century England," *American Archivist,* XXVII, No. 2 (April, 1964), 195–217 is a good survey of the care and use of documents.

Transmitter of State Papers, held this post from April 20, 1752,[28] till his death in 1791. Ramsden stated that his duty consisted of writing "drafts of such Latin letters as occasion may require, from His Majesty to the Sovereign Princes of Europe, but he has seldom been called upon for this purpose, this duty being generally executed by persons in the Secretary of State's Office." The salary amounted to £280, but deductions reduced it to £196.10.0.[29]

John Bruce succeeded Ramsden on November 15, 1792.[30] The salary remained the same, but Bruce regarded the office as connected with the position of Keeper of the State Papers to which he had been appointed at the same time. The duties expanded to encompass the examining of letters written in Latin in order to make reports and catalogs.[31] In effect, the office of Latin secretary served as a sinecure used, first, to reward a retired Undersecretary and, second, to supplement the income of the head of the State Paper Office.

III

The position of translator of the German language, held by William Fraser, Undersecretary in the Foreign Office, since October 6, 1773,[32] was similar to that of Latin secretary in being a complete sinecure. In 1795 it ceased to have a general attachment to the Secretaries, as it was placed on the Foreign Office establishment. The office, worth £300 per annum, was to be abolished at Fraser's death, but survived into the nineteenth century.[33]

IV

The Secretaries of State also had a special connection with the *London Gazette*—since 1665 the official newspaper of the Crown. By the 1780's it was no longer a newspaper, but a "handsomely laid-out

28. "Index to Offices," II, E.407. 29. *First Report, 1786,* Appendix 35, p. 34.
30. Patent Rolls, 19–43 George III, p. 237, C.66.
31. *Sixteenth Report, 1797,* p. 324.
32. *Cal. of H. O. Papers,* IV, 87, No. 304. Fraser was appointed Undersecretary to the Duke of Grafton in the Northern Department about July 23, 1765 (*ibid.,* I, 579, No. 1852); followed Weymouth to the Southern Department, October 21, 1768 (*ibid.,* II, 293, No. 740); returned to the Northern Department December 19, 1770 (*ibid.,* III, 103, No. 385). He retired from the Foreign Office in 1789. He also held the offices of king's patent writer and Writer of the *London Gazette.* He died December 11, 1802. P. M. Handover, *A History of the London Gazette, 1665–1965* (London, 1965), pp. 58, 62. His wife died, aged sixty, on July 26, 1799, *Gentleman's Magazine,* LXIX (Aug., 1799), 718. 33. *Sixteenth Report, 1797,* p. 324.

journal of public announcement and advertising."[34] The *Gazette* printed "news" in the form of letters or extracts of letters about British and continental affairs that came to the many government offices; the offices, of course, controlled their release. The *Gazette* also carried most official announcements, such as the appointment of civil officials, the promotion of military officers, grants or titles, copies of Orders in Council relating to the public (quarantines, for example), notices of debtors to their creditors, grain prices, and other matters.[35]

The Writer of the *Gazette* was theoretically its editor, but the office was a sinecure in the 1780's and 1790's, which brought William Fraser £300 a year—his fixed share of profits from the *Gazette*. Frazer had a deputy, always a clerk in the Foreign Office,[36] who did some small amount of work in return for a salary of £30, paid him by the Writer, and fees amounting to £72 in 1784.[37] The Commissioners in 1786 had recommended that the offices of Writer and his deputy be abolished and that the duties be transferred to the chief clerks in the offices of the Secretaries of State.[38] The Secretaries objected, however, to the added burden on the chief clerks, and protested the abolition of offices constituting one of the few rewards available for faithful officers.[39] The position of the Writer and his deputy remained unaltered.

The real work was most probably done by the king's printer himself. This office, held by patent from the Crown, had been granted in 1756 to Edward Owen for forty years. Upon his death he left the patent to Thomas Harrison for his lifetime, but Owen's

34. Handover, *London Gazette*, p. 59.

35. The Home Office apparently sent all the news, even foreign, which came to either Secretary to the *Gazette*, or the printer collected it from the Home Office. Dispatches had to reach the printer by 2 P.M. on the days of publication, or else an extraordinary *Gazette* had to be issued. Edward Johnston to Nepean, May 31, 1794, New Street, H.O. 42/30.

36. George Aust, clerk in the Foreign Office and Undersecretary 1790–1796, was deputy 1783–1790. His wife Sarah (1744–1811) was a writer on topography (*DNB*, I, 730). He was later Muster Master General.

Francis Moore (1767–1854), brother of Sir John and Sir Graham Moore, was clerk in the Foreign Office from July 1784 to January 1803, Deputy Secretary at War from 1803 to 1809, and Deputy *Gazette* Writer from 1790 to December 31, 1796, when he resigned. *Sixteenth Report, 1797*, p. 319; *Burke's Landed Gentry*, 5th ed., II, 941; *Cornwallis Correspondence*, III, 383–84, n. 2.

Stephen Rolleston, clerk in the Foreign Office 1782–1817, and chief clerk till he retired in 1823, was deputy from January 30, 1797, to December 11, 1802, when he became Writer. He died on November 19, 1828 (Handover, *London Gazette*, pp. 62, 66).

37. *First Report, 1786*, p. 7.

38. *Ibid.*, p. 12.

39. *Sixteenth Report, 1797*, p. 310.

grandson, Edward Johnston, succeeded Harrison in April 1790.[40] Johnston's grant was renewed in 1793 to run till 1810, but he died in 1796. For the remainder of the period in consideration, Andrew Strahan, the king's printer, published the *Gazette*.[41]

The finances of the *Gazette* were fairly simple. The printer and (probably) the deputy Writer kept the accounts. In 1791, the only year for which there is complete information, about 156,000 *Gazettes* were printed, of which about 50,000 were sold, and about 100,000 sent to various public offices. In that year the gross receipts amounted to £2,844. Much of the income came from fees for inserting advertisements rather than from the sale of papers.[42] The printer, as patentee, received sixpence out of each quire (twenty-four) *Gazettes* sold, the extra price paid for the insertion of advertisements of unusual length, and one guinea per night for publication.[43] In 1791 the net income of the printer amounted to almost £400, or £442 if the salary to an assistant is added.[44] The salary of the Writer (£300) and the fees of his deputy (£72 in 1784) also came from the profits of the *Gazette*. The remaining profits (about £600 per annum) were divided equally between the two Secretaries of State, and after 1795 were placed in the general fee fund of each office.[45]

An additional financial connection between the *Gazette* and the Secretaries of State concerned the clerks and chamber keepers in the offices. Each clerk and chamber keeper was entitled to about twelve free *Gazettes* that he could then resell at a price lower than that the printer charged; furthermore, he could mail the papers without

40. *Sixteenth Report, 1797*, p. 325; Johnston to Dundas, March 26, 1792, H.O. 42/20. Harrison, who died on November 4, 1791, had had a paralytic stroke two years previously. He had been alderman of Castle Baynard ward in 1782, and master of the Company of Stationers in 1784. He was "a bon vivant, and was very generally respected by a large circle of acquaintance." C. H. Timperley, *A Dictionary of Printers and Printing, with the Progress of Literature, Ancient and Modern. . . .* (London, 1839), p. 773; *Gentleman's Magazine*, LXI (Nov., 1791), 1067. The last issue of the *Gazette* bearing his name as printer was April 3, 1790. Johnston said that he was indolent and had died in the King's Bench Prison. Johnston to Dundas, March 26, 1792, H.O. 42/20. See Sir Cecil Reeves Harrison and H. G. Harrison, *The House of Harrison* (London, 1914). Edward Johnston was the son of William Johnston, a bookseller in Ludgate Street (died 1804). His father relinquished the business to him about 1770. Edward Johnston inherited a considerable fortune from his maternal grandfather, Edward Owen. Johnston died in Dublin in 1796. Timperley, p. 792.

41. Handover, p. 65. Strahan (1749–1831) was also an M.P. for several different constituencies at various times. *DNB*, XIX, 18.

42. Johnston to Dundas, March 26, 1792, H.O. 42/20.

43. *Sixteenth Report, 1797*, p. 325.

44. Johnston to Dundas, March 26, 1792, H.O. 42/20.

45. *Sixteenth Report, 1797*, p. 302.

paying postage.[46] In 1798, probably to increase the profits of the paper by eliminating the large numbers sent to government offices (almost 100,000 a year), free copies to the clerks in the Home and Foreign Offices ceased. Each clerk received, however, about £75 per annum in lieu of the loss.[47] The chamber keepers, for some reason, retained the privilege of receiving papers, although the printer later bought them at a slightly higher price than the market value.[48]

The last ten years of the eighteenth century witnessed a movement to disentangle the financial accounts of the *London Gazette* from the offices of the Secretaries of State—a movement fully in accord with the financial and administrative reforms of Pitt. In general, the Secretaries interfered very little with the *Gazette,* and it continued as a vehicle of advertisements and public announcements, with a little news gleaned from the public offices.

V

The Secretaries of State acquired an increasing amount of control over the messenger corps. The term "messenger" entailed much more in the eighteenth century than it does now—at least as used by Americans. As one might suppose, the corps carried important dispatches and messages both in the British Isles and abroad, but it also acted as a kind of national police, as the messengers often served as guards and escorts for prisoners (usually state prisoners). When armed with a warrant from a Secretary of State, they had power to search dwellings and to arrest the persons named in the warrant.[49] Warrants later empowered messengers to deport aliens.[50]

The messenger corps appeared as a distinct body in the thirteenth century, attached to the chancery and then to the wardrobe in the royal household. In 1377, in keeping with an increased distinction between household and public affairs, the Exchequer assumed control of the messengers.[51] Later, however, the corps passed under the

46. Johnston to Dundas, March 26, 1792, H.O. 42/20.
47. Handover, p. 62; Contingent Account Book, 1798–1811, H.O. 82/3.
48. The clerks in the War Department seem never to have received *Gazettes,* although the chamber keepers did. Handover, p. 62; *First Report of the Committee Appointed by the Treasury to Inquire into the Fees and Emoluments of Public Offices,* H. of C. 162, pp. 50–53, 58–59; *PP 1837,* XLVI.
49. For example, the warrant Dundas to William Ross, May 12, 1794, H.O. 42/30; H.O. 13/9, p. 497.
50. For example, Dundas to Frederic Courvoisier, Nov. 30, 1793, H.O. 42/27.
51. Mary C. Hill, *The King's Messengers 1199–1377, A Contribution to the History of the Royal Household* (London, 1961), especially pp. 1–19.

control of the Lord Chamberlain of the Household and its forty members became known as Messengers of His Majesty's Great Chamber.

The Secretaries made the greatest use of the messengers, though the Lord Chamberlain's office managed the finances and assignments of the corps. The king needed only a few messengers for his personal service. Although one messenger always attended the First Lord of the Treasury, other offices rarely called on the corps for services. The Clerk of the Cheque in the department of the Lord Chamberlain assigned the messengers to their journeys upon receiving orders from the Secretaries, and examined the bills submitted by the messengers for their services. The messengers always had their bills prepared for presentation by Thomas Ancell, deputy chamber keeper in the Foreign Office. After the Clerk of the Cheque approved the bills, the Treasurer of the Great Chamber paid each messenger once a fortnight.[52]

The demands of the Secretaries for messengers became so constant that in 1772 sixteen of them were detached from the office of the Lord Chamberlain and permanently assigned to the Secretaries. The sixteen messengers waited upon the offices in rotation, which became particularly important to them after the division of the offices into Home and Foreign in 1782, since foreign journeys were more lucrative than domestic ones. In normal circumstances these sixteen were the only messengers to go abroad, but those attached to the Lord Chamberlain sometimes served in Europe. When a Secretary appointed a new messenger, he notified the Clerk of the Cheque who swore him to his duty.[53] The Clerk of the Cheque also continued to examine the bills for foreign journeys, but the chief clerks in the two offices examined the domestic bills submitted by the sixteen messengers. The chief clerks, at least in the Foreign Office, did not pay a great deal of attention to examining the vouchers.[54] The Treasurer of the Great Chamber continued to pay the sixteen messengers as well as the others until July 1, 1782, when Burke's Establishment

52. *First Report, 1786,* pp. 8–9; Wheeler-Holohan, *The History of the King's Messengers,* chaps. i–iv.

53. *First Report, 1786,* pp. 8–9; Sydney to the Lord Chamberlain, April 9, 1784, H.O. 43/1. There are numerous instances of the appointments of messengers extraordinary who were to succeed to the first vacancy among the sixteen. T. Townshend to the Lord Chamberlain, Jan. 3, 1783, H.O. 43/1; Grenville to same, Aug. 29, 1789, April 12, 1791, and June 6, 1791, H.O. 43/3; Dundas to same, Oct. 9, 1793, H.O. 43/4.

54. *First Report, 1786,* pp. 9, 13.

Bill abolished that office, and at the same time reduced the messengers under the Lord Chamberlain from twenty-four to eighteen. Thereafter the messengers attached to the Secretaries received their pay from the chief clerks and later from an officer appointed by the Lord Chamberlain. Unfortunately, the new methods of paying the messengers did not accomplish the purpose efficiently or promptly. Payments fell as much as sixteen months in arrears, and sometimes put the messengers in cruel distress.[55]

Although the commissioners in 1786 did not feel that a reform of the messenger corps properly came within their purview, the Secretaries, on their own volition, made several major alterations in 1795. The Secretaries found sixteen messengers entirely inadequate to meet the needs of their service and suggested that the number be increased to thirty by removing all but four from the control of the Lord Chamberlain. They quite logically pointed out that as they had to entrust matters of greatest importance to the messengers, they ought to have a knowledge of their characters and abilities.

The reform sought by the Secretaries came into being by Order in Council February 27, 1795.[56] From July 5 of that year the three Secretaries took turns in appointing messengers to vacancies. The control of the Clerk of the Cheque ceased entirely over the thirty messengers, who now took their oaths before the Secretaries.[57] The chamber keeper in each office kept a list of those waiting for journeys in a glass case to which he alone had a key. The keeper made an entry of the departure and return of every messenger sent on a journey. At the end of each fortnight Richard Ancell, who succeeded his father as agent for the messengers,[58] received the list, and at the end of every quarter made out the bills for each messenger. (Each messenger paid Ancell two guineas a year for his services, as had been the case with Ancell's father.) The chief clerk, after the Secretary of State signed the bills, paid the messengers.[59]

55. *Ibid.*, p. 9; *Sixteenth Report, 1797*, p. 305.
56. *Sixteenth Report, 1797*, pp. 309–311.
57. A copy of the oath is in the Warrant Book, H.O. 38/6, p. 332.
58. Thomas Ancell died on March 24, 1795, having been agent to the messengers for fifty years. *Gentleman's Magazine*, LXV (April, 1795), 352. Richard Ancell was second clerk in the State Paper Office from 1795 to January 1801, when he resigned to become librarian in the Foreign Office (King to John Bruce, Feb. 6, 1801, H.O. 36/11). The commissioners in 1797 commented that the public was indebted to the Ancells for their "integrity and scrupulous accuracy" (p. 307).
59. *Sixteenth Report, 1797*, p. 305. This part of the reform was not entirely satisfactory, since there were still delays in paying the messengers. As late as April 1796 the messengers had to beg payment for their bills for 1793–1795. H.O. 42/38.

The cost of the messenger corps to the public was considerable. In 1784 the expense for the sixteen totaled over £13,000, or as much as either the Home or Foreign Office for that period.[60] Fourteen additional messengers, plus an increased number of foreign journeys during the war, brought the total expenditure to £23,000.[61] Costs arose from a salary to each messenger of £40 (reduced by deductions to £35.8.) and £25 for maintaining a horse, till 1795, when the allowance became £60 clear of deductions. Each messenger also received 7 shillings 6 pence per day as board wages while on duty in the British Isles or while in waiting for an assignment. Board wages ceased when a messenger went to the Continent, but a daily allowance of up to 10 shillings replaced the board wages.[62] From his salary and board wages alone, each messenger received about £196 per annum (or more than the junior clerks in the Home Office).

The greatest expense came not from the salaries and board wages, which for thirty messengers amounted to only £5,880 per annum, but from the cost of journeys. Set charges existed for trips within twenty-five miles of London—for example, £1 to Hampton Court and £1.8. to Windsor. For journeys beyond twenty-five miles, called posting journeys, the standard rate was sixpence per mile for one messenger with two horses, except to Dublin and Edinburgh, for which a messenger received a flat £40. If a messenger had a prisoner or prisoners, he could charge certain set sums for their maintenance while in his custody. In 1794 the charge per mile for home journeys rose to 1 shilling 3 pence per mile. Although there were set charges for journeys to five areas on the continent—£25 to The Hague and to Bruges, £30 to Paris, £50 to the Groyne, and £60 to Lisbon—the usual manner was to charge a fixed sum per mile, varying according to the mode of travel such as by stagecoach or horseback.[63] Whether the messengers profited from these expense accounts is unknown, but considering the reputation of the Ancells for scrupulousness, it is doubtful if any significant amount of cheating occurred.

These twenty years tend to verify the corps' reputation for competence and bravery. No record indicates that any messenger was dismissed for neglect or any other cause, although Portland once suspended a messenger for at least six weeks for having lost a pris-

60. *First Report, 1786,* p. 13. 61. *Sixteenth Report, 1797,* pp. 305, 306.
62. *First Report, 1786,* Appendix 46, pp. 42–43; *Sixteenth Report, 1797,* pp. 305, 326.
63. *Ibid.*

oner.[64] At least three messengers during this period died on active duty. Samuel Brooks and John Magistri sailed to Calais aboard a packet in September 1797 to take dispatches to Lord Malmesbury at Lille. High winds prevented the packetboat from putting them ashore; consequently, they were lowered into a smaller boat that overturned as they neared shore, and both drowned.[65] William Flint died in 1797 from injuries received when his carriage overturned near Augsburg.[66]

When the messengers became too old or incapacitated for active service, they were granted pensions upon retirement.[67] For example, after a fall from a horse incapacitated Thomas Maclean for duty, Portland granted him a pension of £90 in addition to his salary of £60.[68] The standard pension was generally £150, half of which continued to the widow of a messenger.[69]

During these twenty years the secretaries exerted an increasing control over the messenger corps. They came to appoint, supervise, and pay the messengers, whereas they formerly gave them only their assignments. The changes put the corps on a more rational basis by placing it under the immediate control of the officers that had the greatest use for it. Another administrative body of public servants thus followed the path of logic and moved out of court. The greatest difficulty regarding the messengers lay not with them, but with the government for failing to find a satisfactory replacement for the Treasurer of the Great Chamber in order to facilitate the prompt settling of all accounts and bills.

VI

The Signet Office arose in the fourteenth century later passing under the close supervision of the Secretaries of State for over five

64. Andrew Basilico to Portland, Oct. 19, 1798; same to same, Dec. 9, 1798, H.O. 42/45. Portland dismissed Charles Silvester in December 1795, but immediately restored him upon George III's explaining that Silvester had not been responsible for the negligence that occasioned his dismissal. The relevant letters are in *Later Correspondence of George III*, II, 438–442.

65. *Gentleman's Magazine*, LXVII (Sept., 1797), 806. Their deaths occurred on September 13.

66. Wheeler-Holohan, p. 203.

67. *Sixteenth Report, 1797*, p. 307.

68. Entries for Feb. 26 and March 24, 1801, in the Messenger Book, H.O. 82/5. Maclean had been a messenger since about 1779. Maclean and John Gurnell to Portland, June 20, 1797, H.O. 42/41.

69. *Third Report from the Select Committee . . . on Public Expenditure in Great Britain and Ireland . . . (Relative to Offices, Places, Sinecures, and Pensions)*. H. of C. 331, 161; *PP 1808*, III.

hundred years. As long as the duties of the late medieval Secretaries consisted almost exclusively of functions arising from their possession of the king's personal seal or signet, the four Writers of the Signet formed part of the staff of the Secretaries. After the Secretary's duties acquired an increasingly political hue, the four Writers of the Signet came to form a distinct and separate, though subordinate, office from that of the Secretaries, in which they attended to the drafting and transcribing of documents and warrants signed by the king and countersigned and sealed by the Secretaries.[70]

Although the Signet Office consisted of four writers, or clerks as they came to be called by the eighteenth century, all four generally executed the limited duties of their office by deputy. The clerkships were, in practice, sinecures in the gift of the Secretaries of State. Of the five persons who served as clerks from 1782 to 1801, two had been Undersecretaries of State and two had been clerks in the Home Office.[71] There were usually two deputies at any given time, always clerks in the Home Office.[72] It is not clear whether a deputy acted for two clerks,[73] or whether two of the clerks actually performed some of the limited duties of their offices. The *Royal Kalender* always lists an office keeper, who may have done a good part of the work.

Formal warrants, signed by the king and countersigned by the Secretary, directed the Attorney General or the Solicitor General or both to prepare a bill. (Peerages went only to the Attorney General; grants of offices and most ordinary matters went to the Solicitor General; and grants of charters went to both. Warrants for ordinary church preferments skipped the law officers and went directly to the Signet Office.) After the law officer (or officers) prepared and signed

70. Evans, *Principal Secretary of State,* pp. 194–221.

71. James Rivers (c.1729–1807), son of Dr. Thomas Rivers (d. 1731) prebendary of Winchester, and brother of the fifth and sixth baronets. Thomas Wotton, *The Baronetage of England,* edited by E. Kimber and Richard Johnson (3 vols.; London, 1771), I, 213–14. He was Undersecretary in the Northern or Southern Department, 1754–1765, and Clerk of the Signet from September 17, 1762 (*Cal. of H. O. Papers,* I, 238, No. 751) till his death on August 29, 1807. *Annual Register,* XLIX (1807), 589. William Fraser (d. 1802) was Clerk of the Signet 1782 till his death. John Tirel-Morin was Clerk 1782–1807, and Eardley Wilmot 1797–1801. See Appendix I. Montagu Wilkinson was the fifth Clerk. He was granted the office in reversion on March 20, 1767 (date of warrant) and succeeded on July 26, 1770 (date of oath). *Cal. of H. O. Papers,* II, 263; III, 54, No. 211. He died in Vienna in June 1797. *Gentleman's Magazine,* LXVII (July, 1797), 616.

72. Richard Shadwell served as the Deputy to Rivers, 1769–1785, and thereafter William Pollock. Charles Brietzcke acted as Fraser's deputy until his death in 1795, when William Henry Higden succeeded him. See Appendix I.

73. This was the case in 1837 when Thomas Venables acted as deputy to two Clerks. *PP 1837* (162), XLIV, 139–40.

the bill, a solicitor employed by the interested party brought the bill, called the Attorney General's bill (varying in name according to the law office preparing it), to the Secretary of State, who procured the king's signature. After the king signed the bill the solicitor took it to the Signet Office where, called the king's bill, it was deposited to remain on record. The signet clerk or a deputy made a transcript of the bill, but added a heading directing the Lord Privy Seal to send it to the Lord Chancellor. The signet or king's seal was affixed to this direction to the Lord Privy Seal. (Evidently the signet clerk brought the bill to the Secretary of State to affix the seal or else the Secretary sent the seal to the Signet Office.) The Privy Seal Office affixed its seal to a transcript of the bill addressed to the Lord Chancellor, who eventually signed it. The affixing of the great seal completed the grant—resulting in a letter close or a letter patent.[74]

The Signet Office charged fees for each document that passed through it. An act in 1535 fixed the rate, but prior to 1711 an increase in fees occurred. Thereafter, however, no alteration was made. The clerks, deputies, and office keeper received certain fixed percentages of the fees on each bill that passed through the Office. A duke, for example, had to pay £28.2.0 to the Signet Office for its part in preparing his patent of creation. Each clerk received £2.10.0 (called a perpetuity); each deputy received £1.11.6 as his fee and the same amount as his gratuity; the office keeper received 7 shillings for docketing (abridging) the bill and £3.3.0 for receiving the fees for the Signet Office.[75] The amounts received by the clerks and deputies varied, of course, with the number of documents that passed through the Office. John Tirel-Morin estimated his office to be worth £250 per annum.[76] William Fraser received £218 in 1784.[77] Brietzcke testified that his average receipts as deputy from 1778 to 1783 had been £104, although he made £227 in 1784 under extraordinary conditions.[78] Pollock received £180 as deputy in 1796.[79]

The Signet Office throughout this period, and in fact till its

74. William Pollock's description of the process in 1800 (note to a letter from Eardley Wilmot to the Select Committee, March 10, 1800, *Report on Records,* First Series, XV, Appendix C.4, p. 78) conforms to the description given by Evans, *Principal Secretary of State,* pp. 196–97.

75. *PP 1837* (162), XLIV, 65, 136–38. A complete table of fees charged on each document and the amount to each officer is at pp. 136–38.

76. The documents which the Office handled are deposited in the P.R.O. under the classification S.O. The Signet and Privy Seal Board Wages Account is in H.O. 82/19.

77. *PP 1806* (309), VII, 75. 78. *First Report, 1786,* p. 27.

79. *Ibid.,* pp. 20–21.

abolition in 1851, remained as a vestige of the medieval past—a living relic in the chain of procedure for passing a document through the seals. Except for its value as a record deposit, the office was useful primarily as a source of patronage.[80]

VII

The last office to have a close relationship to the Secretaries of State was the Secret Department or deciphering branch of the Post Office. The Foreign Office used it almost exclusively to decode messages and letters from foreign governments or agents that had been intercepted by the British Post Office or by other means. The Secret Department may also have devised codes for use by the British. In twenty years the Home Office seems to have applied to the two decipherers, Sir Francis and Edward Willis (who were always paid by the Foreign Secretary), only three times—in 1782 regarding a letter intercepted on a vessel coming from Philadelphia,[81] in the same year concerning a letter taken from a Dutch prisoner held in Kent,[82] and in 1799 regarding two French letters seized in Ireland.[83] As Professor Kenneth Ellis has dealt with the Secret Department in a thorough manner in his *Post Office in the Eighteenth Century*,[84] there seems to be little use in pursuing the subject in this study.[85]

80. *Sixteenth Report, 1797*, p. 317.
81. Nepean to Sir Francis Willis, June 14, 1782, Willis Papers, Add. MS 45,519, f. 64.
82. Nepean to Edward Willis, Sept. 6, 1782, H.O. 43/1.
83. Sir Francis Willis to Wickham, May 9, 1799, Chesterfield St., H.O. 42/47.
84. Pp. 127–31.
85. The *Royal Kalenders* list the office of embellisher as subordinate to the Secretaries from 1782 to 1791; thereafter it disappears. The embellisher was T. Holland. He must have been the person whom Pollock described in 1797 as receiving £25.16.0 per annum as "Embellisher of Vellum Skins for the King's Letters to the Eastern Princes, and to the States of Barbary. . . ." *Sixteenth Report, 1797*, Appendix B.6, p. 320.

CONCLUSION

In the twenty years from 1782 to 1801 the Home Office moved further out of court. Although the constitutional relationship between the king and his Secretary of State did not change (and scarcely could while the king ruled as well as reigned), the office itself became more public than royal. The Secretary ceased to pay his staff from his personal funds after 1795; from that time the clerks and other officers became servants of the state rather than servants of the Secretary (and hence the Crown). However great the difference in status between eighteenth-century clerks and modern civil servants, this financial arrangement of 1795 fundamentally altered the standing of the office of Secretary of State. Parliament took a long step toward gaining jurisdiction and supervision over the office when it directly voted (through the civil list) for the maintenance of the establishment. In this respect Parliament began to exceed its classic position, *viz.*, voting supplies and exercising its right to criticize the ministers of the king. It is not without significance that an Act of Parliament was required to appoint the commissioners to investigate the government offices in 1786, whereas a select committee of the House of Commons itself conducted the investigation in 1797. (The concept of public office appears nowhere more clearly than in the designation "public offices" for the police magistrate courts in London after 1792. Parliament directly voted the appropriation to maintain them and could call for a detailed account of expenditures.)

The Home Office and several of the related offices bear witness to the administrative and financial acumen of William Pitt, for it was he who was instrumental in bringing about the reorganization. (He may not, of course, have been cognizant of the far-reaching consequences of his plans.) All the Home Office officials surrendered the greatest part of their incomes in 1795. This move spelled the end of the reliance of individuals upon the medieval system of fees for their stipends and marked the establishment of fixed salaries for public servants. The increased fees received by the Office after 1792 would have meant an appreciable rise in income for the Secretary, Under-secretaries, and chief clerks, but the additional income was instead diverted to defray other expenses of the establishment. In place of the irregular sums from franking privileges, the clerks received specified compensations. Within the Office a regular system of accounting replaced a haphazard arrangement in which the chief clerk carried away the account books when he retired. The regularization of finances marked a significant advance in Pitt's efforts to promote efficiency in government.[1] The old constitutional and administrative system began to die before the dawn of the nineteenth century.

The financial changes were designed and executed by statesmen; yet external pressures brought about equally significant modifications. The Home Office, after 1789, found itself forced to exercise its authority to preserve order to an unprecedented extent. In the counties the Office failed to develop any institutional means to cope with the chronic unrest. The Secretary continued to advise the justices of the peace and other local officials much as his many predecessors had done—though never for so long or so frequently. Occasionally the Office sent investigators into the counties, but no systematic national police network resulted. In London the story was different, for the deterioration of the old judicial system of the city and the increasing turbulence of the population obliged Parliament to place the supervision of the police courts in the hands of the Home Secretary. An even more noticeable involvement in the governing process occurred when the Home Office acquired responsibility for the control of aliens. The creation of an Alien Office marked an institutional response to a new problem. The present scheme of alien registration and passport regulations had their origins in 1793. It was probably the growth of humanitarianism that increasingly involved the Home Office in petitions on behalf of criminals and finally forced Dundas to appoint an officer to deal specifically with the problem. Concomitant with the growth of petitions for mercy was the Home Office's considerable concern both with supervising the hulks where criminals whose death sentences had been commuted to transportation awaited removal and with planning trans-

1. Sir David Lindsay Keir, "Economical Reform, 1779–1787," *Law Quarterly Review*, L (July, 1934), 368–85, is an excellent treatment of administrative reform before 1787.

portation to and settlement in New South Wales. Such unforeseen pressures as these brought the Home Office deeper into the process of governing His Majesty's subjects.

Other changes also affected the Home Office's duties. The creation of a War Department removed responsibility for the foreign secret service and the executive direction of the war. The war also affected relations with the Barbary states, but did not alter the basic British view of those states. The growth of political radicalism increased but did not significantly alter connections with Scotland, Ireland, and the Channel Islands. Interest in the old colonies declined after the death of the Undersecretary Grey Elliott in 1787. Exploration rather than the West Indian possessions received the most imaginative attention.

A certain amount of specialization occurred in order to cope with new developments during the twenty years. The addition of a précis writer and a private secretary reflected the general increase in business of all kinds after 1789. No longer was the Secretary able to keep in touch with all the details of his office. The addition of a librarian signified that the memories of the clerks would no longer suffice as a filing system. The keeper of criminal registers and the Alien Office obviously represented an increase in specialization. The size of the Office itself grew by one-third in twenty years, though there were still under thirty-five persons employed.

Despite the many significant changes in the Office, there was a great deal of continuity. Procedure in 1801 had great similarity to procedure in 1782. Formal business, in particular, scarcely altered. The Home Secretary remained (except in military affairs) the principal channel to and from the sovereign. Basically all duties except those relating to foreign secret service, war, the London police, and the Alien Office remained on the same traditional footing, however much they expanded in volume. The Secretary continued to provide personal supervision over all aspects of Office business, although some of the detail must have escaped his notice. The Secretaries remained boss of the Office throughout the twenty years. Only (possibly) under Lord Sydney did a permanent Undersecretary assume a dominant position.

Although the Office's scope of responsibilities increased, the attitude toward governing did not alter. The Home department did not willingly intrude into the daily routine of local administration. It met problems on a personal level. There was no thought of implementing programs, and nothing that might be called theory of administration. The Office was basically passive—it acted when external pressure obliged it so to do.

In summary, it may be said that the Home Office from 1782 to 1801 competently executed its responsibilities. The Secretaries were all men of ability; only Sydney and North did not excel in industry and conscientiousness. The permanent Undersecretaries and chief clerk were model servants of the public; and most of the lesser officers performed well. No controversies sullied the reputation of the Office nor of any of its personnel.

Appendix I

CLERKS ON THE REGULAR ESTABLISHMENT OF THE HOME OFFICE 1782–1801

[In the text on a clerk a superscript number, say the number 1, may appear more than once. It always refers to the first citation. The method avoids repetition and the imprecision of a summary of sources.]

ADAMS, WILLIAM DACRES (1775–1862) of Bowden, Devon.

Born on Dec. 16, 1775, first son of William Adams (1752–1811), of Bowden, Devon, M.P. for Plympton Erle 1796–1801 and Totnes 1801–1811, by Anna-Maria, daughter of Richard Dacres of Leatherhead, Surrey. Married on March 10, 1804, Elizabeth, second daughter of Mayow Wynell-Mayow of Sydenham, Kent; four sons, one daughter; succeeded his father in 1811.[1] Clerk in the Home Office (extra) by May 17, 1791;[2] permanent from July 11, 1794, to July 30, 1810 (resigned);[3] private secretary to William Pitt 1804–1806, and to the Duke of Portland 1807–1809;[4] commissioner of the Lottery Office, July 21, 1804, to Oct. 1829 (office abolished);[5] commissioner of Woods and Forests, July 31, 1810, to Aug. 1834 (resigned).[6] His salary as commissioner of the Lottery Office was £375, 1804–1807, thereafter £500; pension £375.[5] He transacted business in the Home Office of preparing licenses for British subjects to pay bills in foreign countries, for which he received £200 per annum, but had to pay an extra clerk and rent for apartments.[7] His papers (or rather Pitt's papers that he took with him) are in the P.R.O. He died on June 8, 1862, aged eighty-six.[1]

1. *Burke's Landed Gentry*, 5th ed., I, 4. 2. Grenville to P.O., May 17, 1791, H.O. 43/3. 3. Salary Books, H. O. 82/1. 4. "P.R.O. Class List of Gifts" (index to private papers in the P.R.O., II, 106). 5. *Return of the Length of Service of Several Persons Belonging to the Lottery Office, Entitled to Retired Allowances, 26 April 1830*, H. of C. 298, pp. 388–90; *PP 1830*, XVII. 6. Haydn, *Book of Dignities*, pp. 271–72. 7. Contingent Accounts, H. O. 82/3.

BRADBURY, JOHN (took name of Norton in place of Bradbury on March 21, 1797), of Rye, Sussex.

Clerk in the Plantation Department, December 21, 1783,[1] and thereafter in the Home Office until May 8, 1797 (resigned).[2] In compliance with the will of his relation Catherine Owens, widow of Thomas Owens, formerly secondary of the Court of King's Bench, and daughter of Ralph Norton of Rye, Bradbury took the name of Norton in place of Bradbury, by royal license, March 21, 1797.[3] Norton and his wife Mary held court at the manor of Iden, Goldspur Hundred, in 1797 and in 1805, and also owned other land in Sussex.[4] Ralph Norton (1666–1750) lived at Tower House, Rye, and at his death left his property to his daughter Elizabeth who died without issue in 1781, leaving her property to her sister Catherine, who had married Thomas Owens in 1752. Owens died in 1769. Catherine Owens died without issue in 1797, aged ninety, and left her property to Bradbury, a descendant of her father's sister, provided that he would take the name Norton. Norton apparently died in 1832 or 1833, when his executors are said to have sold his land.[5]

1. *First Report, 1786,* p. 26. 2. Salary Books, H.O. 82/1. 3. *London Gazette,* March 21, 1797. 4. *Victoria History of the Counties of England: Sussex,* edited by William Page and L. F. Salzman (6 vols. but numbered I–IX; London, 1905–53), IX, 153. 5. L. A. Vidler, "Rye Foreign," *Sussex Archeological Collections,* XCII (1954), 150.

BRIETZCKE, CHARLES (c.1738–1795), of St. James's Place.

Born c.1738,[1] a younger son of (?) Daniel (?) Christian Brietzcke,[2] a Prussian, valet de chambre to the second Duke of Grafton (1683–1757),[3] by Elizabeth Catherine,[2] a housekeeper at Somerset House.[3] Married Catherine (?); three sons, one daughter: (1) Richard Betenson (who took the name Dean in place of Brietzcke on May 5, 1801), born on December 29, 1772, died on July 1, 1850; admitted to the Charterhouse Jan. 21, 1784; Oxford, B.A. 1794; Lincoln's Inn, 1792; called to the bar, 1798; commissioner of customs, Sept. 17, 1810, and chairman after September 13, 1823; died July 1, 1850 in Brook St., London.[2] (2) Charles Ware, Lt. R.N. of H.M.S. *Hannibal*; died Oct. 1795 in the West Indies of yellow fever.[4] (3) George Purchas: see next entry. (1) Carolina, married on September 4, 1800, John Edmund Dowdeswell, M.P. of Pull Court, Worcester. She died on May 6, 1845.[5] Clerk in the Northern Department c.1755–September 1763,[6] in the Southern Department and later Home Office, September 1763 to July 10, 1795, when he was retired because of ill health;[7] engrossing clerk in the Alienation Office, January 1763 to July 1765; and from July 1766 to his death; deputy to William Fraser, Clerk of the Signet, from c.1776 to his death.[8] He retired on a pension of £445 per annum, one-half of which was continued to his widow. His will, dated November 16, 1765, and proved June 17, 1795, leaves all his possessions to his wife.[9] She died on August 23, 1830.[7] Her will leaves all possessions to her daughter Carolina Dowdeswell.[10] Brietzcke had been recommended to his initial employment by Lady Harrington,[3] presumably Elizabeth (died 1794), second wife of Sir James Harrington, sixth Baronet. He died on June 5, 1795, at his home in St. James's Place. The *Gentleman's Magazine* wrote: "Charles Brietzcke, esq. aged 57 years, 40 of which he faithfully dedicated to the service of Government, in the Secretary of State's Office."[1]

1. *Gentleman's Magazine,* LXV (June, 1795), 533. 2. Bower Marsh and Frederick Arthur (eds.), *Alumni Carthusiani: A Record of the Foundation Scholars of Charterhouse, 1614–1872* (no place, 1912), p. 110. 3. Shelburne MSS, Vol. 138; printed in Thomson, *Secretaries of State,* pp. 179–80. 4. *Gentleman's Magazine,* LXV (Supplement 1795), 1112. 5. *Burke's Landed Gentry,* 4th ed., I, 363; *ibid.,* 11th ed. (2 vols.; London, 1906),

I, 479. **6.** *Cal. of H.O. Papers,* I, 302–303. **7.** Salary Books, H.O. 82/1. **8.** *First Report, 1786,* p. 21. **9.** Newcastle, 367. **10.** n.d., proved February 9, 1831; written in the margin of a page containing the will of her husband.

BRIETZCKE, GEORGE PURCHAS (died 1817).

Third son of the above. Married on October 4, 1800, Susannah, eldest daughter of Sir Justinian Isham, Br., of Lamport, Northants.; without issue. She died in 1849.[1] Clerk in Home Office from July 11, 1794 to his death, and earlier without salary.[2] His father requested that his third son be placed on the Home Office establishment.[3] An administration of his estate, estimated at under £600, was granted to his wife on June 9, 1817.[4] He died at Bath, April 27, 1817.[5]

1. *Gentleman's Magazine,* LXX (Supplement, 1800), 1286; *Burke's Peerage,* 99th ed., p. 1286. **2.** Salary Books, H.O. 82/1; *Sixteenth Report, 1797,* p. 325. **3.** To Dundas, Aug. 20, 1795, H.O. 44/41. **4.** AA, 1817. **5.** *Gentleman's Magazine,* LXXXVII (May, 1817), 475.

CARRINGTON, GEORGE WILLIAM (died 1801).

Younger son of James Carrington (died 1794), chancellor of the diocese of Exeter, 1757–73; brother of James (died 1825), chancellor of the diocese of Exeter, 1773–1825; brother of William Henry (1754–1813), rector of Holy Trinity, Exeter, 1780–1813, and vicar of Sydbury and Ide, Devon, 1785–1813.[1] Married Jane (?). Clerk in the Southern Department and then the Home Office, November 1768[2] to July 10, 1794, when Dundas forced him to retire on a pension of £210.[3] His widow continued to receive one-half of his pension until June 1827, when she presumably died. He died on May 20, 1801.[4]

1. *Alumni Cantab.,* Pt. I, I, 298; Pt. II, I, 523, 524; James Carrington (died 1794) to Sydney, July 19, 1784, H.O. 42/5. **2.** *Cal. of H.O. Papers,* II, 435. **3.** To Carrington, June 2, 1794, H.O. 43/5. **4.** *Contingent Accounts,* H.O. 82/3.

CHAPMAN, JAMES (1767–1845), of Pauls Cray Hill, Kent.

Born on May 25, 1767, first son of James Chapman (1730–1824) of Pauls Cray Hill, by Jane, daughter of Rev. Preb. Mawe. Married on January 21, 1792, Mary, daughter of William Greenwood. She died in 1837. Two sons, two daughters. Succeeded his father in 1824.[1] Merchant Taylors' School, 1776–79.[2] Clerk in the Home Office from c. July 7, 1784, to July 10, 1794; précis writer in the Home Office, June 8, 1791, to July 11, 1794; private secretary to Dundas from January 1 to July 11, 1794;[3] clerk in the War Department, July 11, 1794, to March 1, 1795; chief clerk March 1, 1795, to April 5, 1824 (retired);[4] secretary, clerk of the council, secretary to Cabildo, and register of deeds in Trinidad, December 1806, to May 1831 (offices abolished);[5] deputy lieutenant of Kent, 1810. His pension upon retiring from the Colonial Office because of ill health in 1824 was £1,000,[4] and from the abolished offices £1,000—the salary having been £1,500.[5] His will, dated March 28, 1839, and proved on January 23, 1846, leaves the bulk of his estates to his eldest son James (1797–1878).[6] His papers are in the Kent County Archives Office. He died on December 16, 1845, aged seventy-eight.[1]

1. Ashworth P. Burke, *Family Records* (London, 1897), p. 154. 2. Mrs. E. P. Hart (ed.), *Merchant Taylors' School Register* (2 vols.; London, 1936), I, no page numbers, but alphabetical. 3. Sydney to P.O., July 7, 1784, H.O. 43/1; Contingent Accounts, H.O. 82/3. 4. *Estimate of the Sum Required to pay the Salaries and Epenses in the Department of Her Majesty's Most Honourable Privy Council and Committee of Privy Council for Trade,* H. of C. 142–III, p. 655; *PP 1839,* XXXI; Young, p. 266. 5. *PP 1834* (494), XLI, 453. 6. Wills, 1846, f. 13.

CHAPMAN, ROBERT.

Probably brother of James Chapman, above.[1] Clerk in the Plantation Office and then in the Home Office, c.1787 to before May 17, 1791 (resigned).[2]

1. A. Burke, *Family Records,* p. 154. 2. Grenville to P.O., May 17, 1791, H.O. 43/3.

CHETWYND, RICHARD (1757–1821), fifth Viscount.

Born on September 27, 1757, fourth but first surviving son and heir of William, fourth Viscount Chetwynd, by Susannah, daughter of Sir Jonathan Cope, first Bt. Married on July 30, 1791, Charlotte, youngest daughter of Thomas Cartwright of Aynho, Northants., and stepdaughter of Stephen Cottrell, clerk of the Privy Council. One son, three daughters. Succeeded his father on November 12, 1791.[1] Clerk in the Southern Department and the Home Office from 1780 to September 1786;[2] clerk to the Board of Trade, 1786 to January 24, 1792 (resigned);[3] clerk to the Privy Council (extraordinary) 1772–1810 and (ordinary) 1810–his death. The estates of the second Viscount had passed to a daughter, and the title to a brother, leaving the third and subsequent viscounts with little wealth, which no doubt accounted for Richard Chetwynd's being in the Home Office. Two elder brothers who reached maturity predeceased their father without male heirs.[1] He found his situation in the Home Office "rather mortifying."[4] In 1793 he wrote to ask Pitt to give him a seat in the House of Commons.[5] He died on February 27, 1821, in Bolton Row, Piccadilly, aged sixty-three. His widow (born 1772) died on April 7, 1845, aged seventy-two.[1]

1. *Complete Peerage,* III, 188–89. 2. Sydney to P.O., Sept. 6, 1786, H.O. 43/2. 3. Minutes of the Board of Trade for that date, Liverpool Papers, Add. MS 38,393. 4. Chetwynd to Charles Jenkinson, Jan. 14, 1784, but probably 1785, Suffolk Street, Charing Cross, *ibid.,* 38,218, f. 273. 5. Oct. 23, 1793, Harworth House, Isleworth, P.R.O. 30/8/122 (Chatham Papers).

COLLETON, JAMES NASSAU (1752–1815), sixth Bt. after July 1801.

Born on March 23, 1752, only surviving son of Robert Colleton, Captain, First Regiment of Foot Guards, third son of the third Bt. Married on December 3, 1778, Susanna, daughter of William Nixon of Lincoln. Three sons, five daughters. Succeeded his cousin Sir John Snell Colleton in July 1801.[1] Clerk in the Southern Department and the Home Office, October 1774[2] to July 10, 1794, when Dundas gave him the option of remaining in the office without advancement or of resigning.[3] His pension was £180. Colleton suffered many setbacks in life. He lost his property in the Carolinas after the American Revolution. When the Assembly of South Carolina granted him £20,000 as compensation, his agent embezzled it and died before Colleton could take action. An old relation died worth £300,000, but unexpectedly left his property to his own wife rather than to Colleton. Lord Rochford, Colleton's relation, placed him in the Southern Department in compensation for the loss of a large fortune which ought to have reverted to him rather than to Lord Rochford.[4] He died intestate in the Old Bailey, January 16, 1815, aged sixty-two.[1]

1. G. E. C[okayne], *The Complete Baronetage, 1611–1800* (5 vols.; Exeter, 1900–1909), III, 163. 2. *Cal. of H.O. Papers,* IV, 245; 3. June 2, 1794, H.O. 43/5. 4. Colleton to Dundas, June 8, 1794, Eaton Street, Grosvenor Place, H.O. 42/31.

DAW, THOMAS (died 1791).

Clerk in the Southern Department and the Home Office by November 4, 1768,[1] to his death before May 17, 1791.[2] Letters of administration for the estate of a Thomas Daw were granted on June 12, 1791, to Mary Dearsgill, cousin german and only relation of Daw, who was a bachelor. Daw's estate was valued at less than £1,000; he lived at Robertsbridge, Sussex.[3] But the Contingent Accounts record a gratuity of £50 per annum paid to the widow of Thomas Daw. The last such payment is dated May 8, 1794. As the payments begin on May 8, that is presumably the day on which Daw died.[4] George, Duke of Montague (1712–90), recommended Daw to his initial employment.[5]

1. *Cal. of H.O. Papers,* II, 435. 2. Grenville to P.O., May 17, 1791, H.O. 43/3. 3. AA, 1791. 4. H.O. 82/3. 5. Montague to Shelburne, April 24, 1782, Lacaita-Shelburne MSS, Clements Library.

DOUGLAS, ROBERT.

Clerk in the Home Office by May 17, 1791[1] to November 11, 1802 (dismissed).[2] Dundas informed Douglas in 1794 that he was withholding promotion from him because of his inattention to his duty and warned him that he would be dismissed if it continued.[3] Lord Pelham discharged him after he had been absent for four months and yet requested some additional time to settle his personal affairs, as he had incautiously taken a house at Bury St. Edmunds, 75 miles from London.[2]

1. Grenville to P.O., May 17, 1791, H.O. 43/3. 2. Sir George Shee to Douglas, Nov. 11, 1802, H.O. 43/13. 3. June 2, 1794, H.O. 43/5.

GODDARD, CHARLES (1771–1845).

Born c.1771, son of Charles Goddard of Westminster. Married in 1812. Seven children. The eldest son, George Frederick, matriculated at Oxford in 1835, aged eighteen; B.A. 1839, M.A. 1859; honorary canon of Rochdale 1856, rector of Southfleet 1854.[1] Matriculated at Christ Church, Oxford, in 1787, M.A. (by degree) 1821, B.D. and D.D. 1821. Clerk in the Home Office by August 22, 1789[2] until sometime in June of 1791.[3] He served as Grenville's secretary and précis writer while Grenville was Secretary of State; Collector and Transmitter of State Papers from January 6, 1795 to his death.[4] Counsul-general at Lisbon, December 21, 1796, to Oct. 31, 1799; pension of £800.[5] Secretary to the embassy in Paris, 1806.

Agent for Upper Canada and deputy ranger of St. James's (?) Park until 1799.[6] Entered holy orders in 1812; prebendary of Lincoln 1814, archdeacon 1817–44; subdean 1844 to his death; rector of St. James's, Garlick Hill, London 1821–36; rector of Ibstock 1836 to his death; chaplain to the Bishop of Rochester. Goddard was a protégé of the Grenville family. He died on January 21, 1848.[6]

1. *Alumni Oxon.*, II, 531–32. 2. Grenville to P.O., Aug. 22, 1789, H.O. 43/3. 3. General Account Book, H.O. 82/1. 4. Patent Rolls 19–43 Geo III, p. 291, C. 66. 5. *Ibid.*, pp 308, 351. Memo by Goddard, Aug. 13, 1841, Ibstock Rectory, Peel Papers, Add MS 40,486, ff. 104–105; memo of WHS, n.d., 40,534, f. 308; memo attached to J. Sinclair to Sir Robert Peel, March 19, 1835, 40,417, ff. 235–37. 6. Obituary, *Gentleman's Magazine*, n.s. 3, XXIX (1848), 555.

GORDON, ADAM (1770–1841) of Manchester Square, Middlesex.

Born c.1770, only son of John Gordon of Charleston, South Carolina, by his second wife, Katherine, daughter of William Smith, judge of the Supreme Court of New York and brother of William Smith (1728–93), Chief Justice of Quebec. John Gordon died in 1778 in Bordeaux, and his wife had died on December 15, 1775.[1] Married Amelia Watts. Died without issue.[2] Educated at a private school of Dr. John Carr in Hertford, which he was attending in 1784.[3] Clerk in the Home Office by May 17, 1791,[4] until July 10, 1794; clerk in the War (and Colonial) Department, March 1, 1795, to April 5, 1824, and chief clerk April 5, 1824, to March 31, 1833 (retired); Naval Officer of Trinidad, March 1801, to Jan. 1826 (office abolished); secretary and clerk of the Council in Trinidad;[5] agent for Demerara, 1804; agent for Lower Canada, 1814.[4] His will, dated August 2, 1839, and proved on April 24, 1841, leaves his property to his wife.[6] His wife's will, dated May 3, 1841, and proved on March 13, 1845, leaves the property to James Gardiner (or Gardiner Wood) of Charleston, South Carolina, and to Gordon Gardiner of the Colonial Office, and an annuity to her brother George Watts.[2] Gordon died on March 29, 1841, in Manchester Square, aged seventy-one.[7]

1. Joseph W. Barnwell and Mabel L. Weber (eds.), "St. Helena Parish Register," *South Carolina Historical and Genealogical Magazine*, XXIII, No. 3 (July, 1922), 103; Mabel L. Weber (compiler), "Death Notices from the South Carolina and American General Gazette, and Its Continuation the Royal Gazette, May 1766–June 1782," *ibid.*, XVII (April, 1916), 93; (Oct., 1916), 149; Lothrop Withington and H. F. Waters (compilers), "South Carolina Gleanings in England," *ibid.*, IV (Oct., 1903), 286–87; A. S. Salley, Jr. (ed.), *Marriage Notices in the South Carolina Gazette and Its Successors, 1732–1801* (Albany, 1902), pp. 32, 44–45. 2. Wills, 1845, f. 203. 3. *Diary of William Smith,* I, 73; II, 43–44, n. 2. 4. Grenville to P.O., May 17, 1791, H.O. 43/3. 5. Young, *The Colonial Office,* p. 266. 6. Wills, 1841, f. 269. 7. *Superannuations,* H. of C. 137, p. 699; *PP 1842,* XXVI; *Gentleman's Magazine,* n.s., XV (June, 1841), 666.

HEPBURN, ROBERT (1766–1846), later spelled HEPBURNE.

Born c.1766, second son of Robert Hepburn of Clerkington (died January 2, 1798), commissioner of the customs in Scotland, June 1786 to his death, by Isabella (died December 18, 1774), daughter of John Mitchelson of Middleton.[1] Married on October 1, 1800, Catherine, third daughter of Alexander Gordon, Lord Rockville (1739–1792), a lord of session in Scotland, who was the fourth son of William, the second Earl of Aberdeen. Her mother Anne (died 1811), was the widow of the Earl of Dumfries and Stair.[2] At least one son and three daughters.[3] (?) Matriculated at St. Andrews University on February 17, 1778.[4] Clerk in the Home Office from July 1775 to 1787;[5] clerk in the board of control 1787–?; private secretary to Dundas by 1788[6] and private secretary in the Home Office, June 8, 1791, to January 1, 1794;[7] master of the mint in Scotland, January 12, 1792,[8] to June 1805; commissioner of stamps in Scotland, June 1805[9] to August 1, 1828, when he retired upon a pension of £600.[10] Lt. First Regiment of Fencible Cavalry, 1798.[8] Dundas recommended him to his initial employment in 1785.[11] He evidently served as Nepean's private secretary upon his first coming to the Home Office.[12] His wife received a pension of £184 on March 16, 1829.[13] In the early 1830's he was forced to flee from Edinburgh to Mt. Holyrood because of financial difficulties.[3] He died on August 5, 1846, aged eighty.[14]

1. Sir Francis J. Grant (ed.), *The Faculty of Advocates in Scotland, 1532–1943, with Genealogical Notes* (Edinburgh, 1944), p. 101; will of Robert Hepburn, dated February, 3, 1783, and registered on March 16, 1793, Vol. 131, Gen. Reg. House. 2. *Burke's Genealogical and Heraldic History of the Peerage, Baronetage, and Knightage* (London, 1928), p. 61. 3. Hepburne to James Chapman, Feb. 24, 1832, Holyrood, Edinburgh, Chapman MSS. 4. James Maitland Anderson (ed.), *The Matriculation Roll of the University of St. Andrews, 1747–1897* (Edinburgh, 1905), p. 26. 5. Hepburne to James Chapman, Oct. 23, 1827, Edinburgh, Chapman MSS, U. 619, c. 14. 6. Hepburn to Nepean. Oct. 6, 1788, Doneira Lodge, H.O. 102/59. 7. Contingent Accounts, H.O. 82/3. 8. *Thirtieth Report of the Select Committee on Finance: The Civil Government of Scotland,* First Series, XIII, 467. 9. *Scots Magazine,* LXVII (June, 1805), 488. 10. *Superannuations,* H. of C. 120, p. 334; *PP 1829,* XV. 11. Dundas to Sydney, July 16, 1786, Wimbledon, Sydney MSS, Brotherton Collection, University of Leeds. 12. *First Report, 1786,* p. 21. 13. *Sum Required for Salaries, &c., heretofore Paid out of the Civil List for England and Ireland, the Hereditary Revenues of the Crown in Scotland, and the Four-and-a-Half per cent Duties, but for which no Provision has been made in the Civil List of His Present Majesty, from the Periods to which the Several Services were last Paid to 5 July 1831,* H. of C. 87, p. 395; *PP 1831,* XIII. 14. *Superannuations,* H. of C. 222, p. 462; *PP 1847,* XXXIV.

HICKS, JOHN (1775–1839) of Upper Wimpole Street.

Born c.1775.[1] Clerk in the Home Office from July 11, 1794, to July 29, 1834 (retired),[2] but in office earlier without salary.[3] He retired on a pension of £946 in 1834 because of age and infirmity.[1] His will is in Vaughn, f. 434. He died on June 20, 1839, aged sixty-four.[4]

1. *PP 1839* (142–III), XXXI, 653. 2. Salary Books, H.O. 82/1. 3. *Sixteenth Report, 1797,* p. 325. 4. *Gentleman's Magazine,* n.s., XII (July, 1839), 98.

HIGDEN, WILLIAM HENRY (1741–1811) of Bridgeroad, Lambeth, Surrey.

Born c.1741;[1] brother of Charles Higden of Curriers Hall in London and of Maryland Point, Stratford, Essex (died February 8, 1818).[2] Married on February 28, 1801, at St. Mary, Lambeth, Ann Jane Fassett or Hassett of Camberwell. Without issue.[3] She married a second time on July 31, 1813, George Byfield.[4] Clerk in the Southern Department and the Home Office by November 4, 1765,[5] to August 15, 1805, when he retired on a pension of £600 after a paralytic stroke;[1] temporary secretary to Sir Robert Ainslie, ambassador to Turkey, 1777; chargé d'affaires in Savoy-Sardinia September 3 to October 9, 1783, and secretary thereafter to John Trevor until about June 16, 1784;[5] deputy Clerk of the Signet, March 11, 1795.[6]

"In the Bridge-road Lambeth, in his 70th year William Henry Higden, Esq. formerly of the Secretary of State's Office for the Home Department; a situation which he held for many years with distinguished reputation for integrity and ability. In the earlier parts of his life he had attended the late Earl of Rochford, Sir Robert Ainsle, and the Hon. Mr. Trevor, in different embassies to France, Spain, Turkey, and Sardinia; and was honoured with the esteem of those illustrious persons. He possessed an extensive knowledge of foreign languages and manners, which accomplished him as a scholar and as a gentleman, while the goodness of his heart rendered his knowledge useful. His character in private life was not less distinguished for philanthropy and benevolence; and it is but an imperfect tribute to his memory to describe him as an affectionate husband, a kind relative, and an indulgent master."[8]

He died May 20, 1811, aged seventy.

1. *PP 1808* (331), III, 264. 2. *Gentleman's Magazine,* LXXXVIII (April, 1818), 379. 3. *Ibid.,* LXXI (March, 1801), 275; Higden's will, Crickett, f. 287. 4. *Gentleman's Magazine,* LXXXIII (Aug., 1813), 186. 5. *Cal. of H.O. Papers,* II, 435. 6. D.B. Horn (ed.), *British Diplomatic Representatives, 1689–1789* (Camden Society Publications, Third Series, XLVI; London, 1932), pp. 127, 155. 7. H.O. 38/6. 8. *Gentleman's Magazine,* LXXXI (May, 1811), 502; cf. *European Magazine,* LIX (May, 1811), 399.

JESSEP, JOHN (possibly JESSUP).

Clerk in the Plantation Department and then in the Home Office, December 1783 till sometime before August 22, 1789 (resigned).[1]

1. *First Report, 1786,* p. 26; Grenville to P.O., August 22, 1789, H.O. 43/3.

JOHNSTON, WILLIAM FRANCIS (died 1799).

Married (?). One child. In 1801 his widow married a second time, a Mr. Falconar. The last payment to his wife was on April 5, 1835.[1] Clerk in the Home Office (extra) February 16 to July 10, 1794, and (permanent) July 11, 1794 to his death.[2] The *Gentleman's Magazine* wrote at his death: "In Buckingham-street, after a long and painful illness, William Francis Johnston. . . ."[3] He died on January 7, 1799.

1. Portland to the Treasury, March 20, 1799, H.O. 36/11; Contingent Accounts, H.O. 82/3. 2. *Sixteenth Report, 1797,* p. 325. 3. LXIX (Jan., 1799), 82; *European Magazine,* XXXV (Jan., 1799), 70.

LEFROY, GEORGE THOMPSON (died 1801).

Born between 1777 and 1782, third son of Anthony Peter Lefroy of Limerick, Ireland, former lt.-col. of the Thirteenth Regiment of Light Dragoons (died September 8, 1819), by Anne Gardiner. Unmarried.[1] Clerk in the Home Office before October 18, 1794,[2] until his death. He was absent with the leave of the Duke of Portland from at least January 5, 1797, until July 5, 1799, but received his salary of £100 per annum. He died on July 9, 1801.[3]

1. [General Sir John Henry Lefroy], *Notes and Documents Relating to the Family of Loffroy. By a Cadet* (Woolwich, 1868), p. 107; Sir Bernard Burke, *A Genealogical and*

Heraldic History of the Landed Gentry of Ireland (London, 1912), p. 393, omits this son. 2. General Account Book, H.O. 82/1. 3. Salary Books, H.O. 82/16.

MATHIAS, GEORGE AUGUSTUS VINCENT (died 1848).

Second son of Vincent Mathias, subtreasurer to Queen Charlotte and treasurer of Queen Anne's Bounty, 1776 to his death on June 15, 1782, by Marianne (November 8, 1724–January 6, 1799), daughter of Alured Popple, secretary to the Board of Trade and governor of Bermuda;[1] brother of Thomas James Mathias (?1754–1835), the Italian scholar.[2] Married on September 2, 1807 (?) Dennison of Curzon Street.[3] Eton College, 1775–79;[4] admitted to Lincoln's Inn, August 7, 1793.[5] Clerk in the Home Office, February 25, 1783,[6] to May 3, 1784 (resigned);[7] messenger to Queen Charlotte, October 1, 1784, till her death in 1818 (pension in 1819 of £71.18.4); inspector in the audit office, October 9, 1806, to April 5, 1826 (abolished), pension of £300.[8] In 1784 Mathias' mother explained to Lord Sydney the reason for her son's resignation: "He sees no prospect of rising in his office, and is desirous of pushing his fortune in another line."[7] He died on June 6, 1848.[9]

1. *Gentleman's Magazine,* XXII (Oct., 1752), 478; LII (June, 1782), 311; LXIX (Jan., 1799), 82. 2. *DNB,* XIII, 47–49. 3. *Gentleman's Magazine,* LXXVII (Sept., 1807), 887. 4. Richard Arthur Austen-Leigh, *The Eton College Register, 1753–1790* (Eton, 1921), p. 359. 5. *Lincoln's Inn Admission Register,* I, 547. 6. Sydney to P.O., Feb. 25, 1783, H.O. 43/1. 7. May 3, 1784, H.O. 44/40. 8. *Return of Persons who Hold Two or More Commissions, Offices, Pensions, Half or Retired Pay or Allowances of any Kind from the Public in Civil and Military Establishments,* H. of C. 479, p. 602; *PP 1830,* XVII. 9. *Superannuations,* H. of C. 155, p. 509; *PP 1849,* XXX.

MEDLEY, RICHARD (1778–1846).

Born c.1778, son of Richard Medley of Brighthelmstone, Sussex, and of Clapham, Surrey (c.1741–August 31, 1823).[1] Clerk in the Home Office, January 22, 1799, to March 24, 1823 (resigned).[2] He died on May 20, 1846, at Walworth.[3]

1. Will of Richard Medley, dated February 24, 1823, and proved September 16, 1823, Wills, 1823, f. 533; *Gentleman's Magazine,* XCIII (Sept., 1823), 284. 2. Salary Books, H.O. 82/16. 3. *Gentleman's Magazine,* n.s., XXVI (July, 1846), 104.

MILLS, FREDERICK RUSSELL (1780–1861) of 11 Cunningham Place, St. John's Wood, Middlesex.

Born c.1780, son of the Rev. Thomas Mills, vicar of Hillingdon, Middlesex (died June 4, 1810).[1] Married (?), at least two sons: (1) Frederick Russell (June 27, 1817–February 16, 1896), vicar of Esholt, near Leeds 1852–77; (2) William (June 3, 1820–September 22, 1877), lawyer.[2] Educated at Harrow, 1775, 1776.[3] Clerk in the Home Office from January 17, 1798, to 1849 (retired); later librarian and précis writer of the Home Office.[4] He died on August 8, 1861.[1]

1. *Gentleman's Magazine,* 2nd n.s., XI (Sept., 1861), 337; *Alumni Oxon.,* III, 959. 2. *Alumni Cantab.,* Pt. II, IV, 419–20. 3. W. T. J. Gun (ed.), *The Harrow School Register, 1751–1800* (London, 1934), p. 106. The entry is apparently Mills, as the information on his sons indicates that their father attended Harrow. M. G. Daughlish and P. K. Stephenson (eds.), *The Harrow School Register, 1800–1911* (London, 1911), pp. 124, 139. 4. Salary Books, H. A. 82/16.

MORIN, JOHN (died 1807). Took the name TIREL before that of Morin on November 10, 1787; of Weedon Lodge, Bucks., and of Hanover Square.

Son of Peter Michael Morin, Undersecretary of State in the Southern Department (died on November 15, 1768),[1] by Jane, granddaughter of John Tirel de Gavré in lower Normandy (died 1787).[2] Married Mary Ann (?); one son, one daughter: (1) John Richard Rose Tirel-Morin (April 5, 1785, to June 1801), Westminster School, 1795; Midshipman R.N.; killed in a fall from aloft on board H.M.S. *L'Heureux* at Martinique;[3] (1) Jane Elizabeth, married on March 12, 1805, Sir Salisbury Humphreys (later Davenport) of Bramall Hall; she died on September 30, 1808.[4] Clerk in the Southern Department by October 11, 1765;[5] in the Home Office to February 25, 1783 (resigned); private secretary to Lord Shelburne;[6] Clerk of the Signet, April 1781 to his death; Keeper of Papers at the Treasury, 1783 to his death (£340 per annum); receiver-general of rents and revenues of Gilbraltar (£300 per annum).[7] Early in the 1800's he purchased the manor of Fleet Marston in Bucks.[8] He also owned the manors of Hardwick and Weedon Lodge in that county.[9] At his death he left his personal property to his wife and his real property to his daughter and her husband.[10] He died at his house in Hanover Square on March 19, 1807.[11]

1. Thomson, *Secretaries of State,* p. 180; *Gentleman's Magazine,* XXXVIII (Nov., 1768), 543. 2. *London Gazette,* Nov. 10, 1787; the will is dated April 6, 1787, and was proved on November 2, 1787, Major, f. 505. 3. Barker and Stenning, *Old Westminsters,* II, 665. 4. *Gentleman's Magazine,* LXXV (March, 1805), 280; George Lipscombe, *The History and Antiquities of the County of Buckingham* (6 vols.; London, 1847), I, 328–29; John Burke and Sir John Bernard Burke, *A Genealogical and Heraldic Dictionary of the Landed Gentry of Great Britain and Ireland* (3 vols.; London, 1846–49), I, 312. 5. *Cal. of H.O. Papers,* I, 607. 6. Morin to Townshend, Feb. 25, 1783, H.O. 42/2; Fitzmaurice, *Life of Shelburne,* I, 43. 7. *PP 1806* (309), VII, 75. 8. *Victoria County History, Buckingham,* edited by William Page (5 vols.; London, 1905–28), IV, 74, 76. 9. Lipscombe, *History of Buckinghamshire,* III, 371. 10. Lushington, f. 449. 11. *Gentleman's Magazine,* LXXVII (April, 1807), 384; *European Magazine,* LI (April, 1807), 317.

NOBLE, RICHARD HATT (1778–1849) of Littlefife House, Middle Scotland Yard, and of Leckhamstead, Berks.

Born c.1778, son of John Noble, mayor of Bristol (1743–1828), by Mary (died 1804). Unmarried. Clerk in the Home Office, July 15, 1797, to January 5, 1849 (retired);[2] Naval Officer of St. John's, Newfoundland, April 1, 1800,[3] to 1827 (office abolished); pension c.£380 per annum.[4] John Noble, father of the subject, wrote to Portland on August 11, 1795: "My Son participating in my heavy Losses, with gratitude & pleasure will accept your Grace's Nomination to a Situation in your Departm[en]t whenever such may offer. . . ."[5] His pension upon retirement was £1,025.[2] At his death he left £5,000 to his nephew William Hatt Noble.[6] He died May 4, 1849, aged seventy-one.[7]

1. Will of John Noble, dated Jan. 24, 1826, and proved Oct. 30, 1828; *Correspondence of Edmund Burke,* III, 74 f. 2. *Superannuations,* H. of C. 171, p. 647; *PP 1850,* XXXIII. 3. C.O. 324/46. 4. *PP 1834* (494), XLI, 452. 5. Portland MSS, PwF 7,201. 6. Wills, 1849, f. 457. 7. *Gentleman's Magazine,* CXXXIV (June, 1849), 665.

NORRIS, JOHN FRANCIS (1785–1854).

Born c.1785, almost certainly the son of John Norris, M.P., by Catherine, daughter of Rev. William Lynch, dean of Canterbury.[1] Married. Two sons, three daughters: (1) John Style; (2) Henry Charles; (1) Lucy Elizabeth Stewart; (2) Henrietta Style; (3) Clara Priscilla Leyester.[2] Clerk in the Home Office, July 9, 1801, to 1841, when he retired on a pension of £660.[3] He died in Wilton Crescent on November 2, 1854, aged sixty-nine.[4]

1. *History of Parliament,* III, 203–204; Norris to Portland, Aug. 10, 1795, No. 17 Panton Square, Portland MSS, PwF 7,218; memo by Portland, July 9, 1801, H.O. 43/13. 2. Will dated May 1, 1852, and proved Nov. 28, 1854, f. 852. 3. *PP 1842* (137), XXVI, 698. 4. *Gentleman's Magazine,* CXXXV (Dec., 1854), 645.

PALMAN, GEORGE LEWIS (? died 1829) of Pimlico.

Son of Frederick Amelia Palman, page of the backstairs to George III (died November 20, 1793)[1] and grandson of John George Palman, page to the mother of George III (died August 12, 1772).[2] Married ? Admitted to Westminster School on October 31, 1775.[3] Clerk in the Colonial Office, 1779, to March 1782,[4] and thereafter in the Home Office until July 1794, when he retired because of ill health with a pension of £150 per annum.[5] The last payment to him is dated June 11, 1829,[6] which is probably the day he died.[7] His widow received a gratuity of £20 on October 15, 1831.[5]

1. Will dated July 15, 1767, and proved April 4, 1794, Holman, f. 220; *Gentleman's Magazine,* LXIII (Nov., 1793), 1061. 2. Administration granted to his son Frederick Amelia Palman, Feb. 26, 1773, AA 1772; *Gentleman's Magazine,* XLII (Aug., 1772), 391. 3. Barker and Stenning, *Old Westminsters,* II, 715. 4. *First Report, 1786,* p. 24. 5. Portland to the Treasury, Oct. 23, 1794, H.O. 36/8. 6. Contingent Accounts, H.O. 82/3. 7. In the margin of the volume containing the will of his mother Anna Margaretta (Bridport, f. 435), dated August 16, 1800, and proved July 5, 1814, is the notation, dated June 12, 1829, that the administration of the will had been granted to G. L. Palman and his sister Sarah Charlotte Elizabeth Findlay, both deceased; the administration was granted to James Henry Charles Findlay of Bath, widower of Sarah.

PLASKET, THOMAS HENRY (1773–1850) of Clifford Street and of Sidcup Place, Footscray, Kent.

Born c.1773.[1] Married. Three sons, two daughters: (1) Captain Thomas Henry of the Thirty-first Regiment; (2) Charles of Henrietta Street, Cavendish Square; (3) Edward; (1) Sophia Parisot Phobbs of Union Crescent, Kent Road; (2) Ellen.[2] Clerk in the Home Office by October 18, 1794,[3] until 1849, when he retired on a pension of £1,432;[1] succeeded as chief clerk in January 1816. He entered the office as fifth clerk, bypassing five who were his seniors—a step taken at no other time in the period 1782–1801. His will, dated April 24, 1847, divided his property, including a wine business in Old Burlington Street, among his wife and children; but a codicil dated February 27, 1850, revoked his former will and left all his property to his eldest son. The will mentions that his mother, brother, and sister were buried at St. James's Chapel in Hampstead Road. He directed that he be buried at the East Chislehurst Church if he died at Sidcup,[2] as he did. He rented the property at Sidcup.[4] He died on October 1, 1850, aged seventy-seven.[5]

1. *Superannuations, PP 1850* (171), XXXIII, 647. 2. Will proved on Nov. 14, 1850, f. 913. 3. General Account Book, H.O. 82/1. 4. Tax Rolls, Kent Co. Archives. 5. *Gentleman's Magazine,* CXXVII (Nov., 1850), 561.

POLLOCK, WILLIAM (1741–1816).

Born c.1741,[1] son of William Pollock, king's messenger.[2] Married before April 18, 1773,[3] Hannah Cowther[4] (c.1740–April 3, 1822).[5] Without issue. Clerk (extra) in the Southern Department, February 1757 to the end of 1758; clerk (extra) at the Admiralty from late 1758 to January 1763; clerk in the Southern Department, January 6 to September 1763; in the Northern Department, September 1763 to June 1766; in the Southern Department, June 1766 to January 1768;[7] chief clerk of the Colonial Office (except for 3 months), January 1768 to March 1782; in the Home Office March 1782 to May 31, 1782, and thereafter chief clerk[6] until he retired in January 1816 on a pension of £1,480.[8] Clerk of the Crown for Quebec, March 16, 1781;[9] deputy Clerk of the Signet, 1785.[6] Both Pollock and his wife are buried in the vault of St. Margaret's Church, Westminster.[1] He died on January 16, 1816, at Lambeth,[10] aged seventy-five.[1]

1. "Register of Burials," St. Margaret's Church, Westminster. Pollock was buried on November 11, 1816 (?), and his wife on April 10, 1822. His age is given as seventy-five and hers as eighty-two. 2. Thomson, *Secretaries of State,* p. 180. 3. Will dated April 18, 1773, Wynne, f. 159. 4. Will dated Nov. 2, 1816, with later codicils, proved April 24, 1822, Herschell, f. 216. 5. *Gentleman's Magazine,* XCII (May, 1822), 475. 6. *First Report, 1786,* p. 19. 7. *Cal. of H.O. Papers,* I, 302; II, 54–55. 8. General Account Book, H.O. 82/1; note on Portland to Treasury, June 16, 1795, H.O. 36/9. 9. C.O. 324/44. 10. *Gentleman's Magazine,* LXXXVI (March, 1816), 282, gives the date of his death as February 17, 1816, but the Account Book (H.O. 82/1) is probably correct in stating it as the 16th.

PORTER, JOHN (1755–1833).

Born c.1755.[1] Clerk in the Plantation Department, December 1783[2] until August 1786, when he moved to the Board of Trade;[3] clerk and eventually chief clerk at the Board until 1832, when he retired on a pension of £1,000.[1] He died on December 13, 1833, aged seventy-eight.[4]

1. *Superannuations,* H. of C. 735, p. 694; *PP 1833,* XXIII. 2. *First Report, 1786,* p. 26. 3. Cockroft, *Life of Chalmers,* pp. 84–85. 4. *Superannuations,* H. of C. 160, p. 424; *PP 1834,* XLI.

RANDALL, GEORGE (died 1798) of Mount Row, Lambeth, Surrey.

Son of William Randall, by Mary (died 1777).[1] Unmarried.[2] Clerk in the Southern Department and the Home Office by September 25, 1767,[3] until his death. He left his property to the widow and two daughters of his late brother William. He also left instructions that he be interred with his parents at Hornsey.[2] He died on January 16, 1798.[4]

1. Rev. Daniel Lysons, *The Environs of London, Being an Historical Account of the Towns, Villages, and Hamlets, within Twelve Miles of the Capital* (6 vols.; London, 1792–1811), III, 55. 2. Will, dated Feb. 7 and proved Feb. 1, 1798, Walpole, f. 130. 3. *Cal. of H.O. Papers,* II, 187. 4. *Gentleman's Magazine,* LXVIII (Feb., 1798), 173; *European Magazine,* XXXIII (Feb., 1798), 142.

SHADWELL, RICHARD (1718–1785) of Ringmer, Sussex.

Born c.1718,[1] eldest son of Thomas Shadwell of Ripe, Sheplake, Sussex (died 1730), by Susan, daughter of Richard Gunn of Middleham, Ringmer, Sussex (died 1744).[2] Married Mary Barlow[3] (died 1777).[4] At least one son: Henry Thurloe (c.1757–October 1, 1807), army officer.[3] Matriculated at University College, Oxford, November 11, 1735; admitted to the Middle Temple, November 15, 1732; called to the bar, 1741.[1] Clerk in the Northern Department, 1752 (?)–September 1763; in the Southern Department, September 1763 to August 1766; Northern Department, August 1766 to 1775 (?);[5] chief clerk in the Southern Department and Home Office, 1775 (?) to May 31, 1782, when he retired on a pension of over £700.[6] Deputy Clerk of the Signet, April 1769 until his death.[7] A marble mural in memory of him and his wife is in the west end of the parish church at Ringmer.[8] He died at Bath, June 1, 1785, aged sixty-seven.[9]

1. *Alumni Oxon.*, IV, 1278. 2. William Berry, *County Genealogies: Pedigrees of the Families of the County of Sussex* (London, 1830), p. 369. 3. Barker and Stenning, *Old Westminsters,* II, 835–36. 4. Lysons, *Environs of London,* III, 252, indicates that she is buried in the Marybone churchyard. 5. *Royal Kalenders; Cal. of H.O. Papers,* I, 302–303; II, 67; III, 556. 6. Sydney to the Treasury, March 28, 1783, S.P. 44/333. 7. Warrant to act as deputy dated April 13, 1769, *Cal. of H.O. Papers,* II, 560. 8. Fane Lambarde, "Coats of Arms in Sussex Churches, Part IV," *Sussex Archeological Collections,* LXX (1929), 163. 9. *Gentleman's Magazine,* LV (June, 1785), 490.

WILMOT, EARDLEY (died 1801).

Third and youngest son of Sir John Eardley Wilmot (1709–1792), chief justice of the common pleas 1766–1771.[1] Unmarried.[2] Admitted to Derby School, 1760.[3] Engaged in commerce in London in 1767.[1] Clerk in the Colonial Office from early 1773 to March 1782; in the Home Office from March 1782[4] to August 8, 1788, when Lord Sydney was forced to retire him because of ill health on a pension of £150.[5] Clerk of the Signet in reversion, July 15, 1782;[6] succeeded in June 1797.[7] His obituary records that he was "esteemed and beloved by all who knew him, particularly by his inferiors and dependants [*sic*], whom he considered and treated with unbounded friendship and humanity. He had long laboured under a painful disease, which he bore with true Christian patience."[8] His will (by which he left most of his property to his brother Sir John Eardley Wilmot) directed his physician to open and examine his urethra and bladder, from which he had so long suffered, so that the knowledge might be of use to his fellow creatures.[2] He died on January 2, 1801.[8]

1. John Wilmot [later Sir John Eardley Wilmot, Bt.], *Memoirs of the Life of the Right Honourable Sir John Eardley Wilmot, Knt.* (2nd ed.; London, 1811), p. 215. 2. Will undated, proved Feb. 19, 1801, Abercrombie, f. 174. 3. B. Tacchella (ed.), *The Derby School Register, 1570–1901* (London, 1902), p. 16. 4. *First Report, 1786,* p. 23. 5. Sydney to the Treasury, Aug. 8, 1788, H.O. 36/6. 6. Patent Rolls 19–43 George III, p. 67, C. 66. 7. Succeeded Montague Wilkinson, who died in Vienna, June 1797. *Gentleman's Magazine,* LXVII (July, 1797), 616. 8. *Ibid.,* LXXI (Jan., 1801), 90; *European Magazine,* XXXIX (Jan., 1801), 78.

WOOD, EDWARD (1778–1824).

Born on June 10, 1778, second son of Thomas Wood (died 1835), whose father had been treasurer of the Inner Temple, by Mary, only daughter and heir of Sir Edward Williams, fifth Bt. Died without issue.[1] Clerk in the Home Office by Oct. 18, 1794,[2] to May 22, 1795.[3] By 1799 he had entered the East India Company's service as assistant under the subtreasurer at Madras;[4] chief secretary to the government at Madras until his death.[1] He died of cholera in late 1824, aged forty-six.[5]

1. *Burke's Landed Gentry* (17th ed.; London, 1952), p. 2774. 2. General Account Book, H.O. 82/1. 3. Salary Book, H.O. 82/16. 4. Robert Hudson (compiler), *The New East India Calender for 1801* (London, 1801), p. 105. 5. *Gentleman's Magazine,* XCIV (Dec., 1824), 574.

WOOD, ROBERT RICHARD (1780–1856).

Born on February 13, 1780, third son of Thomas Wood; brother of Edward Wood. Died without issue.[1] Clerk in the Home Office from May 22, 1795, to May 23, 1835 (retired);[2] Naval Officer of Grenada, pension £200; Vendue Master of Malta, October 1809 to June 1813 (office abolished), pension £1,000.[3] He died on March 19, 1856,[1] at Putney, aged seventy-seven.[4]

1. *Burke's Landed Gentry,* 17th ed., p. 2774. 2. Salary Books, *H.O.* 82/16. 3. *PP 1834* (494), XLI, 452, 453. 4. *Gentleman's Magazine,* n.s., XLV (May, 1856), 547.

Appendix II. EMOLUMENTS OF HOME OFFICE PERSONNEL IN 1784

Name	*Rank*	*Salary*	*Fees*	*Gratui-ties*	*Perqui-sites*	*Franks*	*Parlia-mentary grants*	*Total net*
Sydney	Secretary	3,680	2,520		237			4,271
Townshend	Undersecretary	500	266	149	50			878
Nepean	Undersecretary	500	427	149	50			1,079
Pollock	Chief clerk			425	55		100	850
Brietzcke	2nd clerk	175			5	190	163	533
Randall	3rd clerk	120			5	105	100	340
Higden	4th clerk	120			5	95	90	310
Carrington	5th clerk	65			5	85	100	265
Daw	6th clerk	65				75	140	280
Wilmot	7th clerk	60				60	35	155
Colleton	8th clerk	45				55	45	145
Chetwynd	9th clerk	45				45	20	110
Palman	10th clerk	50				40	20	150
Chapman	11th clerk	50					20	70
Lucas	Arabic interpreter				80			80
Kirby	Chamber keeper	20	65		39			220
Doudiet	Chamber keeper	20	65					52
Emmitt	Housekeeper	48			46			28
Plantation Office								
Elliott	Undersecretary	500						500
Bradbury	1st clerk	120						120
Porter	2nd clerk	100						100
Jessup	3rd clerk	80						80

SOURCE: *First Report, 1786*, Appendix 42, pp. 38–39. Sydney had an additional £695 in fees that he had not received. Nepean received £450 as Naval Officer of Grenada, £500 from a government commission, and £318 as a commissioner of the privy seal. Pollock received £250 as clerk of the Crown in Quebec. Brietzcke received £81 as clerk in the Alien Office, and £277 as Deputy Clerk of the Signet. Elliott also had his pension of £250. All figures are in pounds, and are rounded off.

Appendix III. EMOLUMENTS OF HOME OFFICE PERSONNEL IN 1796

Name	*Rank*	*Salary*	*Franks*	*Gifts*	*Perquisites*	*Total*
Portland	Secretary	6,000				6,000
King	Undersecretary	1,593		2	50	1,646
Greville	Undersecretary	1,406				1,459
Pollock	Chief clerk	1,000		7	53	1,058
Randall	2nd clerk	650	54	5		709
Higden	3rd clerk	450	40	5		495
Norton	4th clerk	300	11	5		316
Plaskett	5th clerk	200	20	5		225
Douglas	6th clerk	160	13			173
Adams	7th clerk	140	14			155
Johnston	8th clerk	130	19			149
Hicks	9th clerk	120	21			141
Brietzcke	10th clerk	110	60			170
Lefroy	11th clerk	100				100
Wood	12th clerk	80	13			93
Carter	Private secretary (1/4)	75				75
Moss	Précis writer	300				300
Gander	Chamber keeper	100		12	166	278
Hancock	Chamber keeper	100		12	166	278
Drinkwater	Housekeeper	100				100
Tully	Arabic interpreter	80				80
Peace	Librarian	200	34			234
Raven	Register of felons	200				200
Carter	Supt. of Aliens	500				500
Lullin	Clerk to the above	150				150

SOURCE: *Sixteenth Report, 1797*, Appendix B.1, pp. 317–18. King received £300 as law clerk. Pollock received £250 as clerk of the Crown in Quebec, and £180 as Deputy Clerk of the Signet. Peace received a pension of £90. Carter was both private secretary and Superintendent of Aliens. All figures are in pounds and are rounded off.

Appendix IV

UNPUBLISHED LETTERS OF GEORGE III

THE KING TO [HENRY DUNDAS]

[Weymouth, August 29, 1792, 4:30 P.M.] Colonel Delancey seems to have executed the business of Constructing for Barracks at Manchester, Nottingham and Sheffield with every proper caution local circumstances naturally occasion some proving more expensive than others. [H.O. 42/20]

THE KING TO [THE DUKE OF PORTLAND]

[Queen's House, May 22, 1798, 7:40 A.M.] The last Evening I received the Duke of Portland's Note transmitting Mr. King's letter from Maidstone to Mr. Wickham, by which it seems that the preparatory steps to the trials of the persons accused of High Treason met with every kind of chicane, consequently that the business will probably prove very tedious; the ill advised zeal of the Revd. Mr. Arthur Young appears to have been very properly noticed by the Attorney General which I trust will remove any impression it might otherwise have justly occasioned. [H.O. 42/43][1]

1. See Portland to the King, May 21, 1798, *Later Correspondence of George III*, III, 65.

A SELECTED BIBLIOGRAPHY

Note on Sources

The great body of manuscripts used in this book are in the classification Home Office in the Public Record Office. The in-letters (H.O. 42) and the out-letters H.O. 43) provided the richest source for the general operation of the Office. I examined with care all 57 bundles (containing about 100 letters each) of H.O. 42 and the 13 volumes (of about 500 pages) of H.O. 43. The other H.O. classifications yielded varying amounts of useful information. Some, such as the correspondence between the Home Office and the Admiralty (H.O. 28) did not warrant close study; the correspondence with the Treasury (H.O. 36) proved much more rewarding. I could not examine the 103 bundles of Irish correspondence (H.O. 100) with any pretext of thoroughness.

Other classification of manuscripts in the Public Record Office contained correspondence that had once been in the Home Office. The Colonial Office papers from 1782 to 1801 are now classified by colony in the C.O. series. All papers relating to the Barbary states are now in the F.O. series. The W.O. classification has many of the documents that relate to the Home Secretary's participation in the war in 1782–1783 and 1793–1794. Other groups of departmental papers provided various bits of information. The Chatham Papers, which contain the correspondence of the younger Pitt, had a considerable amount of miscellaneous information. The private papers of the Secretaries and Undersecretaries varied as to their worth. Shelburne's papers in the Clements Library did not have much concerning his brief tenure as Home Secretary; I could not examine the collection that is at Bowood, Wiltshire. North's papers for this period seem to be lost. Sydney's papers at the Clements Library provided some information, but those in the Brotherton Collection, University of Leeds, were thin. I saw only the printed letters of Grenville. The collection of Melville MSS at both the General Register House and the National Library of Scotland proved disappointing for his years as Home Secretary. Portland's papers at the University of Nottingham were full only for the years 1794 and 1795. To my great disappointment, I could not locate the papers, if they survive, of either Nepean or King. Nepean's Secret Service Account Book, in the Clements Library, proved especially valuable; but it was the only remnant of his papers that I could locate except those relating to his years as governor of Bombay, which are in the Commonwealth Office Library. The Spencer Bernard MSS yielded the most useful information of any of the collections, and indicated a great deal about the routine of office. Wickham's papers related mostly to Ireland or to his intrigues on the Continent. The British Museum had only scattered letters of value to me. The Secret Service records of Nepean under Dundas were read after the above was written. They are in the Dundas Papers in Duke University Library, Manuscripts Division.

MANUSCRIPTS

In the Public Record Office (P.R.O.)

Alien Office (A.O.).
Chancery (C.).
Colonial Office (C.O.).
Exchequer (E.).
Foreign Office (F.O.).
Home Office (H.O.).
Privy Council (P.C.).
Treasury (T.).
War Office (W.O.).
Chatham Papers (P.R.O.).
William Dacres Adams Papers (P.R.O.).

In other collections

Chapman MSS. Kent Archives Office, Maidstone.
Hardwicke MSS. British Museum.
Huskisson MSS. British Museum.
Keith MSS. British Museum.
Lacaita-Shelburne MSS. William L. Clements Library, Ann Arbor, Michigan.
Liverpool MSS. British Museum.
Melville Castle Muniments. General Register House (Public Record Office of Scotland, Edinburgh).
Melville MSS. National Library of Scotland, Edinburgh.
North MSS. Kent Archives Office, Maidstone.
Peel MSS. British Museum.
Pelham MSS. British Museum.
Pitt MSS. William L. Clements Library.
Portland MSS. Division of Manuscripts, University of Nottingham.
Shelburne MSS. William L. Clements Library.
Spencer Bernard MSS. Nether Winchendon House, Aylesbury, Buckinghamshire.
Sydney MSS. Brotherton Collection, University of Leeds.
Sydney MSS. William L. Clements Library.

Wentworth Woodhouse Muniments. Sheffield City (Central) Library, Sheffield.
Wickham MSS. Hampshire Record Office.
Willes MSS. British Museum.
Copies of wills deposited in the Prerogative Court of Canterbury. Somerset House, London.
Copy of will of Robert Hepburn. General Register House, Edinburgh.
Parish Register of St. Margaret's Church, Westminster.

Printed Sources: Books, Articles, and Government Documents

[Adams, John] *The Adams Papers: Diary and Autobiography of John Adams.* L. H. Butterfield, editor in chief. 4 vols. Cambridge, Mass., 1961.

Anderson, Bern. *Vancouver: A Life, 1757–1798.* New York, 1931.

Anderson, James Maitland (ed.). *The Matriculation Roll of the University of St. Andrews, 1747–1897.* Edinburgh and London, 1905.

Anderson, M. S. "Great Britain and the Barbary States in the Eighteenth Century," *Bulletin of the Institute of Historical Research,* XXIX (May, 1956), 87–107.

Andrews, Charles M. *Guide to the Materials for American History to 1783 in the Public Record Office of Great Britain.* 2 vols. Washington, D.C., 1912.

Anson, Sir William. *The Law and Custom of the Constitution.* Vol. II: *The Crown.* 4th ed. edited by A. B. Keith. 2 pts. Oxford, 1935.

Armitage, Gilbert. *The History of the Bow Street Runners, 1729–1829.* London, [1932].

Aspinall, Arthur. "The Cabinet Council, 1783–1835," *Proceedings of the British Academy,* XXXVIII (1952), 145–232.

——— (ed.). *The Early English Trade Unions.* London, 1949.

———. *Politics and the Press, c. 1780–1850.* London, 1949.

———, and E. Anthony Smith (eds.). *English Historical Documents, 1782–1832.* English Historical Documents, XI, David C. Douglas, editor in chief. London, 1959.

Austen-Leigh, Richard Arthur. *The Eton College Register, 1753–1790.* Eton, 1921.

Aylmer, G. E. *The King's Servants: The Civil Service of Charles I, 1625–1642.* New York, 1961.

Bagot, Josceline (ed.). *George Canning and His Friends.* 2 vols. London, 1909.

Balteau, J., and others (eds.). *Dictionnaire de Biographie Française.* 28 vols. to date. Paris, since 1933.

Barker, G. F. Russell, and Alan H. Stenning (eds.). *The Record of Old Westminsters.* 2 vols. London, 1928.

Barnes, Donald Grove. *History of the English Corn Laws from 1660 to 1846*. London, 1930.
Barnwell, Joseph W., and Mabel L. Weber (eds.). "St. Helena's Parish Register," *South Carolina Historical and Genealogical Magazine*, XXIII, No. 3 (July, 1922), 102–204.
[Barthélemy, François] *Mémoires de Barthélemy, 1768–1819*. Edited by Jacques de Dampierre. Paris, 1914.
———. *Papiers de Barthélemy, 1792–97*. Edited by Jean Kaulek. 6 vols. Paris, 1886–1910.
Bayse, Arthur Herbert. *The Lords Commissioners of Trade and Plantations: Commonly Known as the Board of Trade, 1748–1782*. Yale Historical Miscellany, XIV. New Haven, 1925.
Beckett, J. C. "Anglo-Irish Constitutional Relations in the Later Eighteenth Century," *Irish Historical Studies*, XIV (March, 1964), 20–38.
Bemis, Samuel Flagg. "British Secret Service and the French-American Alliance," *American Historical Review*, XXIX, No. 3 (April, 1924), 474–95.
———. *The Diplomacy of the American Revolution*. Rev. ed. Edinburgh and London, 1957.
Berry, William. *County Genealogies: Pedigrees of the Families in the County of Sussex*. London, 1830.
Binney, J. E. D. *British Public Finance and Administration, 1774–92*. Oxford, 1958.
Black, Eugene Charlton. *The Association: British Extraparliamentary Political Organization, 1769–1793*. Harvard Historical Monographs, LIV. Cambridge, Mass., 1963.
Bolton, G. C. *The Passing of the Irish Act of Union: A Study in Parliamentary Politics*. Oxford, 1966.
[Boswell, James] *Boswell's Life of Johnson*. Edited by George Birkbeck Hill and rev. and enlarged by L. F. Powell. 6 vols. Oxford, 1934–64.
Brown, Philip Anthony. *The French Revolution in English History*. London, 1918.
Buckingham and Chandos, Duke of. *Memoirs of the Court and Cabinets of George III*. 2nd ed. rev. 4 vols. London, 1853–55.
[Burges, Sir James Bland] *Selections from the Letters and Correspondence of Sir James Bland Burges, Bart*. Edited by James Hutton. London, 1885.
Burke, Ashworth P. *Family Records*. London, 1897.
[Burke, Edmund] *The Correspondence of Edmund Burke*. Edited by Thomas Copeland and others. 5 vols to date. Cambridge and Chicago, since 1958.
Burke, John, and John Bernard Burke. *A Genealogical and Heraldic Dictionary of the Landed Gentry of Great Britain and Ireland*. 3 vols. London, 1846–49.
Burke's Genealogical and Heraldic History of the Landed Gentry. 5th ed. 2 vols. London, 1871.

———. 11th ed. 2 vols. London, 1906.

Burke's Genealogical and Heraldic History of the Landed Gentry Including American Families with British Ancestry. 16th ed. London, 1939.

Burke's Genealogical and Heraldic History of the Landed Gentry. 17th ed. London, 1952.

Burke's Genealogical and Heraldic History of the Landed Gentry of Ireland. London, 1912.

Burke's Genealogical and Heraldic History of the Peerage, Baronetage, and Knightage. London, 1928.

———. 99th ed. London, 1949.

Candler, Allen D. (ed.). *The Colonial Records of the State of Georgia*. 25 vols. in 28. Atlanta, Ga., 1904–1916.

Chatwin, Philip D. (ed.). *The Records of King Edward's School, Birmingham*. [Vol. V] Publications of the Dugdale Society; Vol. XXV. Oxford, 1963.

Clarke, William Bordley. *Early and Historic Freemasonry of Georgia, 1733/4–1800*. Savannah, Ga., c.1924.

Clutterbuck, Robert. *The History and Antiquities of the County of Hertford*. 3 vols. London, 1815–27.

Cobban, Alfred. *Ambassadors and Secret Agents: The Diplomacy of the First Earl of Malmesbury at the Hague*. London, 1954.

———. "The Beginning of the Channel Isles Correspondence, 1789–1794," *English Historical Review*, LXXVII (Jan., 1962), 38–52.

———. "British Secret Service in France, 1784–1792," *English Historical Review*, LXIX (April, 1954), 226–261.

Cobbett, William (compiler). *The Parliamentary History of England from the Earliest Period to the Year 1803*.

Cockroft, Grace Amelia. *The Public Life of George Chalmers*. Studies in History, Economics and Public Law, No. 454. New York, 1939.

Cohen, Emmeline W. *The Growth of the British Civil Service, 1780–1939*. London, 1941.

C[okayne], G. E. *Complete Baronetage, 1611–1800*. 6 vols. Exeter, 1900–1909.

———. *The Complete Peerage of England, Scotland, Ireland, Great Britain, and the United Kingdom*. New ed. rev. by Vicary Gibbs and others. 12 vols. in 13. London, 1910–1959.

Colson, Percy. *The Strange History of Lord George Gordon*. London, 1937.

Conn, Stetson. *Gibraltar in British Diplomacy in the Eighteenth Century*. New Haven, 1942.

Connell, Brian. *Portrait of a Whig Peer: Compiled from the Papers of the Second Viscount Palmerston, 1739–1802*. London, 1957.

Copeland, Thomas, and Milton Shumway Smith. *A Checklist of the Correspondence of Edmund Burke*. Cambridge, 1955.

[Cornwallis, Charles, Marquis] *Cornwallis Correspondence*. Edited by Charles Ross. 3 vols. London, 1859.

Cox, Cynthia. *The Enigma of the Age: The Strange Story of the Chevalier d'Eon.* London, 1966.
Cubbon, William (ed.). *A Bibliographical Account of Works Relating to the Isle of Man.* 2 vols. London, 1933–39.
Dalzel, Andrew. *History of the University of Edinburgh from Its Foundation.* 2 vols. Edinburgh, 1862.
Daughlish, M. G., and P. K. Stephenson (eds.). *The Harrow School Register, 1800–1911.* London, 1911.
Deane, Phyllis. *The First Industrial Revolution.* Cambridge, 1965.
Debreet, John (compiler). *The Parliamentary Register or History of the Proceedings and Debates of the House of Commons [and the House of Lords].*
Dugdale, George S. *Whitehall Through the Centuries.* London, 1950.
Eagleston, A. J. "Wordsworth, Coleridge and the Spy," *Coleridge: Studies by Several Hands on the Hundreth Anniversary of His Death.* Edited by Edmund Charles Blunden and Earl Leslie Griggs. London, 1934.
Ellis, Kenneth. *The Post Office in the Eighteenth Century: A Study in Administrative History.* London, 1958.
Evans, Florence M. Grier (Mrs. C. S. S. Higham). *The Principal Secretary of State: A Survey of the Office from 1558 to 1680.* Publications of the University of Manchester: Historical Studies, XLIII. Manchester, 1923.
Fay, C. R. *The Corn Laws and Social England.* Cambridge, 1932.
———. *Huskisson and His Age.* London, 1951.
Fieldhouse, David. "British Imperialism in the Late Eighteenth Century: Defence or Opulence?," *Essays in Imperial Government Presented to Margery Perham.* Edited by Kenneth Robinson and Frederick Madden. Oxford, 1963.
Fisher, Sir Godfrey. *Barbary Legend: War, Trade and Piracy in North Africa, 1415–1830.* Oxford, 1957.
Fitzmaurice, Lord Edmund. *Life of William Earl of Shelburne, Afterwards Marquess of Lansdowne.* 2nd ed. rev. 2 vols. London, 1912.
Fitzpatrick, W. J. *Secret Service Under Pitt.* 2nd ed. London, 1892.
Fortescue, Sir John. *A History of the British Army.* 13 vols. in 14. London, 1906–30.
Foster, Joseph (ed.). *Alumni Oxonienses: The Members of the University of Oxford, 1715–1886.* 4 vols. London, 1888.
Furber, Holden. *Henry Dundas, First Viscount Melville, 1742–1811.* London, 1931.
[George III] *The Correspondence of King George the Third, from 1760 to December 1783.* Edited by Sir John Fortescue. 6 vols. London, 1927–28.
———. *Later Correspondence of George III.* Edited by Arthur Aspinall. 5 vols. in progress. Cambridge, since 1962.
[George, Prince of Wales] *The Correspondence of George, Prince of*

Wales, 1770–1812. Edited by Arthur Aspinall. 3 vols. to date. Oxford, since 1965.

George, M. Dorothy. "The Combination Laws," *Economic History Review,* VI, No. 2 (April, 1936), 172–78.

———. "The Combination Laws Reconsidered," *Economic History,* I (May, 1927), 214–28.

———. *London Life in the Eighteenth Century*. London, 1925.

Gibb, D. E. W. *Lloyd's of London: A Study in Individualism*. London, 1957.

Ginter, Donald E. "The Loyalist Association Movement of 1792–93 and British Public Opinion," *Historical Journal,* IX, No. 2 (1966), 179–90.

Glover, Richard. *Peninsular Preparation: The Reform of the British Army, 1795–1809*. Cambridge, 1963.

Grant, Sir Alexander. *The Story of the University of Edinburgh During its First Three Hundred Years*. 2 vols. London, 1884.

Grant, Sir Francis J. (ed.). *The Faculty of Advocates in Scotland, 1532–1943, with Genealogical Notes*. Edinburgh, 1944.

Great Britain. Parliament. House of Commons. *Journals.*

———. *Parliamentary Papers.*

———. [*Official Returns of the*] *Members of Parliament*. 2 vols. London, 1878.

Great Britain. Public Record Office. *Calendar of Home Office Papers of the Reign of George III, 1760–1775*. 4 vols. London, 1878–99.

Great Britain. *Journal of the Commissioners for Trade and Plantations from January 1759 to December 1763*. London, 1935.

———. *Journal of the Commissioners for Trade and Plantations from January 1776 to May 1782*. London, 1938.

———. *Statutes at Large.*

Green, Edward J., and Gomer H. Redmond. "Comments on a General Theory of Administration," *Administrative Science Quarterly,* II (1957/58), 235–43.

[Greville, Charles Cavendish Fulke] *The Greville Memoirs, 1814–1860*. Edited by Lytton Strachey and Roger Fulford. 8 vols. London, 1938.

[Greville, Robert Fulke] *The Diaries of Colonel the Hon. Robert Fulke Greville, Equerry to His Majesty King George III*. Edited by F. McKno. Bladon. London, 1930.

Gun, W. T. J. (ed.). *The Harrow School Register, 1571–1800*. London, 1934.

Hallett, Robin. *The Penetration of Africa: European Enterprise and Exploration Principally in Northern and Western Africa up to 1830*. London, 1965.

——— (ed.). *Records of the African Association, 1788–1831*. London, 1964.

Hammond, John Lawrence, and Barbara Hammond. *The Skilled Labourer, 1760–1832*. London, 1919.

Hancock, P. D. *A Bibliography of Works Relating to Scotland, 1916–1950.* 2 vols. Edinburgh, 1959–60.

Handover, P. M. *A History of the London Gazette, 1665–1965.* London. 1965.

Harlow, Vincent Todd. *The Founding of the Second British Empire, 1763–1793.* 2 vols. London, 1952–1964.

Harrison, Sir Cecil Reeves, and H. G. Harrison. *House of Harrison.* London, 1914.

Hart, Mrs. E. P. (ed.). *Merchant Taylors' School Register, 1561–1834.* 2 vols. London, 1936.

Haydn, Joseph. *The Book of Dignities.* 3rd ed. revised by Horace Ockerby. London, 1894.

Higgins, Mrs. Napier. *The Bernards of Abingdon and Nether Winchendon: A Family History.* 4 vols. London, 1904.

Hill, Mary C. *The King's Messengers, 1199–1377: A Contribution to the History of the Royal Household.* London, 1961.

Historical Manuscripts Commission. "Manuscripts in the Posession of Sir Edward Strachey, Bart., &c &c, Sutton Court, Somersetshire," *Sixth Report, Part I,* pp. 395–404. London, 1878.

———. "The Manuscripts of Captain Howard Vicente Knox," *Report on the Manuscripts in Various Collections,* VI, 81–296. 6 vols. London, 1901–1909.

———. *Report on the Manuscripts of His Grace the Duke of Rutland, K. G., Preserved at Belvoir Castle.* 4 vols. London, 1888–1905.

———. *Report on the Manuscripts of J. B. Fortescue, Esq., Preserved at Dropmore.* 10 vols. London, 1892–1927.

[Hobhouse, Henry] *The Diary of Henry Hobhouse (1820–1827).* Edited by Arthur Aspinall. London, 1947.

[Holland, Henry Richard Vassall Fox, third Baron] *Memoirs of the Whig Party During My Time.* Edited by Henry Edward, fourth Baron Holland. 2 vols. London, 1852–54.

Horn, D. B. (ed.). *British Diplomatic Representatives, 1689–1789.* Camden Society Publications, Third Series, XLVI. London, 1932.

Hudson, Robert (compiler). *The New East India Calendar for 1801.* London, 1801.

Hughes, Edward. "The Scottish Reform Movement and Charles Grey, 1792–94: Some Fresh Correspondence," *Scottish Historical Review,* XXV, No. 1 (April, 1956), 26–41.

[Huskisson, William] *The Huskisson Papers.* Edited by Lewis Melville. London, 1931.

Jacobs, Phyllis M. *Registers of the Universities, Colleges and Schools of Great Britain and Ireland.* London, 1964.

Johnson, Allen, and Dumas Malone (eds.). *Dictionary of American Biography.* 20 vols. and supplements. New York, since 1926.

Johnston, Edith M. *Great Britain and Ireland, 1760–1800: A Study in*

Political Administration. St. Andrews University Publications, LV. Edinburgh, 1963.

Jones, E. H. Stuart. *The Last Invasion of Britain*. Cardiff, 1950.

Keir, Sir David Lindsay. "Economical Reform, 1779–1787," *Law Quarterly Review*, L (July, 1934), 368–85.

[Knox, William] *Extra Official State Papers*. London, 1789.

Lambarde, Fane. "Coats of Arms in Sussex Churches, Part IV," *Sussex Archeological Collections*, LXX (1929), 134–64.

Langford, John Alfred. *A Century of Birmingham Life*. 2 vols. Birmingham, 1868.

Lee, Hilda I. "The Supervising of the Barbary Consuls During the Years 1756–1836," *Bulletin of the Institute of Historical Research*, XXIII (Nov., 1951), 191–99.

[Leeds, Francis Godolphin (Osborne), fifth Duke of] *The Political Memoranda of Francis Fifth Duke of Leeds*. Edited by Oscar Browning. Camden Society Publications, n. s., XXXV. Westminster, 1884.

[Lefroy, General Sir John Henry] *Notes and Documents Relating to the Family of Loffroy. By A Cadet*. Woolwich, 1868.

Linglebach, Anna Lane. "The Inception of the British Board of Trade," *American Historical Review*, XXX, No. 4 (July, 1925), 701–27.

Lipscombe, George. *The History and Antiquities of the County of Buckingham*. 6 vols. London, 1847.

Litchfield, Edward H. "Notes on a General Theory of Administration," *Administrative Science Quarterly*, I, No. 1 (June, 1956), 3–29.

London County Council. *The Parish of St. James, Westminster, Part One: South of Piccadilly*. Survey of London, XXX. London, 1960.

———. *The Parish of St. Margaret, Westminster, Part One*. Survey of London, X. London, 1926.

———. *The Parish of St. Margaret, Westminster, Part Two: Neighborhood of Whitehall*, Vol. I. Survey of London, XIII. London, 1930.

———. *The Parish of St. Margaret, Westminster, Part Three: Neighborhood of Whitehall*, Vol. II. Survey of London, XIV. London, 1931.

Lonn, Ella. *The Colonial Agents of the Southern Colonies*. Chapel Hill, N.C., 1945.

Lucas, Reginald. *Lord North, Second Earl of Guilford, K. G. 1732–1792*. 2 vols. London, 1913.

Lysons, Reverend Daniel. *The Environs of London, Being an Historical Account of the Towns, Villages, and Hamlets, within Twelve Miles of the Capital*. 6 vols. London, 1792–1811.

Mackaness, George. *The Life of Vice-Admiral William Bligh*. 2 vols. in 1. New York, 1931.

Madden, A. F. McC. "The Imperial Machinery of the Younger Pitt," *Essays in British History Presented to Sir Keith Feiling*. Edited by H. H. Trevor-Roper. London, 1964.

Madden, Richard Robert. *The United Irishmen, Their Lives and Times*. 7 vols. Dublin, 1842–46.

Mahoney, T. H. D. *Edmund Burke and Ireland.* Cambridge, 1960.

[Malmesbury, James (Harris), first Earl of] *Diaries and Correspondence of James Harris, First Earl of Malmesbury.* Edited by James Howard, third Earl of Malmesbury. 4 vols. London, 1844.

Manning, Mrs. Helen Taft. *British Colonial Government After the American Revolution, 1782–1820.* Yale Historical Miscellany, XXVI. New Haven and London, 1933.

Manning, Owen, and William Bray. *History and Antiquities of the County of Surrey.* 3 vols. London, 1804–14.

Marsh, Bower, and Frederick Arthur (eds.). *Alumni Carthusiani: A Record of the Foundation Scholars of Charterhouse, 1614–1872.* Privately printed, 1913.

Marshall, Dorothy. *English People in the Eighteenth Century.* London, 1956.

———. *The Rise of George Canning.* London, 1938.

Meikle, Henry W. *Scotland and the French Revolution.* Glasgow, 1912.

Meyer, George W. "Wordsworth and the Spy Hunt," *American Scholar,* XX (Winter, 1950/51), 50–56.

Minet, William. *Some Accounts of the Huguenot Family of Minet.* London, 1892.

[Miranda, Francisco de] *Archivo del General Miranda. . . .* Edited by Vicente Davala. 24 vols. Caracas, Venezuela, 1929–50.

Mitchell, Austin. "The Association Movement of 1792–3," *Historical Journal,* IV (1961), 56–77.

Mitchell, Harvey. *The Underground War Against Revolutionary France: The Missions of William Wickham, 1794–1800.* Oxford, 1965.

Morris, Richard. *The Peacemakers.* New York, 1965.

Mullett, Charles F. "The 'Better Reception, Preservation, and More Convenient Use' of Public Records in Eighteenth Century England," *American Archivist,* XXVII, No. 2 (April, 1964), 195–217.

Munk, William. *The Roll of the Royal College of Physicians of London.* 2nd. ed. 4 vols. London, 1878–1955.

Namier, Sir Lewis. *Crossroads of Power.* New York, 1962.

———, and John Brooke (eds.). *The History of Parliament: The House of Commons, 1754–1790.* 3 vols. London, 1964.

Newsam, Sir Frank. *The Home Office.* The New Whitehall Series. London, 1954.

Norris, John M. "The Policy of the British Cabinet in the Nootka Crisis," *English Historical Review,* LXX (Oct., 1955), 562–80.

———. *Shelburne and Reform.* London, 1963.

Nys, Ernest. *Le Droit Romain, le Droit des Gens et le Collège des Docteurs en Droit Civil.* Brussels, 1910.

O'Brien, Eris. *The Foundation of Australia (1786–1800): A Study in English Criminal Practice and Penal Colonization in the Eighteenth Century.* 2nd ed. Sydney and London, 1937.

Omond, George W. T. *The Arniston Memoirs: Three Centuries of a Scottish House, 1571–1838*. Edinburgh, 1887.

Pargellis, Stanley, and D. J. Medley (eds.). *Bibliography of British History: The Eighteenth Century, 1714–1789*. Oxford, 1951.

Parker, Harold T. "French Administrators and French Scientists During the Old Regime and the Early Years of the Revolution," *Ideas in History: Essays Presented to Louis Gottschalk by His Former Students*. Edited by Harold T. Parker and Richard Herr. Durham. N.C., 1965.

Parkinson, C. Northcote. *Edward Pellew Viscount Exmouth, Admiral of the Red*. London, 1934.

Pemberton, W. Baring. *Lord North*. London, 1938.

Powicke, Sir Maurice, and E. B. Fryde (eds.). *Handbook of British Chronology*. Royal Historical Society Guides and Handbooks, No. 2. 2nd ed. London, 1961.

Pritchard, Earle Hampton. *The Crucial Years of Early Anglo-Chinese Relations, 1750–1800*. Pullman, Washington, 1936.

Pryde, George S. *Scotland, 1603 to the Present Day*. London, 1962.

Radzinowitz, Leon. *A History of English Criminal Law and Its Administration from 1750*. 3 vols. to date. New York, 1948–57.

Records of the Honourable Society of Lincoln's Inn. Admissions from A.D. 1420 . . . A.D. 1893, and Chapel Registers. 2 vols. London, 1896.

Records of the Honourable Society of Lincoln's Inn. The Black Books, 1422–1845. 4 vols. London, 1897–1902.

Reed, Joseph W., Jr. "Boswell and the Major [J. G. Semple]," *Kenyon Review*, XXVII, No. 2 (March, 1966), 161–84.

Rose, John Holland. *Pitt and Napoleon: Essays and Letters*. London, 1912.

———. *William Pitt and National Revival*. London, 1911.

———. *William Pitt and the Great War*. London, 1912.

Rose, John Holland, and others (eds.). *The Cambridge History of the British Empire*. 7 vols. Cambridge, 1929–40.

Rose, R. B. "The Priestley Riots of 1791," *Past and Present*, No. 18 (Nov., 1960), pp. 68–88.

Salley, A. S., Jr. (ed.). *Marriage Notices in the South-Carolina Gazette and Its Successors 1732–1801*. Albany, New York, 1902.

Sanders, Charles Richard. *The Strachey Family, 1578–1932*. Durham, N.C., 1953.

Saunders, A. C. *Jersey in the 18th and 19th Centuries*. Jersey, 1930.

Shaw, A. G. L. *Convicts and the Colonies*. London, 1966.

[Sheridan, Richard Brinsley] *The Letters of Richard Brinsley Sheridan*. Edited by Cecil Price. 3 vols. Oxford, 1966.

Shortt, Adam, and Arthur G. Doughty (eds.). *Documents Relating to the Constitutional History of Canada, 1759–1791*. 2nd ed. rev. 2 vols. Ottawa, 1918.

[Simcoe, John Graves] *The Correspondence of Lieut. Governor John*

Graves Simcoe. Edited by E. A. Cruinkshank. 5 vols. Toronto, 1923–31.

Smith, E. Anthony. "Earl Temple's Resignation, 22 December 1783," *Historical Journal,* VI (1963), 91–97.

[Smith, William] *The Diary and Selected Papers of Chief Justice William Smith, 1784–1793.* Edited by L. F. S. Upton. Publications of the Champlain Society, XLI and XLII. 2 vols. Toronto, 1963–65.

Spector, Margaret Marion. *The American Department of the British Government, 1768–1782.* New York, 1940.

Stanhope, Philip Henry (Stanhope), fifth Earl. *Life of the Right Honourable William Pitt.* 4 vols. London, 1861–62.

Stephen, Sir Leslie, and Sir Sidney Lee (eds.). *Dictionary of National Biography.* 21 vols. and supplements. London, since 1885.

Stevens, Benjamin Franklin (compiler). *B. F. Stevens's Facsimiles of Manuscripts in European Archives Relating to America, 1773–1783.* 25 vols. London, 1889–1898.

Strutt, Austin. "The Home Office: An Introduction to Its Early History," *Public Administration,* XXXIX, No. 2 (Summer, 1961), 111–30.

Tacchella, B. (ed.). *The Derby School Register, 1570–1901.* London, 1902.

Thomas, F. S. *A History of the State Paper Office.* London, 1849.

———. *Notes of Materials for the History of Public Departments.* London, 1846.

Thompson, E. P. *The Making of the English Working Class.* New York. 1963.

Thomson, Mark A. *The Secretaries of State, 1681–1782.* Oxford, 1932.

Timperley, C. H. *A Dictionary of Printers and Printing, with the Progress of Literature, Ancient and Modern . . . .* London, 1839.

Todd, F. M. *Politics and the Poet: A Study of Wordsworth.* London, 1957.

Tomline, George. *Memoirs of the Life of the Right Honorable William Pitt.* 4 vols. London, 1821.

Troup, Sir Charles Edward. *The Home Office.* The Whitehall Series. London, 1925.

Tully, Miss. *Letters Written During a Ten Years' Residence at the Court of Tripoli Published from the Originals in the Possession of the Family of the Late Richard Tully, Esq., the British Consul.* New ed. with introduction and notes by Seton Dearden. London, 1957.

Turberville, Arthur Stanley. *A History of Welbeck Abbey and Its Owners.* 2 vols. London, 1939.

Valentine, Alan. *Lord North.* 2 vols. Norman, Okla., 1967.

Venn, John, and J. A. Venn (eds.). *Alumni Cantabrigienses: A Biographical List of All Known Students, Graduates and Holders of Office at the University of Cambridge, from the Earliest Times to 1900.* 10 vols. Cambridge, 1922–54.

Victoria History of the Counties of England: Buckingham. Edited by William Page. 5 vols. London, 1905–28.

Victoria History of the Counties of England: Sussex. Edited by William Page and L. F. Salzman. 6 vols. numbered I–IX. London, 1905–1953.

Vidler, L. A. "Rye Foreign," *Sussex Archeological Collections,* XCII (1954), 125–56.

Wade, John. *The Black Book; or, Corruption Unmasked.* 2 vols. London, 1820.

Webb, Sidney, and Beatrice Webb. *English Local Government.* 9 vols. London, 1906–1929.

Weber, Mable L. (compiler). "Death Notices from the South Carolina and American General Gazette, and Its Continuation the Royal Gazette, May 1766–June 1782," *South Carolina Historical and Genealogical Magazine,* XVII (April, 1916), 87–93 and (Oct., 1916), 147–66.

Werkmeister, Lucyle. *The London Daily Press 1772–1792.* Lincoln, Nebraska, 1963.

Western, J. R. *The English Militia in the Eighteenth Century: The Story of a Political Issue, 1660–1802.* London, 1965.

———. "The Formation of the Scottish Militia in 1797," *Scottish Historical Review,* XXXIV (April, 1955), 1–17.

———. "The Volunteer Movement as an Anti-Revolutionary Force, 1793–1801," *English Historical Review,* LXXI (Oct., 1956), 603–14.

Wharton, Francis (ed.). *The Revolutionary Diplomatic Correspondence of the United States.* 6 vols. Washington, D.C., 1889.

Wheeler-Holohan, Ambrose Vincent. *The History of the King's Messengers.* London, 1935.

[Wickham, William] *The Correspondence of the Right Honourable William Wickham from the Year 1794.* Edited by William Wickham. 2 vols. London, 1870.

Wickwire, Franklin B. "Admiralty Secretaries and the British Civil Service," *Huntington Library Quarterly,* XXVIII (May, 1965), 235–54.

———. *British Subministers and Colonial America, 1763–1783.* Princeton, N.J., 1966.

———. "King's Friends, Civil Servants, or Politicians," *American Historical Review,* LXXI (Oct. 1965), 18–42.

Wilmot, John. *Memoirs of the Life of the Right Honourable Sir John Eardley Wilmot, Knt.* 2nd ed. London, 1811.

Wilson, Carolina Price (ed.). *Annals of Georgia.* Vol. I: *Liberty County Records and A State Revolutionary Pay Roll.* New York, 1928.

[Windham, William] *The Diary of the Right Hon. William Windham, 1784 to 1810.* Edited by Mrs. Henry Baring. London, 1866.

Withington, Lothrop, and H. F. Waters (compilers). "South Carolina Gleanings in England," *South Carolina Historical and Genealogical Magazine,* IV (Oct., 1903), 286–95.

Wotton, Thomas. *The Baronetage of England.* Edited by E. Kinber and Richard Johnson. 3 vols. London, 1771.

[Wraxall, Nathaniel William] *The Historical and the Posthumous Memoirs of Sir Nathaniel William Wraxall, 1772–1784 [1789]*. Edited by Henry B. Wheatley. 5 vols. New York, 1884.

Wright, Charles, and C. Ernest Fayle. *A History of Lloyd's from the Founding of Lloyd's Coffee House to the Present Day*. London, 1928.

Young, D. M. *The Colonial Office in the Early Nineteenth Century.* Imperial Studies, No. XXII. London, 1961.

Newspapers and Magazines

Annual Biography and Obituary
Annual Register
European Magazine and London Review
Gentleman's Magazine
London Chronicle
London Gazette
Royal Kalender
Scots Magazine
The Times

INDEX